W9-DEF-580

The Marvelous Pigness of Pigs

Also by Joel Salatin

Folks, This Ain't Normal
Pastured Poultry Profits
Salad Bar Beef
You Can Farm
Family Friendly Farming
Holy Cows and Hog Heaven
Everything I Want to Do Is Illegal
The Sheer Ecstasy of Being a Lunatic Farmer
Fields of Farmers

The Marvelous Pigness of Pigs

OR, Does God care?

Respecting and Caring for All God's Creation

JOEL
SALATIN

New York   Boston   Nashville

Copyright © 2016 by Joel Salatin

Cover design by Jody Waldrup
Cover photo by Dean Dixon
Cover copyright © 2016 by Hachette Book Group, Inc.

All rights reserved. In accordance with the U.S. Copyright Act of 1976, the scanning, uploading, and electronic sharing of any part of this book without the permission of the publisher constitute unlawful piracy and theft of the author's intellectual property. If you would like to use material from the book (other than for review purposes), prior written permission must be obtained by contacting the publisher at permissions@hbgusa.com. Thank you for your support of the author's rights.

FaithWords
Hachette Book Group
1290 Avenue of the Americas
New York, NY 10104
faithwords.com
twitter.com/faithwords

First Edition: May 2016

FaithWords is a division of Hachette Book Group, Inc.
The FaithWords name and logo are trademarks of Hachette Book Group, Inc.

The publisher is not responsible for websites (or their content) that are not owned by the publisher.

The Hachette Speakers Bureau provides a wide range of authors for speaking events. To find out more, go to www.hachettespeakersbureau.com or call (866) 376- 6591.

Unless otherwise noted, all Scripture quotations are taken from the King James Version of the Holy Bible.
Scripture quotations noted AKJV are taken from the American King James Version.
Scripture quotations noted ESV are taken from the The Holy Bible: English Standard Version®, copyright © 2001 by Crossway, a publishing ministry of Good News Publishers. Used by permission. All rights reserved.
Scripture quotations noted HNV are taken from the Hebrew Names Version.
Scripture quotations noted KJ21 are taken from The Holy Bible, 21st Century King James Version (KJ21®), copyright © 1994. Used by permission of Deuel Enterprises, Inc., Gary, SD 57237. All rights reserved.
Scripture quotations noted NIV are taken from The Holy Bible: New International Version® NIV®. Copyright © 1973, 1978, 1984, 2011 by Biblica, Inc. Used by permission. All rights reserved worldwide.
Scripture quotations noted NKJV are taken from the New King James Version®. Copyright © 1982 by Thomas Nelson. Used by permission. All rights reserved.

Library of Congress Cataloging-in-Publication Data has been applied for.

ISBNs: 978-1-4555-3697-9 (hardcover); 978-1-4555-3696-2 (ebook); 978-1-4789-0913-2 (audio book); 978-1-4789-0914-9 (downloadable audio book)

Dedicated to God's Creation

Contents

Foreword

I'm a Christian. Jesus is my Lord. Joel Salatin is a Christian. That makes him my brother. But should Joel, or someone like him, be my farmer? Does it matter who grew my steak or my potatoes?

Most Christians don't know how to begin to answer this question. We don't know what the Bible has to say on the subject. We've not had a sermon on the biblical ethic of food. We can't articulate the theology of eating too much of the wrong things or too little of the right. Gluttony is one of the seven deadly sins, and temperance is the cardinal virtue that counteracts it. But how many Christians think about what the Bible says when they walk into a grocery store or restaurant and cast a vote with their wallet for what they want the world to be like? How many know about the curses placed on Levi and Simeon in Genesis because they maimed a farm animal? How many of us have had a sermon on agriculture—not a reminder about how the Bible is set in an agrarian culture, but agriculture today?

This book is a clarion call to connect what you ingest three times a day with what you say you believe in. Like me, Joel believes that the Bible is the inspired word of God, and he looks to the Good Book rather than corporate America for directions. For many, both inside and outside the church, it will be eye opening to find out that there's a sustainable and unchanging farming ethic to be found in Scripture. But again, one might ask, "Does it matter who grew my meal? Don't Christians have bigger things to worry about right now?" I would answer that the Bible says God will give us great things to look after if we are faithful in the little things.

Three-quarters of Americans are overweight. Obesity isn't something that happens to us in our sleep. It comes from eating too much or working too little. In religious terms these issues have been talked about using the terms *gluttony* and *sloth*. They are not pretty terms, but ignoring them is literally leading us into large problems.

And weight isn't the only problem that comes from bad nutrition and industrial farming. On several occasions, I've asked people in a congregation to raise their hands if someone in their family has had cancer. A sea of hands go up. Then I've asked how many have heard a sermon on cancer. No hands are raised. There's a disconnect between what we're dying from and what we're hearing about in church. The book you're holding connects your faith and your food.

It's not just physical health that results from un-anchoring ourselves from God's plan for our lives. When all we do is look for the most at the cheapest price, we lose track of the world that can surprise us with its beauty. Joel's vision of the world is alive! It's a picture of wonderment. As he says, "One breath gets recycled through an apple tree leaf and then into an earthworm and then into a red clover leaf and then into your teenager." His insights act as an antidote to the increasingly mechanistic world that threatens to reduce the meaning of human life to that of profit and loss. Joel's dream of what our world could be seems to be much more in keeping with what I read in Scripture.

God could have worked His plan through the builders of ancient Egypt or the scientists of Babylon. Instead, He chose the tribe of Jacob, who traveled with their sheep and cattle. He brought their descendants to farmland and gave them agricultural laws that included rest for the animals. God didn't leave sustainable agriculture to chance for His people. He even gave His nation of farmers ordinances on pruning fruit trees, for heaven's sake! Joel asks, and I wonder with him, "How did the people of God get so disconnected from God's plan?"

Jesus wasn't born by accident. He was the most planned baby in history. It is not by chance that the Son of God spent His first night surrounded by farm animals and visited by shepherds. The Bible says that "all creation groans" as a result of human sin and failings. How appropriate that the baby Jesus should be attended by the creatures He came to restore to the right relationship with us. I've visited modern factory farms and I've been to Joel's Polyface Farm; there is no question in my mind which farm is in God's will for us and His creatures. There is no question which offers a picture of dignity and hospitality.

If you don't think the Bible has anything to say about food, consider that Adam and Eve ate the wrong thing and it got them thrown out of the garden. Abraham and Sarah were made the parents of many nations because they served strangers a meal. Jesus taught for five chapters over a meal in the book of John, and then He offered Himself as the bread of life. He died and was resurrected, and what He did to calm His disciples and show them He was real was to eat with them. The centerpiece of heaven is the Tree of Life that yields fruit and heals the nations.

My prayer is that this book and Joel's work will bring us one step closer to what we pray to our Father God, that "thy kingdom come, thy will be done, on earth as it is in heaven." As Joel would say: Dear friends, let that be food for thought. Amen.

Matthew Sleeth, MD
Blessed Earth founder and creation care author

1·22·22

Introduction

This is my coming-out book. Number ten seemed to be a good one for that. My mantra as a Christian libertarian environmentalist capitalist lunatic farmer has always generated some chuckles, and I've never shoved my Christianity down people's throats. I don't wear it on my sleeve, but people whose radars are up perceive that I'm a Christian.

So far, I've been able to bridge the creation worshippers and the Creator worshippers. This book has grown out of the tension between those two camps. I have deep, deep friendships in both camps. Often my liberal creation-worshipping environmental friends ask: "How can you believe what you do and be a Christian?"

By the same token, my Christian friends wonder how I can identify with so many liberal environmental ideas. This book is targeted to the 34 percent of Americans who call themselves evangelicals, the religious right, Christians, or members of the faith community. My biggest concern is that those will not be the ones who read it because "my people" have not been my constituency. But they're moving, and that's exciting to see.

Let me say a word to my non-Christian friends and constituency. I hope you'll indulge this book. My utmost hope is that it presents God's biblical view of things, not human interpretations of God's view. That said, I'm sure I've missed some things and made some mistakes. In no way is this book meant to offend my non-Christian friends. Rather, I hope it gives you an understanding of God's heart in earth stewardship. And if the full impact draws you to an interest in seeking more biblical insight, wonderful. That said, it's hard to write a book for everyone, so I've targeted Christians with this one. But I invite you to listen in on our conversation.

I've purposely used biblical phraseology so that Christians will know I'm not a radical liberal creation-worshipping environmentalist masquerading as a believer. Think of this as a sermon that's been a long time coming. For some, it will be the purest breath of fresh air you've inhaled for a long time. For others, it will challenge the very foundation of your assumptions.

In truth, I've grown weary of apologizing for Christian abuse of God's property. While Christians aren't the only ones abusing God's creation, to be sure, we are the ones who should do it least. Society should have to strain things to accuse us of abusing God's stuff. The sad fact is that by and large Christians deserve the accusations.

The thesis of this book is simple: all of God's creation, the physical world, is an object lesson of spiritual truth. Object lessons for children have been part of spiritual instruction for a long, long time. Jesus' parables were object lessons. The Jewish tabernacle during the wilderness wanderings was an object lesson.

Francis Schaeffer routinely asked: "How shall we then live?" Of all the great Christian apologists, he dared to wrestle with the physical/spiritual connection. While many theologians and academics have written books about earth stewardship, I've always found them lacking when the question "How shall we then live?" gets asked. As a full-time Christian farmer, I wanted to offer an extremely practical apologetic for earth stewardship.

The question, then, is, what does a food and farming system look like that exemplifies spiritual truths? What does a forgiving farm look like, a faith farm? What does a "whosoever will" food system look like? More than just asking if there is a right or wrong way to farm and feed ourselves, I've attempted to explain how God's mind shows itself in real life. If we can't grasp or understand truth in the life we see, how in the world are we supposed to practice it in the life we can't see?

I do not see any conflict between the physical and the spiritual. In fact, I see symbiosis between the two. Each chapter, then, juxtaposes a farm and food system that illustrates biblical truth versus its opposite. I don't purport to have all the answers, but I think we as Christians owe it to our world, our neighbors, our credibility, and especially to God to represent Him well. How we represent Him should not be taken lightly.

My prayer is that God will use this book to stir the hearts of His people to a renewed stewardship mandate. To God be the glory.

Joel Salatin
November 2015

Who Am I?

I have been a stranger in a strange land.

Exodus 2:22

"If you enter a health food store, you've just joined a cult." I could scarcely believe the words. I put the magazine down, hoping my dormitory roommates did not notice the angst etching my face. Could it be true? Was I a cultist?

It was 1978; I was a senior at Bob Jones University in Greenville, South Carolina. The university's professional and slick magazine, *Faith for the Family*, arrived in every dorm room each month—one for each student. The chancellor, Dr. Bob Jr., had written the cover story about the emerging food fad—organic, health food, compost—environmentalism's latest permutation on our culture's landscape.

Not only was I a student, I was also a student leader. Appearing in *Who's Who Among American College Students*, president of my society (BJU's alternative to fraternities), prayer captain (in charge of three dorm rooms), official campus tour guide for visitors. I was no slouch. I was a good foot soldier and considered myself a model of everything the university stood for. Indeed, I embraced the tenets and intended to promote the BJU vision for the rest of my life. I was a member of the religious right before anybody invented the term.

In modern parlance, I had drunk the Kool-Aid. But I had this other part of my life—my family and home. A farm nestled in Virginia's Shenandoah Valley, about six hours north. It wasn't just any farm; it was a non-chemical compost-centric, free-range chicken, homemade raw milk organic-embracing place. In fact, when the first health food store came to our town of Staunton, my parents immediately began buying things there.

Adelle Davis, early maven of heritage-based non-industrial food, was a household name. Her books *Let's Eat Right to Keep Fit* and *Let's Cook It Right* received plenty of attention in our house. Interestingly, she never could break her smoking habit and eventually died of lung cancer. I remember when I was about fifteen years old and my dad tried to eat brewer's yeast. I was leaning over the kitchen counter, wide eyed, watching him try yet another healthy concoction.

Remember, these were early days in the integrity food movement. McDonald's had not yet become a national brand. My dad took a spoonful of straight brewer's yeast and promptly blew it all over the kitchen. Have you ever tried eating flour? It's like trying to swallow sandpaper wood dust. One of his other early trials was flaxseed tea. I assumed my normal position as spectator, protected by the kitchen counter while he stayed in the kitchen on the other side.

He tried to spoon some of the flaxseed tea out of the cooking pot. It was like melted plastic. Every time he'd get some and try to get it to his mouth, it would snap back into the pot. It was like silly goo in a children's toy store. Children like me who grow up on farms have distinctly intimate and memorable experiences with life's greatest wonders, not the least of which is birthing. I blurted to Dad: "It looks like afterbirth."

He and I both started laughing so hard he couldn't continue trying to eat it. Obviously, something had gone wrong in the brewing. It was absolutely inedible. It was pliable but more like a rubber band. I took the pot out to my chickens, known for their ability to eat anything. Used to eating our kitchen scraps, the hens came running when I entered the yard with the pot. I poured it into their slop pan and they peered in sideways—their eyes make it difficult to see straight ahead. They circled the pan, first looking at the concoction with one eye, then tilting their heads the other way to study it with the other eye. Then they walked away.

I couldn't believe it—I went running back into the house to exclaim to Dad the most amazing news of the day: "Even the chickens won't eat it!" I'd never seen the chickens turn their beaks up at anything. The nastiest, most spoiled meat, milk, or whatever went down their throats like homemade ice cream. In my experience, the more mold and weird stuff hanging on food scraps, the more the chickens liked them. But not Dad's flaxseed tea! I don't think he ever tried to make it again. But he did make Tiger's Milk, Adelle Davis's nutritional milk shake concoction. Friends at church called it Panther Puke.

Our house was full of Rodale's *Organic Gardening and Farming* magazines and *The Mother Earth News*. Plowboy interviews in the front of the magazine introduced me to permaculture. Another start-up in those days, *ACRES U.S.A* magazine provided a steady diet of eco-farming information.

My teen years during the early 1970s saw the rise of the hippie movement. Our family enjoyed entertaining hippie friends, some of whom arrived engulfed in an acrid, sweet-smelling perfume that we knew was not from tobacco. We enjoyed and embraced these back-to-earthers, discussing evil corporate American companies, the Vietnam War, compost, natural food, and alternative wellness like acupuncture and chiropractic. These folks formed our support network—yes, you could call it a tribe—in our environmental farming ventures.

All this time, I equally enjoyed my role as leader in the Bible Memory Association (BMA), kind of a precursor of today's AWANA (Approved Workmen Are Not Ashamed) organization, which is also a

Bible memory program. At the time, I did not feel a tension between practical earth stewardship, alternative health, and the Bible. These elements seemed to complement each other.

Our family actually would visit Eco-Village in North Carolina on the way to Bob Jones University. To my mind, both places were equally inspiring. So imagine my chagrin when, as a senior, student leader, and devotee of this beloved university, I suddenly realized that my family and I were branded cultists. I could scarcely finish the article. I was in a fog the rest of the day.

The university prohibited students from attending movie theaters. In fact, if you went to one during holiday or summer breaks, you faced disciplinary action if administrators found out. I had a sinking feeling, like I was a criminal among the righteous. I couldn't confess—that would jeopardize my standing. I suddenly had this deep, dark secret. And it was more than just my problem.

My mother had been the first women's health and physical education professor for Bob Jones College—when it was still in Cleveland, Tennessee. In fact, she was on the faculty during the transition from Tennessee to South Carolina. Our family had deep roots in the school. Had our family betrayed this legacy? As a senior, as supposed leader of several dorm rooms' worth of guys, was I a sham, a wolf in sheep's clothing, because we shopped at the health food store?

At that point, I realized how different I was. It all started to make sense. The health fooders, as a subset of the greater environmental movement, essentially embraced evolution and worshipped creation. You didn't have to read hippie material very long to realize that God had little equity in their ranks. God was the problem, not the solution. Creation? Forget it. It all came from a haphazard big bang.

Christians responded aggressively. These environmentalist hippie whackos were anti-God, anti-Christian, anti-Bible—a cult, in fact. The lines were drawn. Each side despised the other, blaming the other for all sorts of sins. Environmentalists pointed to the Crusades and the conquistadors. Rigidity, hypocrisy, Phariseeism, and judgmentalism—the Bible birthed it all.

Christians pointed to drugs, free love, sex, and saving baby whales while ripping out thinking, hearing, responding human babies in abortion. *Roe v. Wade* burst on the cultural scene and further polarized these camps. Stereotypes form easily, and as the religious right under Jerry Falwell's Moral Majority gained political traction, conservatives generally and Bible-thumpers specifically carried the blame for every environmental disaster. The environmentalists had their enemy—conservatives and the religious right.

In fact, I spoke at the University of Guelph in Ontario several years ago, part of a panel in a town meeting format. The instructions were clear: the three of us had an opening five-minute monologue and then we would entertain questions from the students for two hours. I arrived and sat down in my designated seat next to a professor-looking gentleman who placed a Bible on the table in front of him. I saw it and wondered what it was for—this was unusual.

He was the first to speak, and, holding the Bible aloft, he began a five-minute rant that went something like this: "You students need to understand that every ecological disaster, every polluted river, every smog-filled city, every toxic waste site, is due to this book." He went on and on this way, blaming Jesus, the prophets, Moses, creation thinking—you name it. He left no stone unturned in the vitriolic diatribe. He didn't know that I carry a Bible in my luggage because I love it, not because I loathe it.

I was next. I simply said: "I appreciate this remonstrance, but the blame is not on the Book, the blame is on misinterpretations and misapplications of the Bible." This was simply one of many similar situations. I was speaking at another conference and we sat down at round banquet tables. Normally everyone introduces themselves around as the meal starts and the small talk ensues.

This time we all sat down, and, before introductions could be enjoyed, the guy next to me—another speaker—announced loudly:

"I hate Christians." *Oh, boy, here we go again,* I thought. Turns out he had just returned from six months of filming in Africa and watched local economies displaced by containers of missionary clothes and trinkets. The displaced entrepreneur class became the warlords featured prominently in Western news media—the guys who held up Red Cross trucks with submachine guns, extorting payments in order for the aid truck to proceed. He viewed Christian charity as the cause of warlords and cultural misery.

As my own position as a mouthpiece of environmentally friendly farming and local food grew, I found the tension at every turn. I realized I was living in two very different worlds. My environmentalist friends, largely liberal Democrats, loved my evangelical passion for promoting the pigness of pigs, compost, and food with integrity. But they quickly became embarrassed that I opposed abortion, wanted smaller government, and toted a Bible when I traveled. I loved these tree-hugging cosmic-worshipping, Gaia-promoting, big-government evolutionists. Many were and are closer friends than my Christian friends.

I was equally distanced from my Christian friends, and that was frustrating. When I attended services with these friends, I blanched at potluck dinners where parishioners brought Kentucky Fried Chicken. An elder who was a farmer had Tyson chicken houses. That made for strained conversations. Children's programs featured sugary snacks and genetically modified organism (GMO) crackers. My Christian friends loved conservative talk radio, whose hosts laughed at the notion of animal rights: "Can they write a constitution?" Har, har, har. Rush Limbaugh's perfunctory audio execution of monkeys in the rain forest—that wasn't funny to me. My Bible says that God knows when a sparrow falls, that God feeds the ravens and clothes lilies with a glory greater than Solomon's. Wow!

Then, of course, there are the prayer requests for sickness after sickness after sickness. Go to parishioners' homes and you'll find cartons of high fructose corn syrup drinks, candy bars, industrial food, microwavable breaded chicken nuggets loaded with artificials and un-pronounceables. And drugs. Drugs. Drugs. It dawned on me that the biblical narrow way that leads to truth and the broad way that leads to destruction are not just spiritual: they're all-encompassing.

When the faith community pontificates on spiritual matters, it generally hides behind the Augustinian premise of duality: spiritual is good; physical is evil. But God made a world and proclaimed it good. Indeed, He promised the Israelites a land flowing with milk and honey—that doesn't sound like a place of invisible spirit to me. It sounds like a place you can see, touch, drink, eat, taste, and feel.

Francis Schaeffer asked the question: "How shall we then live?" Memorizing verses and the catechism is fine, but how does it translate into practical living? Does God care if we use Styrofoam or paper plates at the church potluck? Does God care if we stop for Happy Meals on our way to a sanctity-of-life rally?

Those of us on the religious right can't even find words to describe the inconsistency of a save-the-tree crusader who cares little about saving life other places, like in the womb. The birth canal does not make life. I've delivered a lot of calves in my life. When you reach into that cow to assist, you grab for a front leg and if it's alive, the calf will instinctively pull away. Your first emotion when that happens is an exultant: "It's alive!" It's not fetal tissue. It's a responding, thinking, living being that just hasn't passed through the birth canal yet. If it doesn't pull away, you feel the loss, realizing it's dead, and now the deed is just to save the mother. This is not a focus group thing or academic blathering—this is real life.

I cannot for the life of me wrap my head around the thinking that elevates keeping a chain saw away from a tree over keeping a vacuum pump away from an unborn human baby. I don't have words for it. And every red-blooded religious rightist can now say: "Amen!"

Okay, brothers and sisters, are you ready for the other side? When we stop off for Happy Meals on our way to a sanctity-of-life rally, the other side sees us as equally inconsistent. Why? Because Happy Meals represent everything Christians should oppose. From encouraging families to not eat together to factory farming to pollution to government subsidies to money being more important than anything else—it's an icon of anti-Christian thought and practice. How could you stop there? Now, how many of you Christians can say, "Amen!"?

I had an epiphany several years ago when I was asked to speak at UC Berkeley, hotbed of liberalism and fount of godlessness. I had a standing-room-only crowd of graduate students and did what I call my stem-winder presentation—pictures of our farm and how we produce things in an environmentally enhancing way. I didn't back down from my libertarian Christian beliefs, and even told the students I was a six-day creationist and sanctity-of-lifer. When I finished, the students erupted in a standing ovation.

The host professors and I went out for ice cream after the talk. As soon as we were outside the auditorium, they stopped me in front of a streetlamp and almost breathlessly said they had a confession to make. My mind spinning, I wondered what this was all about. I mean, there are confessions and then there are confessions.

What they confessed was that they were scared to death for me and they were elated that it had gone so well. You see, they explained, Berkeley developed a hissing technique during the Vietnam era to show their displeasure to speakers who said something unacceptable. Forget common courtesy; this is the apex of American political evolution, remember. Goodness, I love those guys. Anyway, these professors said they had never in their many years on faculty heard a speaker use the word *God* reverently without getting hissed.

Or course, if you used it in a cursing way, or damning way, that was fine and acceptable. I had used *God* several times, completely reverently and completely within the religious right context, and not only had the students not hissed, they had responded with a standing ovation. The professors admitted great relief and it seemed funny, after the fact, that they were distressfully tense and concerned before the event.

I've thought a lot about that incident over the years, and I've come to the conclusion that I may have been the first religious right person these students had ever heard who extended biblical beliefs to physical creation care. That talk-walk consistency resonated positively with the students and they were willing to respect or appreciate that I was a fuddy-duddy otherwise.

I think the faith community has squandered its moral high road. Back in the early 1980s I attended a sustainable agriculture conference with an Amish friend. As we walked out to retrieve our lunch, another attendee passed us on the sidewalk. He had dreadlocks, a hubcap-size peace symbol pendant dangling from his neck, earrings, and a burlap blouse, and he was wearing sandals without socks even though it was a cold day. Two buttons adorned his smock: "Co-exist" and "My Karma just ran over your Dogma." My Amish friend glanced at me and whispered wryly: "Why are they the ones who appreciate that creation is fearfully and wonderfully made?" Indeed.

I am at home both places, but not at home either place. My Christian friends embarrass me with their cavalier attitude toward resource use, toxicity, pollution, animal care, and stewardship. They hold Monsanto's GMOs up as a perfect example of dominion and human innovation, an expression of cerebral technological prowess. The assumption is that anything we're capable of doing comes under the blessing of taking dominion over the earth and subduing it.

In the movie *Jurassic Park*, you may remember the euphoric scientist exulting over his accomplishment while his resurrected dinosaurs wreaked mayhem on civilization—eating people, cars, and so on. The journalist dared to ask the scientist: "But sir, just because we can, should we?" That is a pregnant question and worthy of our attention every day. As a Greco-Roman Western reductionist compartmentalized fragmented disconnected democratized individualized systematized parts-oriented culture, we've become great at figuring out the how of things, but not the why.

It's the why that creates an ethical framework around the how. Otherwise, we're inventive and sharp enough with our big brains

and opposing thumbs to innovate things we can't spiritually, emotionally, physically, or mentally metabolize. Suddenly we find ourselves devoting most of our innovative capacity to solving problems
we created with our amoral innovation.

Why is it that in all the things pastors and evangelists decry,
from alcoholism to abortion, they cannot find room to decry junk
food, pharmaceutical dependency, and plastic islands floating in
the ocean? Any mention of the seven hundred dead zones in and
around the United States? Any mention of concentrated animal
feeding operations that destroy neighborhoods with their stench and
water pollution? No way; the religious right sends our kids to the
best colleges so they can land high-paying jobs at big companies that
pillage the earth. Oh, I mean that practice dominion. Yeah, right.

I'm fascinated by the notion that most Christians happily patronize cheap food that destroys creation in its production, impoverishes
third world countries, and supports oligarchical interests, all in order
to have more money to put in the offering plate for missionaries.
Does that make God happy? Endorse the broad way in every facet
of life in order to wiggle through the narrow way in one small part.

Enter the homeschooling movement. As the new millennium
turned and alternative schooling gained momentum, I saw the glim-
mer of a shift. In the 1990s more than half the visitors to our farm
were of the creation-worshipping variety. But after 2000, that ratio
flipped the other way. Suddenly thousands of families—conservative
libertarian Christians—began talking about food quality, land stewardship, and farm righteousness.

Certainly the Y2K phenomenon fueled this conservative back-to-
the-land movement, but I believe the fuel for the whole shift came
from homeschooling. This grassroots educational innovation occurred
as a result of parents' disenchantment with government institutional
education. They didn't like the curriculum, the violence, the philoso-
phy, the institutionalization, the temptations, or the reduced academic
standards replaced by condom-toting teachers and values adjustment
exercises.

By the thousands, families like ours said "Enough!" and opted out of the government schools. The exodus was huge and continues today. Some started homeschooling. Others went to parochial schools. Many used correspondence. Whatever the alternative, for the most part these parents found it refreshing and deeply satisfying. When a person takes an alternative path and finds it satisfying, that happiness stimulates alternative thinking in other areas of life.

By 2010, a groundswell of homeschoolers had added a kitchen grain mill, milk cow, and farmette to their opt-out lexicon. The conversation went like this: "Now that I've opted out of education's wide gate, found the narrow gate of alternative learning and found it satisfying, what other narrow gate can I find? Where else can I opt out?" Along came Christian health insurance, home business entrepreneurship seminars, and appointments with chiropractors—imagine that. What parents had called quacks these opt-out homeschoolers embraced as truth dispensers.

Moms began reading about nutrition and started seeking raw milk. They planted gardens and kept honeybees. Go to any homeschooling convention today and you'll be amazed at the self-employment homesteading alternative therapy presence. It's huge. Some of these outfits even began asking me to come and speak at their conferences. Me, an environmentalist beyond organic weirdo.

Indeed, the first time I formally articulated the basic themes of this book was at Patrick Henry College, the brainchild of Michael Farris, founder of the Home School Legal Defense Association. How fitting that my first public apologetic for these concepts came at the official American homeschool college. As wonderful as that was, however, I noted that the college did not spend any time talking about food or farming. Those were non-issues compared to making sure American military muscle stayed well financed and Monsanto stayed free to spew GMOs around the landscape. This was not a slight oversight; it was a purposeful and necessary disregard because to wrestle with earth stewardship was to question the axiom: folks who hug trees are anti-God.

During the 1980s Focus on the Family did a multiday series on the plight of the American farmer. My dad was still alive and we listened to the heart-wrenching stories of these Christian farmers who went bankrupt. James Dobson empathized and cried foul with them. Lending institutions, market boards, machinery dealers, chemical companies—oh, the wailing and gnashing of teeth that erupted from the studio over the predations of these uncaring and manipulative entities. Farmers were victims of an insidious agenda beyond their control.

Dad wrote a kind letter to James Dobson describing how our farm avoided dependency on these entities. He explained that we made our own compost for fertilizer, direct marketed our products to local customers, grazed our cattle on perennials, and built ponds for dependable water. We were making good money and doing fine, thank you very much, because we had gone through a narrow gate instead of a wide one. We never even got a reply.

For the record, I deeply appreciate Focus on the Family, Patrick Henry College, Bob Jones University, and anyone else I've singled out in this personal saga of who I am. I use these real-life situations not to disparage, but to illustrate the depth of the neglect. The fact is that the religious right has neglected earth stewardship and given it over to creation worshippers instead of owning it as Creator worshippers.

What would make Satan happier than to paint environmental care and alternative health as his domain so that Christians would not adopt healing and stewardship practices? So that Christians could be branded as earth rapists and pillagers, and lose all their credibility? Making the Christian community impotent in argument and hypocritical in lifestyle blunted God's message. What a great victory. In our self-righteousness, Christians could make jokes about animal rights, organic farmers, and fruit and nut eaters, all while holding our Bibles in one hand and gobbling Hot Pockets with the other.

Lest anyone think I believe Christians are the most destructive people on the planet, let me quickly say that the story of civilization, unfortunately, is generally one of destruction. All kinds of religions and all kinds of people have made a mess of their surroundings; Christians certainly don't have a corner on that. But I'm concentrating on Christians in this book because that's the group I want to challenge and encourage. If it sounds like I'm only picking on Christians while giving Muslims or Shintos or Hindus or Druids a pass, a book on everyone's sins would be too big to print. Today, I'm dealing with my people. I'll let those others deal with the sins of their people.

The bottom line for me, and theme of this book, is that creation is an object lesson of spiritual truth. Just like object lessons for children point them to biblical principles, so the physical universe is supposed to point us to God. "THE HEAVENS DECLARE THE GLORY OF GOD," the psalmist says in Psalm 19:1 (NIV). Indeed. If that is the case, then what does a forgiving farm look like, a beautiful farm, an ordered farm, a neighbor-friendly farm? And not just a farm, but an entire foodscape.

Is a foodscape that hurts people godly? Is a farming system that destroys soil and makes it more fragile forgiving? Shouldn't our food and farming models be more resilient, creating healing and abundance rather than sickness and scarcity? Those are the issues we'll be looking at in the rest of this book, and I hope at the end you'll agree with me that John 3:21 is one of the hardest admonitions in Scripture: "BUT HE WHO DOES THE TRUTH COMES TO THE LIGHT" (NKJV).

I don't know about you, but I'd much rather talk about truth than do it. I'd rather catechize it. I'd rather make it the subject of a Sunday school class or focus group. I'd rather preach about it. I'd rather write books about it. I'd rather do a word study, research the etymology, and systemize it. I'd rather have any relationship with truth than to do it. Please, no, that's too hard. Doing truth makes it visible, practical. Doing truth is what truth looks like—it's physical. Oh, so truth is something you can see? Yes. Clearly, God is interested in the physical manifestation of things, not just cerebral concepts.

So what does food and farming as an object lesson of spiritual truth, that viscerally shows the world what Christians believe, actually look like? That's what this book is all about.

In 2009, with all this background, imagine my utter amazement at receiving "Alumnus of the Year" from my alma mater, BJU. I was beyond humbled and honored to receive it. Certainly I've been privileged to speak and carry a God-centric persona into places perhaps no other graduate has penetrated—because of the bridges I've built around food and farm integrity. But I did have to chuckle at the notion that a cultist had received such a coveted honor.

To be sure, in all my work I've tried to remain true to the biblical principles of this great school. BJU had much to do with shaping who I am, and I'll be forever grateful for the opportunity to have graduated from there. Great people, great education, great debate program (Dad always said I majored in debate and minored in everything else). But like all of us and our institutions, it had some blind spots. I hope that all of us can embrace the challenges of the following pages, like the words of a friend encouraging us to think and do better. We can all use that.

When I was younger, after I did something good, my dad used to say: "That's good; now let's see some more." In other words, don't assume you've arrived at perfection just because you've done a good job. Stay with it and continue refining. As the apostle Paul admonished: "Press on." Let's do that, shall we?

/-22-22

Biological vs. Mechanical

The glory of all lands...

Ezekiel 20:6

Is life fundamentally biological or mechanical?

Intuitively, we understand that life is biological, and yet Western thought tilts decidedly toward the mechanical. The fundamental difference between the two is that living things have feelings and the capacity to communicate, heal, and forgive.

One of my dad's most common sayings was: "Remember, machines don't forgive." What he meant was that machines have no remorse. If a chain saw cuts off your leg, it has no feelings, no sorrow. I've had several accidents with machines and tools, and I guarantee you not a single one is sorry that it hurt me.

If you go on a trip and suddenly a terrible thumping sound comes from your front right wheel bearing, you can stop the car, get out, and beg forgiveness for not lubricating it properly. You can weep: "I'm so sorry I didn't grease you soon enough. Oh, I'm so sorry. Do you need a rest? I'll let you rest." You can let that wheel bearing sit for five years to rest and recuperate, but when you get back in to start down the road, guess what it will do? You got it—thump, thump, thump.

Fortunately, living things can heal and forgive. We can all be grateful for that. You can say an unfit word to your spouse and then apologize and things can be as good as they were before.

Not so machines. They have no feelings, no emotions, no remorse, and cannot offer forgiveness after abuse or misuse. They are inanimate. And material is similar. Clay, plastic, metal, wood—we can fashion it into whatever shape we want to without disrespecting its clayness, plasticness, metalness, or woodness. How many times have you seen a potter smash down a bowl and start over? We don't cry over the poorly formed first attempt. It's inert substance. It has no life, no specialness, except in how we form it.

Contrast that with a pig. I can't make a pig. I can't sculpt a pig out of wood or clay and give it life. The miracle of birth is still very much a miracle. Breeding is a miracle. Starting from that fertilized egg, a pig begins to develop. From the chromosomes to the mitochondria, the cells multiply and that little pig grows. It never looks like an alligator or a tomato. It stays distinctively pig.

In fact, with pigs, several piggies grow simultaneously—even a dozen—inside the sow. As a farmer, I've seen lots of things birthed: calves, lambs, pigs, chicks. A reverent hush always settles over a birthing, a sacredness that almost begs worshipping something bigger, grander than anything we can see: God perhaps?

One of my favorite joys is stepping across the electric fence to commiserate with a group of our pastured pigs. We control them in their pastures with electric fence. My special treat is to sit down, preferably on an old stump, get real quiet and still, then just wait. Sure enough, those pigs eventually ease over to check me out. They snoodle up and down my pants, pushing their wet noses into the creases. Others nip at my shoelaces and chew at the soles of my shoes. Some come up behind me and begin nipping at my pockets or the multi-tool I carry in a leather case attached to my belt.

The friendliest and most docile sidle up alongside and place a chin on my knee, waiting for a rub. Pigs universally like to be rubbed and scratched just above their tails. They straighten out their tails in response and lean into me, like a cat that's being petted. If I begin scratching a pig's belly, he'll often flop down right there on his side, making the exercise even easier. The point here is that the pigs and I can respond to each other.

When you wash and wax your car, does it ease over next to you to demonstrate its happiness and appreciation of your attention? Does the steering wheel turn sideways and rest on your lap when you turn it gently? Animals are not machines. They have distinctive personalities. Even in an eight-pig litter, some will be aggressive and others timid. Some will be a little on the wild side and others will be docile. Some will be more curious and others will hold back when confronted with something new.

But the cars that come off an assembly line show no differences that way. Yes, I know, someone might get a lemon, but that's not a factor of the car's personality. Cars don't have personality. Plants have personality. Ever sit under a magnificent tree? I've cut a lot of trees in my life, but I always have this little gnawing inside about taking a life. Grasping the responsibility that I'm taking a life so that other trees will live better, or so that the world functions better, helps me make a wise decision about which ones to cut (kill) and which ones to keep.

Life has specialness that nonliving things don't. We all can appreciate that living things occupy a special place. But God even ascribes specialness to nonliving things. Let's look at the word *glory* as it pertains to specialness, whether the thing is living or nonliving. What does the word *glory* mean? When we say "the glory of God," what does that mean? Moses wanted to see God's glory. When God's glory departed from Israel, what did that mean? We don't use the word *glory* much today. It's a spiritualized word reserved for church services and theological discussions. The *Westminster Shorter Catechism* is clear: "Man's chief end is to glorify God."

In 1 Corinthians 15:39–41, the apostle Paul writes: "ALL FLESH

IS NOT THE SAME FLESH: BUT THERE IS ONE KIND OF FLESH OF MEN, ANOTHER FLESH OF BEASTS, ANOTHER OF FISHES, AND ANOTHER OF BIRDS. THERE ARE ALSO CELESTIAL BODIES, AND BODIES TERRESTRIAL: BUT THE GLORY OF THE CELESTIAL IS ONE, AND THE GLORY OF THE TERRESTRIAL IS ANOTHER. THERE IS ONE GLORY OF THE SUN, AND ANOTHER GLORY OF THE MOON, AND ANOTHER GLORY OF THE STARS: FOR ONE STAR DIFFERETH FROM ANOTHER STAR IN GLORY." What do we mean when we speak of the glory of all these things?

Isaiah 10:18 speaks of the "GLORY OF HIS FOREST," and we know Solomon "IN ALL HIS GLORY" was not arrayed as beautifully as a lily (Matthew 6:29). Proverbs 17:6 says, "GRANDCHILDREN ARE THE CROWN OF THE AGED, AND THE GLORY OF CHILDREN IS THEIR FATHERS" (ESV). How about Proverbs 20:29: "THE GLORY OF YOUNG MEN IS THEIR STRENGTH"? Even whole cultures have a glory according to Isaiah 35:2, which mentions "THE GLORY OF LEBANON." A concordance listing for "glory" is huge—it's used many different ways and for many different things. What does it mean?

It means the distinctiveness of something, the specificity and uniqueness. That's the common thread throughout all of these uses. *Webster's* defines it as "honor," which is okay as far as it goes, but clearly in all these uses far more than honor is involved. We could certainly agree that honoring something requires appreciating its distinctiveness, its specialness. And so the glory of God is His uniqueness, just like the glory of the pig is its uniqueness. The glory of the stars, the forest, old men, and entire countries is wrapped up in distinctiveness.

Think about God's attributes, codified succinctly in *Unger's Bible Dictionary*:

Spirituality (God is Spirit)
Infinity
Eternity
Immutability

Self-sufficiency
Perfection
Freedom
Omnipotence
Omnipresence
Omniscience
Justice
Truth
Love
Mercy
Grace

I'm surprised the list did not include holiness, but anyway, can we agree that this list is absolutely divine? That no human, no animal, no plant, no angel, no rock, stone, or flower possesses these attributes perfectly? They are unreservedly and distinctly divine. Only God can be described with this list.

That means if the chief end of man is to show forth God's glory, then our lives should honor God in these respects. But notice how many times the Scripture uses the word *glory* for things other than God, showing a deep respect and honor for the uniqueness of all created beings—and things. The point is that the sum and substance of our lives should point toward the Godness of God. And He wants us to understand that how we extend that respect and honor to His creation indicates our level of honoring His specialness.

Who would want to serve a God who is like anything else? That wouldn't be a transcendent deity; it would simply be another something. Glory speaks to uniqueness; what makes God God, you you, and me me. And a pig a pig. With respect to glory, biblically speaking, God's glory inherently is no more special than a forest, a pig, or a civilization. Respecting the glory of each encourages a respect for the glory of all. We could call this whole idea: Glory Consistency.

If we can't appreciate the pigness of the pig, we can't appreciate the Godness of God. Yet, in modern America, no credible scientist would conceive of such a silly notion. Indeed, our research and farming practices are predicated on growing everything faster, fatter, bigger, cheaper, without regard to respecting and honoring distinctiveness. We grab that dominion mandate and run like a bunch of swashbuckling conquistadors right into the sacred domain of life, whacking and flailing, altering, snipping, and inserting as if all of life is some sort of inanimate protoplasmic structure to be manipulated however cleverly hubris can imagine to manipulate it.

As if pigs are no more special than extruded plastic dolls or polyethylene pipe fittings. I would suggest that a culture that views its pigs as just mechanical objects to be reprogrammed and manipulated will view its citizens the same way, and ultimately God the same way. A deity to be manipulated and formed into something of our liking. God becomes either nonexistent or a doting grandpa dispensing goodies to whoever has the most clever sales pitch. Or worse, a fairy that can poof anything into anything in the blink of an eye.

Education always involves learning the rudimentary things first. You don't learn about suffixes and prefixes until you learn the ABC's. You don't learn about logarithms until you learn that two plus two equals four. You don't study rocket propulsion until you learn the simple principle: "For every action, there is an equal but opposite reaction." I would suggest that learning what it means to bring God glory is far more advanced than what it means to bring pigs glory. Honoring the pigness of pigs is far more elementary than honoring the Godness of God.

The same principle applies person-to-person. If we are going to create an ethical framework on which we honor the glory of Tom and the glory of Mary—realizing that this is the object lesson for the glory of God—it starts with honoring the pigness of pigs. I've read bulletins that current research is under way in our land-grant universities to isolate the stress gene in pigs so that we can abuse them even more aggressively in our concentrated animal feeding operations (CAFOs), but they won't care anymore.

In CAFOs, farmers cut off the pigs' tails—called docking—to

intentionally make them sore and tender. Pigs are active and enjoy being busy. When pigs in such confined quarters can't act out their pigness like rooting in the soil, romping, looking for bugs and cavorting, they become bored and stressed. When bored, these pigs gnaw and bite each other, especially tails. Being sore and tender, the pain is more intense and the assaulted pigs quickly move away rather than tolerating the aggressive biting long enough to open a bloody wound. If the tails were not sore and tender from being cut off, the pain of being bitten would not be intense enough to make the attacked pig move away from the aggressor. Once blood flows, the other pigs—remember, they're omnivores—will see that wounded pig as lunch and consume him. I'm not making this up.

By what sort of ethical or moral stretch can anyone make a case for docking tails in order to keep pigs alive in such anti-pig production arrangements? Gentle people, it is how we protect the least of these—pigs in this case—that creates an ethical framework around how we protect the greatest of these—people and then God's reputation. Our children can't see God, but they can see pigs.

Our friends can't see God. But they can see pigs. When we honor the pigness of pigs, we create a philosophical imperative that we can see. Suddenly the spiritual mandate to bring glory to God has an object, something physical in which to participate. Pigs munching on acorns, chowing down on grass, digging up roots, and gamboling around a silva-pasture (tree-dotted grassland) do things that not another living being on the face of the earth can do. None. If we deny the pig that chance, and put it on a slatted floor in a cage in a confinement house, it can't act out its uniqueness. That keeps us from being able to enjoy the pig's special qualities.

The obvious question, then, is: How do we honor the pigness of pigs? How do we create a farm and food system that respects the pig's glory? What are the distinctives, the special attributes of the pig? What is the essence of the pig? First of all, it's an animal. Animals, as opposed to plants, are supposed to move around. Have you ever heard of a stationary animal?

Yet the modern swine industry, with gestation crates and CAFOs, operates under the supposition that animals don't need to move around. They assume that it's utterly respectful to confine sows in crates so that the pigs cannot even turn around—ever. How about laying hens in industrial houses? Imagine a twenty-two-inch by sixteen-inch cage with seven laying hens in it—less space per bird than a sheet of copy paper. The birds cannot stretch their wings and have to take turns moving around because not enough space exists for all of them to move at the same time.

In order to crowd these birds in such confined conditions and keep them alive, farmers cut off their beaks to blunt what would otherwise be too sharp for such confined conditions. Does this sound like something that honors the chickenness of the chicken? By the way, you should see the spell-check lines under all these words like *pigness, chickenness,* and more on the way. My computer screen is lit up with red underlines, but I'll leave them because they convey the strength of meaning better than anything else. Thankfully, the English language is malleable.

Chickens are birds and as such need room to flit, perch, spread their wings, strut, and stretch their necks and legs. This is just common courtesy. Now, back to pigs.

Second, pigs have a wonderful plow on the end of their noses. In this, they are truly distinctive. This means the glory of the pig is in its ability to move things around, to till things, and disturb soil. On our farm, we use pigs to build compost. When we feed hay to the cows in the winter, we bed the cows with wood chips, straw, peanut hulls, or any other kind of carbon we can find, creating a carbonaceous diaper to absorb the fifty pounds of nutrients dropping from the cow's back end every day.

We add corn to this deepening diaper and elevate the hay feed boxes to keep things level as the diaper rises. The cows tromp the oxygen out of the bedding, making it anaerobic. The diaper, or bedding, ferments. When the cows go back out to graze fresh grass in the spring, we put pigs in those vacated hay feeding areas and the pigs seek out the fermented corn imbedded in the carbonaceous diaper. As the pigs till through the bedding, it is aerated, converting it from anaerobic material to aerobic compost. We call these pigs pigaerators because they aerate the bedding and rotovate it.

Not only does this make economic sense because we're letting appreciating animals do the work rather than depreciating machinery, but it also fully honors the pigness of the pig. We're not asking the pigs to do something they don't want to do. They're in hog heaven. Nothing suits them more than to rip and tear into this bedding and eat the fermented morsels buried there.

At this point, the pigs are not just tenderloin and ribs; they are co-laborers in our land-healing ministry. They are team players. Suddenly our spiritual resonance, respect, and appreciation for the glory of pigs completely change our relationship. They are no longer protein stuff, but primarily fellow workers, sharing common vision and visceral participation in the needs of the farm. They are part of an intricate choreography that pulls its dance moves from millennia of porcine glory. This is the fabric of pork legend from time immemorial.

Now, lest you think I'm putting pigs on too high a pedestal, it is sobering to realize that if I climbed into that pigaerating work site and fell asleep, they would just as happily consume me as that fermented corn. In fact, when children come to the farm to visit and invariably want to pet the pigs, I'm always happy to oblige with permission, but I give a warning: "Keep moving. These guys are omnivores, remember. They start with your toes, then your fingers, and within a couple of hours they'll be onto your liver and pancreas. So keep moving."

It's a lighthearted way to remind us all that these are animals. They don't sign treaties. We don't have an armistice agreement with them. They're pretty simpleminded: if it tastes good, eat it. And human flesh is as good as cow poop and fermented corn. Yum.

Now imagine the life of a pig in a CAFO. Crammed in there with literally thousands of other pigs, no sunlight, no fresh air—the floor is slats over a slurry manure pit, which vaporizes ammonia into the air to mix with the fecal particulate for breathing air—in small cubicles without any work to do. Would you go mad, too? Absolutely. And yet Christians routinely grow pigs this way and even send our children to good colleges so they can land high-paying jobs with agribusiness corporations to promote, design, and research more anti-pig models.

Rather than displaying our kids' graduate degrees in these bastions of anti-pigness, we should be repenting in sackcloth and ashes.

On our farm, when the pigs are finished with the compost, and during most of the season, we put them out in pig pastures and acorn finishing glens in the woods. Using electric fence to control them, we move them from paddock to paddock every few days so they enjoy fresh ground and plenty of salad in their diet. Pigs like a varied diet: they are omnivores, remember. They like bugs and worms as much as chickens—that has a double meaning, by the way. Still don't get it?

Okay: The first meaning is that chickens like bugs, too. The second is that pigs like chickens—as in munch, munch. Tasty drumsticks. Sooooo, pigs like bugs and worms as much as chickens. Whew!

In these outdoor rotated paddocks, we provide them with all the feed they want, clean water out of a special drinker they can't soil, and shelter either in trees or with portable nursery shade cloth contraptions. They can tear up roots, eat different kinds of plants, eat Japanese beetles or any other kind of protein they can find. Perhaps one of the most profound statements ever uttered to me came from the mouth of a chef. He wanted to see the farm so I took him on a quick tour, and when we got to the pigs, he confessed he'd never been with live pigs. Ever. After enjoying their antics and natural behavior for a few mesmerizing minutes, he said simply: "If I were a pig, this is how I'd want to live."

Folks, that is exactly the point. Because our farm puts that kind of attention on maintaining the sanctity and dignity of the pig—the glory of the pig—we have a credible launchpad to a bigger discussion about defending the glory of God. Putting the pig in this position does not make God smaller; it makes God bigger and more awesome. This is not theologically demeaning; it's theologically affirming. Do you see how the two ideas complement each other? Because we care about the pigness of pigs, we care about the Godness of God. What does that look like? Suddenly, a whole new discussion occurs.

To the greater Christian community, however, a phrase like *pigness of pigs* conjures up notions of animal worship and environmental flakes. It's the kind of statement you'd expect from vegans and animal rights whackos. But I would argue that our view toward the animals is a direct manifestation of our view toward each other and to God.

The Scripture is full of animal rights, conservative pundits and talk radio notwithstanding. From "THOU SHALT NOT MUZZLE THE OX WHEN HE TREADETH OUT THE CORN" (Deuteronomy 25:4) to "THOU SHALT NOT PLOW WITH AN OX AND AN ASS TOGETHER" (Deuteronomy 22:10), the Bible is full of animal rights. Jesus clearly said it was okay to relieve a distressed animal on the Sabbath, even though the Sabbath was a day of rest. Indeed, Adam's directive to name the animals shows that God was not interested in just a bunch of "its." God feeds the ravens—an especially nasty bird—and knows even when a sparrow falls.

Animals are viewed throughout the Pentateuch as an extension of personhood. My paraphrase of Exodus 21:28 and following says that if an animal you own hurts someone, you're not guilty *unless* the animal has a reputation for aggression. If it has that reputation and you have not dealt with it, the animal is an extension of your body—you are as responsible for the violence as if you had committed it with your own body. Wow. That's significant.

The point is that God neither looks kindly on abusive treatment of animals nor on viewing animals as machines and tools. They occupy an amazing space, subject to humans, dependent on human care and mercy, yet exhibiting their own distinctiveness and glory. It's a unique position, one that it would behoove us to wrestle with until we arrive at a place that ultimately pleases God.

So here's a question: If we assume there is a right way and a wrong way to care for or produce domestic livestock, what might a list that articulates the two look like? I would suggest that anything that honors and respects the animal is right, and anything that equates the animal with machines and tools is wrong. When you enter a factory farm situation—a Tyson chicken house, Smithfield hog factory, Iowa Beef Packers feedlot—does what you're seeing strike you as bringing glory to that animal? Or does it seem more like a machine? Later in this book we'll deal with the naysayers: protection, feeding the world, disease, efficiency. Right now I'm zeroing in on the life vs. nonlife issue. We'll get to the other things later.

A helpful question may be this: If I were an animal, would I want to live like this? I can feel the pushback from my friends who see such a question as anti-human because it sounds anti-dominion. Remember, I slaughter lots of animals. This is not about turning animals into people. But it bears asking: Is this environment, if I were this animal, the kind of habitat I'd like? Is it the way I'd want to be treated? I think that can go a long way toward discovering the answer.

Perhaps a big issue we need to deal with at this point is the pushback that if life is so special, what gives us the right to kill and eat? How does killing the pig honor its glory? How is the pigness of the pig reverenced when we enjoy bacon for breakfast? That's certainly a valid question. First, let's look at this biblically. Nowhere does the Bible even hint that eating animals is wrong. The patriarchs ate animals. The prophets ate animals. The kings and peasants all ate animals. The feasts included animals. Jesus ate animals. The disciples and apostles ate animals.

How does killing and eating animals add strength to their glory? Because life requires death. While it's true that killing a carrot, in the big scheme of things, is no different from killing a chicken, when the blood flows and the eyes go dim, it's far more graphic and real. The typology

of sacrifice preceding life occurs throughout the Old Testament and cul-
minates, of course, in the ultimate sacrifice of God's Son as the perfect
lamb to take away the sins of the world.

Every time we kill something, whether seed embryo (wheat), vegetable, or animal, in order to live, it should remind us not only of the
sacrificial death of Jesus that enables us to partake of eternal life, but
also how precious life is. Life is so precious that it requires death.
The goal of radical animal rightists working through research scientists to grow nonliving meatlike substances from human feces or
primal slime in petri dishes is a denial of this foundational principle
that life requires death.

Jesus uses the principle of a seed being planted, and dying, before
sending forth the new shoot. Unless it dies, the new shoot can't
come forth. Everything, everything, everything requires death in
order to create life. And lest anyone think I'm skipping the Edenic
period where nothing died, we're not in Eden anymore, Toto. We
don't have perfect bodies; we live in a fallen world in which bringing
glory to God includes appreciating the cost of life in Him. It is precious enough to require death. Eating reminds us of that with every
chomp of our jaws.

Our sustenance is completely and utterly dependent on taking
life, be it plant or animal. That alone should drive us to appreciate
the sanctity and precious value of life. That means we don't hurt
people and things unnecessarily. We're all one step away from our
last breath. Every breath is a gift, borrowed, or snatched, from the
hands of death.

That's the biblical part. Now let's go to the ecological part. Everything is eating and being eaten. If you don't believe it, go lie naked
in your flower bed for three days and see what gets eaten. Watch any
nature documentary and you'll be struck by all the consumption
and death going on. From microbes including bacteria and nematodes to viruses, amoebas, and elephants—all of life is eating, biting,
chewing.

Unfortunately, our techno-sophisticated culture's love affair with

Disney has Thumpered and Bambied us to the point that most people feel completely segregated from this visceral death reality. Our skins die. Our blood cells die. Microbes live in our bedsheets, chomping dead skin. Does this make you shiver? I think it's hilarious.

All that being said, I would suggest that what makes the sacrifice of any being sacred is how it was honored in life. To take that one step further, I would even suggest that only when we've honored the life do we have the right to make the sacrifice. In other words, someone who has abused the life, disrespected the life, looked at it as just inanimate stuff, does not deserve to kill and eat. The right to participate in that sacred act must be earned.

Think about the worship surrounding biblical sacrifices. Every one entailed a hush, a God-centric demeanor. Sacrifices were not a place to exalt the dominion of man, but a place to humbly appreciate the cost of life. And of course altar sacrifices show the cost of forgiveness, which is the door into eternal life.

Viewing life as mechanical, like industrial farming does, cheapens it, which in turn cheapens the death. Is it any wonder that our culture is wrestling with increased violence among humans when we cheapen life through CAFOs and a cheap food policy, which is actually a cheap life policy? Food is life; food must live in order to die.

Families who spend extra on high-quality food, who emphasize sacrificial value in food, create a beautiful platform for explaining the cost of salvation. If our food goal is the cheapest stuff available, what does that say about the cost of physical life? By extension, what does it say about the cost of eternal life? Please don't construe my meaning beyond its intent. I'm not suggesting that we be careless about shopping and comparing prices. But price is definitely not the number one criterion: glory—does this food honor life's distinctiveness?—is the number one criterion. After that's been met, then be frugal.

Living food should rot. Mechanical things don't rot. Have you noticed the shelf life of Velveeta cheese? You can squirt a dab on a table and it will sit there for a year. It doesn't grow mold. It doesn't get dry. It doesn't do anything. It just sits there, inert, like protoplasmic sludge. It's not alive. Only life can die and give you life.

We're the first culture in the world that routinely eats things that have never lived. In spiritual parlance, we're ingesting things that are an abomination to our bodies—and then requesting prayer for the ailments that result. God set up life and death, living food and its decomposition and digestion, as visceral object lessons, daily, of our dependence on Him. Ecology does not give us the liberty to deny its principles and neither does God.

Attend any meat conference sponsored by the USDA and their industrial fraternity partners and you won't hear about butchering, you'll hear about "protein fabrication." Even the language is trying to sanitize the reality that something had to die in order for us to eat. What a disingenuous term, that cutting muscle and sinew is simply protein fabrication, rather than what it really is, which is participating in the most fundamental rule of life: death.

I've watched animal rights– and animal welfare–type videos in which people—even pastors—use the term *convenient violence* to describe eating animals. I suppose Jesus used convenient violence when He prepared the Passover and cooked the fish on the beach fire? The problem is that these folks elevate animals above other beings, and that's incorrect. All life is sacred. And all life requires sacrifice.

That is why when we sacrifice ourselves for each other in servant-hood, putting each other above ourselves, we become more fully alive as humans. What a great way to explain the importance of Christian servanthood to children. Want to really live? Then be a servant and take out the trash for Mom and Dad. Help with the yard work. Carry in your little sister's art project for her. That's how we show we're living, and not machines.

I heard one radical animal rightist lament that the fish on his plate didn't look much like it was expressing its fishness. He has it all wrong. The assumption is that the fish ceased expressing its fishness when it died. Nothing could be further from the truth—when it became food for something else, whether human or predators, it gave the ultimate gift, the gift of life, to another being. I can imagine that some of you Christians are now thinking that I'm heading off into la-la land, but I'm trying to create the balance here.

Think about the care and domestic husbandry required to produce a lamb for an Israelite sacrificial altar. Many think the shepherds on Bethlehem's hills who first received the angelic announcement of the Messiah's birth were caring for special temple sacrificial lambs. Maybe so. Remember, those lambs had to be without spot or blemish. That means they had to be protected from brambles, happy enough not to fight with each other, and healthy and of excellent genetic stock, which takes many generations to perfect. That's a lot of investment on the farmers' part.

Many radical animal welfarists view farm animals as oppressed, as if farmers who choose to be responsible for them are not oppressed in taking on this responsibility. It's a two-way street of mutual interdependence. Farmers are caretakers. Pure capitalists need not apply. The problem is that modern American CAFOs are where amoral science and pure capitalism take you, and it's far away from nurturing and caretaking.

Sometimes animal sanctuary crusaders and vegans present a self-righteous spirit that they live a life with less violence since they don't eat animals. How much violence to the ecology is necessary to keep animals alive artificially, unable to perform their function of perpetuating life? These capriciously salvaged animals deprive humans of food and take precious human effort—and food—to maintain a totally superficial facade.

If we turn livestock areas and pastures into wild lands, deer and rabbits will proliferate, to be eaten by foxes, coyotes, and wolves. As much as we may want to wash our hands of death's reality, we can't escape it. God beckons us to participate to maintain our own common sense, our own balanced emotions and reality about how the environment really functions. It's an eating and being-eaten world, no matter how we wish it weren't. Living things eat living things.

Tractors don't eat tractors. Cars don't eat cars. Hammers don't eat hammers. I know when you have children helping you with chores and misplacing tools sometimes it seems like something is eating hammers, but trust me, nothing is eating your hammer. And God, in His infinite plan, offers me the distinct privilege to participate in His object lesson that illustrates God's ultimate lifeness—caretaking and then eating enjoyably things that once lived, and now offer me life.

How I view them and how I treat them say everything about how I cherish and view God's glory. I'll finish with this. It's 1 Corinthians 10:31: "WHETHER THEREFORE YOU EAT, OR DRINK, OR WHATEVER YOU DO, DO ALL TO THE GLORY OF GOD" (AKJV). You know, if I were writing that, I'd make it really religious—like singing, or memorizing the catechism, or how you wear your clothes. Goodness, I'd come up with something far less mundane than eating and drinking. But the apostle here shows the extent of God's penetrating care into the affairs of our lives by extending it to eating and drinking—food, if you will.

None of us are exempt from food. If this isn't a universal mandate, I don't know what is. Obviously, none of us are exempt from bringing Him glory. We're all expected to do it. But beyond that, everything comes under His purview. Even our food is supposed to bring Him glory.

Having looked at what God's glory means, and having applied it to other beings, can we all agree that how our food and drink bring glory to their respective distinctiveness forms a framework to honor this command to the Corinthian believers? That modern Christians by and large refuse to even discuss meat and drink that brings glory to God is tragic.

Too often, the discussion stops with spiritualization only—as long as the heart means well, all is well. It's just about the heart. It's amazing what you can dismiss by claiming that the attitude was good. As if a whistling, happy, smiling bank robber is a great guy.

Dear friends, this is why the Scripture is permeated with the word *do*. It's not about liking the truth, it's about doing truth. The psalmist says God takes vengeance on the inventions of man (Psalm 99:8). Want another one? A few pages later, Psalm 106:29 says: "THUS THEY PROVOKED HIM TO ANGER WITH THEIR INVENTIONS."

The fact is that everything we clever God-imaged humans are capable of is not acceptable. We're not free to create and do anything we can. If indeed God sets parameters around our inventiveness, perhaps it's time to have a meaningful discussion about which inventions bring glory to Him. In that, we fulfill our great objective: bringing glory to God.

Christians who preach and believe that food and life are fundamentally biological rather than mechanical garner consistent credibility when preaching God's specialness. In order for our faith message to resonate and carry weight, others must see us promoting a consistent view toward life in general. If God is the ultimate giver of life, Christians should be the ultimate defenders of that life. Promoting and protecting the pigness of pigs is the visceral starting point in our mission to the Godness of God—His glory.

1 - 23 - 22

Pattern vs. Caprice

In all things showing yourself to be a pattern of good works...
Titus 2:7 (NKJV)

A study of truth is always a study in patterns. Even criminologists spend a lot of time developing patterns of behavior. Where will the bad guy attack next? Certainly military commanders look for patterns in the enemy—what he will do, where he will move. Strategy is all about trying to see patterns and adjust to them.

God is a being of patterns. Biblical typology is a study of patterns. The threads that run through Scripture use types and patterns consistently. Throughout His earthly ministry, Jesus referred to types in the Jewish historical record. He said He would be lifted up like the serpent Moses fashioned in the wilderness that would take away the scourge if people looked on it.

Of course, the whole sacrificial system pointed to the Messiah's ultimate atonement for sin. The tabernacle was full of typology, from the ark of the covenant to the outward badger skin covering, hiding the beauty inside reserved only for those who approached God. Remember, Jesus was not physically appealing; His kingdom was on the inside. And yet how did He proclaim His divinity? With physical manifestations of His power and attributes.

The miracles, including raising people from the dead, corroborated His divinity. That's the point, dear people. Our interaction with the physical defines and establishes our relationship with God. Our stewardship of things we can see illustrates our stewardship of things we can't see. I don't see how the pattern can be stated more simply.

One pattern Christians promote is the pattern of the family. Man, woman, husband, wife, children, with chain of command. Bride and groom, courtship. Such a beautiful picture of Christ the groom courting the bride church. The heavenly marriage feast of the lamb. This relationship is supposed to be pleasurable, not painful. These are all wonderful patterns of our relationship with Christ.

The life-and-death pattern we saw in the previous chapter is certainly a pattern. When we look at nature, we also see patterns.

Perhaps the single most important pattern is the carbon cycle. All of us have studied this in biology. Sunbeams—those mystical and esoteric energy rays falling freely on us from space—convert to biomass through photosynthesis. The biomass decomposes to feed the soil in order to increase fertility in order to grow more plants in order to more efficiently capture more solar energy. The biomass inhales carbon dioxide and exhales oxygen. Biomass in the soil, a form of stored carbon, slowly decomposes, releasing carbon dioxide, which rises up through the soil encountering water and creating carbonic acid, which breaks rocks into their mineral elements so that miles of root filaments and bacteria can transport these minerals into the plants.

I've always thought it magical that something as mystical and esoteric as sunbeams can be captured by plants. You can feel the sun energy on your face, but if I tell you to bring me in some sun energy, you can't do it. You can see sunbeams streaming through your kitchen window. Indeed, if things are kind of dusty they look real enough to grab. But if you try, they slip through your fingers, regardless of how you try to hold on. And yet those sunbeams power the entire planet.

Plants can grab those sunbeams. They actually can hold on to them and convert them into something that has weight, that responds to gravity, that you can hold in your hand, give to some-body else, throw through the air. Isn't that cool? Think of all that sun energy coming to the earth since the beginning of time. That's brand-new energy striking the surface of the earth. Every day, day after day. The earth therefore is actually on a weight gain program. It's supposed to be gaining biomass at the rate of sunbeams strik-ing its surface being converted to plant material. What an astound-ing thought. The pattern is that this limitless sun energy converts to decomposable vegetation, driving all the air, ocean, wind, and atmospheric cycles on the earth.

What that means is that one of the primary goals of ethical cre-ation stewardship is leveraging carbon. The history of civilization, of course, is a legacy of carbon abuse. As Sir Albert Howard wrote in his iconic *An Agricultural Testament*, it is the temptation of every generation to take what nature spent a thousand years building, and turn it into cash.

Some 75 percent of all material that has ever gone in a U.S. land-fill is decomposable biomass. This is a fundamental violation of the carbon leverage principle. If all that biomass had been allowed to decompose along nature's pattern, it would have gone a long way toward maintaining soil fertility without artificial amendments. These chemical fertilizers, of course, take large amounts of petro-leum to produce.

Not only does nature run on carbon, it builds soil with carbon and doesn't move carbon around very much. About the farthest car-bon travels is as far as the wind blows leaves off the trees. Or as far as a bird can fly after eating and then poop somewhere. Or as far as a buffalo can travel after eating and then poop somewhere. Interest-ingly, animals have two roles in this carbon cycle.

The first is as a nutrient spreader. The only way nature can move the fertility created by biomass against gravity is with an animal. Otherwise, all biomass decomposition would move downhill, leaving hillsides and hilltops depleted. Fortunately, predators force animals that would otherwise hang out in the fertile valleys back up onto the hilltops as protection against prey. These high lookout spots receive the blessing of manure from valley fertility and help spread around the abundance.

The second reason for animals is to prune the biomass for more aggressive growth. The pattern of pruning is not only biblical, but comes right out of nature. If you want abundant growth on anything, you prune it. The Bible is replete with examples of beneficial pruning in vineyards and fruit trees. Grass is the same. It goes through three growth phases: early, middle, and late. It's in the shape of an S that starts slowly, grows quickly and aggressively in the middle, then slows down toward senescence. To make the picture easier to understand, I call these phases diaper, teenage, and nursing home. Obviously if we want to metabolize more solar energy into biomass, we will manage the forage so that it is in that sweet middle fast growth spot more often than not.

That is why on our farm we move the cows every day to a new paddock. We call this mob stocking herbivorous solar conversion lignified carbon sequestration fertilization. Lest you think that's something new, it's a mirror image of how bison, wildebeests, Cape buffalo, and every other herbivore in nature functions. Rather than being the scourge of the earth, herbivores are actually the most efficacious soil-building and carbon-sequestering partners out there. But if we allow continuous grazing and overgrazing, they are the most destructive partners out there.

Following this God-ordained pattern requires humility rather than hubris. We're looking at what is best for the soil and the animals, not what is easiest for the human. Interestingly, when we have that caring-for-others attitude in the first place, we actually receive the blessing of more profit and production. This carbon-centric system is a beautiful picture of true value accumulation. It has staying power if we shepherd it. But it can be quickly depleted if we neglect it and refuse to participate.

Any food system that depletes carbon assaults God's pattern for ecology. Carbon, of course, is closely related to organic matter and humus—earth dust, if you will. What is man made of? Human and humus come from common roots. God wants us to build humus, to be humus focused. God is humus focused—He is human focused. Get the parallels?

What destroys humus? Number one is tillage. Remember the Jewish seventh-year fallow? Perennials build soil; annuals deplete it. On a grand scale, U.S. food policy subsidizes annuals: corn, wheat, soybeans, sugarcane, rice, and cotton. Stated bluntly, U.S. farm policy encourages soil depletion. It is anti-humus. Anti-human.

The second thing that destroys humus is chemical fertilizer. It burns out humus. When the Europeans arrived on the shores of America, most agronomists believe the average organic matter was at least 8 percent. Today, it averages 1 percent. If you took that much wealth that fast from anyone, they'd say they'd been robbed. So when are we going to quit robbing God's creation?

You see, God's patterns work very well. They aren't broken. They don't need us to fix them. They only want us to massage them. Why can't we caress creation rather than pillage it? When we despise the carbon-centric system, we thwart God's plan for the earth's weight gain.

Psalm 78:41b says they "LIMITED THE HOLY ONE OF ISRAEL." That's sobering, that I can limit what God really wants to do. I know some of you reformed folks and Calvinists will need to choke back nervous twitches here, but I believe we can thwart or circumvent God's plan A. The fall in Eden was plan B. Aaron was plan B. Israel getting a king was plan B. Goodness, it's not God's will "THAT ANY SHOULD PERISH, BUT THAT ALL SHOULD COME TO REPENTANCE" (2 Peter 3:9). Fortunately, God is powerful enough to accomplish His ultimate will even when we can exercise ours.

Listen, when your daughter runs off with a druggie and gets

pregnant at the age of, that's not God's will. When I say an unkind word to Teresa, that's not God's will. If I throw all of my money away on lottery tickets, that's not God's will either. I weary of God getting blamed for sin, stupidity, and foolishness with the flippant phrase: "It's fine, God's in charge." Let me tell you, when you're sleeping with a woman who's not your wife, that's not God in charge. That's you in charge, and to say God's in charge of that mocks His holiness.

In the Lord's Prayer, Jesus requests that God's "will be done on earth, as it is in heaven." If God's will is always being done, what's the point of this request? I suggest that this request proves that God's will is NOT being done on the earth. God's orders are not being followed, and so Christ implores God to intervene in the affairs of men. Indeed, it seems to me like a blanket yearning of the soul, that God's will would permeate the planet rather than things that aren't His will.

In heaven, God's will rules everything. Not so on the earth.

God's ideal is for His sunbeams to be accumulating as much carbon as possible, to build as much fertile soil as possible. He wants good ground in which the sower can sow seed. Good soil grows plants that bear fruit. You can't bear productive fruit on poor ground. Our heart, our inner person, should be accumulating God's wealth, God's knowledge, God's desires—that's spiritual carbon. The physical is sun powered; the spiritual is Son powered. A farming system that mines out or depletes humus, that reduces or misuses carbon, breaks the heart of God.

When I drive through the countryside and see field after field receiving soil-harming chemical fertilizers, being continuously grazed and overgrazed, plowed and pillaged, my heart breaks. To see God's creation abused, rejected, and raped is no less tragic than seeing people abused, raped, and pillaged. Why is it that to have such a creation stewardship attitude is branded as pagan and romantically flaky? In our churches we present seminars on protecting our kids from Internet predators, handling money properly, investing in our marriages—I beg you, why do most Christians blanch if I mention caring for the soil outside the building? Why is that taboo?

I received a call the other day from an assistant pastor in a Kansas megachurch. He had just preached a sermon on some of these principles, and the backlash from the farmers in his church was so overwhelming he was afraid he would have to flee. These chemical-wielding farmers who feed the ever-increasing dead zone in the Gulf of Mexico should be repenting in sackcloth and ashes for desecrating such a beautiful piece of God's handiwork and the fisheries that should be there. Why is it taboo to cry out against this abuse, to shed a tear?

If someone treated one of these farmers' daughters—goodness, forget the daughter, how about a cow?—like these farmers are treating the Gulf of Mexico, and some six hundred other riparian dead zones around the United States, they'd be calling the sheriff and forming posses to bring the perpetrators to justice. They might even call a special prayer meeting, with a time of fasting, to ask direction for finding the scumbag.

I can hear the petitions: "Oh God, may justice be done. Suffer not this abuse on Your people." And everyone says: "Amen." And then everyone goes home, opens the refrigerator, and snacks on earth-raping life-disrespecting body-damaging industrial pseudo-food. Have we no shame? Have we no conscience? Dear folks, it's time to connect these dots.

Creation destruction goes on and on and it's just called the cost of business, or collateral damage from feeding the world. It's excused because to speak about it labels you an earth-worshipping pantheistic heathen. Regardless of the labeling, God's pattern does not involve spreading chemicals mined and concocted from faraway places. It's building soil, in situ, from sun-powered biomass accumulation nearby. That's the pattern. So does the food in your refrigerator build humus, increase soil carbon, or deplete it? And yes, the answer is a moral question that ultimately defines how you care for God's stuff. Remember, how you care for God's physical stuff reflects how you care for His spiritual stuff.

Ready for another pattern? Let's talk about the cow. Any grade school student knows the difference between an herbivore, carnivore, and omnivore. When we host school tours here at the farm I ask the children to explain what those designations mean. Then I point to the cow and ask: "What is that?" A chorus of "herbivore!" greets me. They know the cow is not an omnivore or a carnivore. This is grade school material.

Then I ask them: "If all of you know that, can you tell me why our country's most educated academic experts at the USDA promoted feeding dead cows to cows for thirty years? And today, they're still promoting feeding dead chickens and manure to these herbivores?" After some initial giggles at my theatrics, the students shake their heads in wonder. Indeed, any twelve-year-old knows you don't feed carrion to cows, and yet official Western world (not Eastern) policy for several decades promoted that.

Farmers like me who refused to go along with the USDA scheme were summarily dismissed as Luddites, anti-science, barbaric Neanderthals who wanted to return to some prehistoric era. Christian scientists generally thought my aversion indicated weak spiritual awareness toward the "dominion" mandate. They saw me slipping down the slope toward liberalism, environmentalism, socialism, veganism, and finally pantheism. Not a pretty picture.

How could anyone be a Christian and not revel in scientific discoveries like feeding dead cows to cows? Goodness, this was the breakthrough of the ages. Of course, we all know what eventually happened: bovine spongiform encephalopathy, known in the vernacular as mad cow disease.

Our family did not embrace this scientific campaign not because we hated the USDA or science, but because we searched the world for a pattern where herbivores eat carrion, and we couldn't find it. This is the problem with amoral science. Today in our techno-sophisticated culture we don't think God through nature has ordered anything. Everything we can manipulate is fair game to manipulate.

How many Christians in the USDA conducted research and seminars promoting this idea? Hello, did any of them ask whether or not this was appropriate, whether it fit God's pattern? No, because the only question was: "Can we?" If the answer is yes, then it's up to us great large-brained dominion-empowered humans to do it. Never mind that it breaks every pattern of God's order.

The herbivore is essentially a portable four-legged fermentation tank. You and I can't eat what an herbivore eats. We can't eat stubble and grass and hay and survive. The glory of the cow is that she can turn cellulose into nutrient-dense products that feed people. But beyond that, the reason the planet enjoys such a variety and volume of herbivores is to prune the biomass to keep it efficiently converting sunbeams.

I call the herbivore God's biomass accumulation restart button.

But are you ready for the next cool thing? In the continuum of solar-to-biomass conversion, grass is number one, bushes number two, and trees number three. I know this sounds counterintuitive when you look at a forest and see all that carbon standing there. But actually, you're seeing the accumulation of many years, all visible at once. In a grass system, you're only seeing a portion of a year at any one time. If you could see forty years' worth of grass biomass accumulation at one time, it would be far more than the forest.

What is most interesting is that when grass reaches its deceleration growth point, it's the most palatable and offers the highest nutrition to herbivores. In other words, the herbivore and grass want to meet at precisely the time that results in both fully leveraging their glory— their distinctiveness. The role of the shepherd, nomad, farmer, rancher is to manage this meeting for maximum grass growth and maximum animal performance.

I think it's befitting that the Israelites were graziers, where staying in tune with grass growth and completely dependent on the seasons created almost a mystical bond and appreciation for a world bigger than themselves.

This game of life, gentle people, is not a romp in the park. It's for all the marbles. It's the real deal, the only deal. We have one crack at it and then eternity for remorse or joy. So that we're clear, plenty of us who engaged in earth rape or bodily harm through cheap industrial food will still be saved by grace—grace is big enough to cover even this sin. But as we mature in understanding, we need to manifest our spiritual growth by doing the truth. Something as simple as leading animals to greener pastures is part of doing the truth and instills a worshipful spirit.

Some people ask me if farming is more godly than, say, fixing electric motors. The answer is no, absolutely not. But I do think that gardens and earth connections draw us closer to God, perhaps easier than anything else. In other vocations, we have to work a little harder at cultivating the proper awe. Does that make sense? God built a garden for humanity to start (Eden), chose a people known for nomadic agrarianism rather than metallurgy (like the Philistines), retreated to a garden (Gethsemane) in His final earthly hours, and invites us to His heavenly garden, walled and secluded. This is a picture of Persian kings who invited special people into their private gardens— God invites us there.

The fact that Lot lost respect and his family when he chose Sodom is not a coincidence. Abram (later Abraham) and Lot were both nomadic shepherds. Remember the story of their separation, and how Lot "pitched his tent toward Sodom." Abram, in contrast, pitched his tent among the oak trees at Mamre. Lot and his family became completely corrupted. Abram stayed faithful. What was Lot doing living in a city? What about his herds? Who was taking care of them? Lot didn't take care of business; Abram did. Abram stayed out with his herds, keeping his pulse on the intricate choreography of God's provision for his livestock.

*   *   *

One of creation's most basic patterns is that perennials build soil; annuals use accumulated fertility in a seasonal flush of production. That in modern times we think we can circumvent this pattern, take the herbivores off the land, plow up the perennials indefinitely, and substitute with chemicals is an insult to God's pattern.

Here in the Shenandoah Valley where we live, the European set- tlers displaced the Native Americans and plowed up the entire area's tall grasslands and converted them into grain production. What had been a silva-pasture of eight-foot grass among intermingled trees became a plowed "breadbasket of the Confederacy," if you'll recall from your history books. During that 150 years, some three to eight feet of topsoil washed off these fields, exposing shale and limestone rock that still dominate the pastures today even a hundred years after the breadbasket moved west.

Where were the sermons in those Lutheran, Methodist, Pres- byterian, Baptist, and Anglican churches of that day, decrying the land's degradation? Those farmers happily turned creation's wealth into cash, putting it dutifully into missionary offerings while they destroyed their fields and yards. Is it any wonder the environmental- ists view Christians with disdain?

In 1 Chronicles 4:40 we see documented a wonderful group of peo- ple, the people of Ham. Notice what it says: "AND THEY FOUND FAT PASTURE AND GOOD, AND THE LAND WAS WIDE, AND QUIET, AND PEACE- ABLE; FOR THEY OF HAM HAD DWELLED THERE OF OLD" (AKJV). What a wonderful commendation. Leaving the land better than they found it. Is that not the test of stewardship? And yet during revivals and even the Great Awakening of the 1800s, of all the things that could have been talked about, nobody mentioned how these farmers' fields were wash- ing into the river.

When we came to our farm in 1961, it would scarcely support twenty cows. Today it supports one hundred. That is not bragging; it's a testament to the healing ability of nature under proper care.

My prayer is that our family would be like Ham, leaving a land of fat pasture and good. Revelation 11:18 offers a strong statement that God will "DESTROY THOSE WHO DESTROY THE EARTH" (NKJV). Why isn't that lumped with the seven deadly sins or the preaching about gambling and pornography?

We Christians can't lump it with the other things we love to rail against because as soon as a Christian starts talking about earth stewardship he's branded a Democrat liberal commie pinko earth muffin. I know. We make jokes about it all the time. Unfortunately, the radical environmental fringe has also hijacked noble earth stewardship and turned it into foolishness like criminalizing building a pond in a swamp. But that gives even more reason for those of us who know the whole game plan to express it from a biblical perspective that includes personal responsibility and the whole litany of biblical patterns we appreciate. How much more important that we discuss these things and appreciate our earth stewardship responsibility than letting this issue be hijacked by creation worshippers.

Interestingly, a whole movement is afoot in environmental circles to embrace the role of the herbivore and grass in world ecology. I don't want to get into a debate about global warming or climate change. I honestly think we know too much today. Whether we're heating up or cooling down, the truth is that the pattern of herbivore-grass-perennial-soil building, that essential carbon-centric system, is right regardless of the planet's current state of affairs. As Christians, rather than getting all fired up about climate change and global warming, Al Gore and the Kyoto Summit, we should be quietly and peaceably devoting ourselves to soil development and promoting God's patterns. That's where the point of our spear should be.

Now, one more pattern and we'll leave it. In the Genesis creation account, God commands the earth to bring forth "GRASS, AND HERB YIELDING SEED AFTER HIS KIND, AND THE TREE YIELDING FRUIT,

WHOSE SEED WAS IN ITSELF, AFTER HIS KIND: AND GOD SAW THAT IT WAS GOOD" (1:12). We see here God stamping two patterns on His creation.

First, plants were to yield seed, and this seed was in the plant. In other words, the plant was self-contained for propagation. It did not require any manipulation outside of itself. All the genetic material and life energy needed to procreate was in that seed. Sterile plants, or seedless plants, are a violation of God's pattern. Even if we could, in our cleverness, create such a plant, it absolutely violates this basic principle of life continuity established in creation.

The second point is that it was to reproduce after its kind. In other words, an apple did not produce a pear. An orchard grass plant did not produce red clover. Each seed produced true to its parent. This purity of kind is important and has many spiritual ramifications. When Jesus says you know people by their fruit, this is a related point. If plants didn't produce true to genetics, imagine what kind of hodgepodge we'd have. The reason we've been able to classify living things according to genus and species is because of this pattern, a pattern of sublime order.

Prior to the Edenic fall, nothing died. Plants lived in a perfect eternal state. The lion lay down with the lamb. Death was nonexistent. The entire life-death-decomposition-regeneration cycle had not yet occurred. In fact, it is not until the second chapter of Genesis that we learn where grains and other annuals came from: God created the earth with the seeds in the ground, but until tillage, they did not sprout. "THESE ARE THE GENERATIONS OF THE HEAVENS AND OF THE EARTH WHEN THEY WERE CREATED, IN THE DAY THAT THE LORD GOD MADE THE EARTH AND THE HEAVENS, AND EVERY PLANT OF THE FIELD BEFORE IT WAS IN THE EARTH, AND EVERY HERB OF THE FIELD BEFORE IT GREW: FOR THE LORD GOD HAD NOT CAUSED IT TO RAIN UPON THE EARTH, AND THERE WAS NOT A MAN TO TILL THE GROUND" (vv. 4–5).

Did you catch that? Until rain and tillage, these plants remained in the ground. God's creative process was completed on the sixth day, but He made unexpressed seeds available to sprout that did not germinate until after rain and tillage occurred. Both of these things did not occur until after the fall. In this passage, *herb* is the Hebrew word *eseb*, which is the word for annuals. This is further explained in Genesis 3:18, which of course is after the fall and explaining the ramifications of Adam and Eve's sin: "BOTH THORNS AND THISTLES IT SHALL BRING FORTH FOR YOU, AND YOU SHALL EAT THE HERB OF THE FIELD" (NKJV). In other words, prior to the fall, wheat, barley, thistles, and brambles did not exist. Remember, Adam and Eve could eat of every tree of the garden: they were not milling wheat into flour.

One of the reasons this is so important is that God's initial plan for creation was different from what we see today. Annuals and death only came after the fall; these were not part of the original Edenic state. What we don't know about this eternal state would fill a library, but we know Adam and Eve had no need to procreate during this time. Children came after the fall. Plants did not need to procreate, either. In His sovereignty, God set it up so that it would still function even if sin occurred. He had the seeds in the ground and the breeding system in place in case sin and death marred Eden.

Now, how God granted free will and still chose us before the foundation of the world and prepared His Son, Jesus, to be the Messiah, I don't have a clue. That's when I retreat to Deuteronomy 29:29: "THE SECRET THINGS BELONG UNTO THE LORD OUR GOD: BUT THOSE THINGS WHICH ARE REVEALED BELONG UNTO US AND TO OUR CHILDREN FOR EVER, THAT WE MAY DO ALL THE WORDS OF THIS LAW." Sorry, I can't help it. Notice the "do" here, not just itemize, preach, catechize, or memorize. It's all about DO, my friends.

The carryover of divine pattern is intact from before to after the fall. The primary difference now, and of course it's pretty big, is Death. Adam and Eve did not need a compost pile. They did not bake bread. They did not plant a garden. They did not eat flesh. Eating flesh was another 180-degree shift from pre-sin. That was the reminder of what sin caused: death.

The seed-bearing fruit and after-its-kind pattern carried through after the fall and actually protected everything from chaos once this whole new group of plants sprouted. It set a pattern, an order, for time immemorial.

Now consider genetically modified organisms (GMOs). That's an incredibly hot topic today. I'm amazed at how many people, especially among Christians, have never even heard of this. For those who don't know, GMOs are genetically altered beings. Now that the clever human mind has been able to learn about DNA and peer into the genetic code, we can splice genetic material from one species into another. In other words, we can take a trait from pigs and put it into tomatoes.

We can take a trait that makes a plant immune to a herbicide like Roundup, ingredient glyphosate, and put it into a plant that is susceptible, creating immunity where it didn't exist before. Suddenly we can spray a genetically altered field of corn, for example, and kill weeds without killing the corn. Aren't we clever? If you've never heard of Dr. Don Huber, retired professor emeritus from prestigious Perdue University, you owe it to yourself to watch at least one of his presentations on YouTube.

If that doesn't shake you up, read *Seeds of Deception* by Jeffrey Smith. If our bodies are the temple of God, does it not behoove us to keep adulteration out? In many ways, GMOs are far more insidious and destructive than alcohol or tobacco, yet since this is a greenie and foodie subject, Christians can't talk about it. Folks, GMOs are wreaking havoc in our gene pool and human health. They've been linked by some one hundred studies and growing every year to everything from infertility to autism to cancer.

Rather than engage in a protracted debate about GMOs, however, I'd like us to turn our attention to God's pattern: seed bearing after its kind. Those two things. Forget the science for a moment. Realize that in order to patent these seeds and protect their intellectual property, the companies who develop and sell GMOs often if not usually insert a sterilizing gene. The most common one is called "Terminator" and keeps the grain from reproducing.

That's a direct violation of the pattern. This is not Mendel's peas, where he tried different varieties of peas to develop a hybrid. A caveat is in order here: some purists, and I vacillate on this one, say that even hybrids are anti-God. I'm not sure about that and don't see it as cut and dried like GMOs. Perhaps I'll come to that position someday. I'm not sure how narrow the "like kind" is. Even open-pollinated varieties don't always have children that look exactly like the parent. So I'm not ready to throw out hybrids. At least they are within varieties of the same species.

But GMOs combine species or genetic material that would never be created without blasting the DNA with gene cannons. This technology is born out of violence and hubris, and more studies are showing that kind of response in the animals and people who eat GMOs—sassier and more violent. Remember the people of Ham who left their landscape peaceable? At any rate, not in a billion years would a piece of pig DNA end up in a tomato. I like to say that if the sexual plumbing doesn't match, it ain't right.

God's design has erected many barriers to this kind of crossover. The only one allowed, apparently, is crossing a donkey with a horse, which gives a mule, which happens to be sterile. It's like God says: "You can go this far, and no more." So now we have a mix-up of kinds. The proliferation of food allergies has coincided perfectly with the rise of GMOs in the nation's food supply.

Regardless of how many *Star Trek* or other sci-fi videos we may watch, we are still fundamentally like our great-great-great-great-great-great-great-grandfathers. Our digestion and our intestinal bacteria share far more commonality with Abraham than with Spock. GMOs, both in germination and in trueness to kind, egregiously violate God's pattern.

Why is God so interested in these two principles? He's obviously interested in succession and procreation because that's the whole plan of evangelism and spreading the good news of the gospel. The New Testament is all about successful replication. Jesus making disciples is a case in point.

What about kind? At the end, God separates sheep from goats, weeds from wheat. Staying true to kind is a pattern that runs throughout Scripture. If you believe in God, then act like it. The whole new birth experience, being reborn through faith in Christ's death, burial, and resurrection as all-sufficient for heirship with Messiah, is about germination and faithfulness. Jesus asks, rhetorically, if a spring can bring forth both bitter and sweet water. "CAN TWO WALK TOGETHER, EXCEPT THEY BE AGREED?" (Amos 3:3).

GMOs violate the Genesis pattern for life sustenance and succession. That is enough for me. That the U.S. Supreme Court would allow life to be patented and therefore owned, like so many clever widgets, was a decidedly dark day in our culture. We've moved from owning humans to owning life. Unbelievable. And nary a whimper from the pulpits of our country. For shame, for shame.

God works with patterns, not caprice. That's how we can trust Him. Patterns work every day. They work in every place, every culture, every time period. As we study nature's patterns, we see revealed the consistency and plan of almighty God and we can rest easy at night knowing that His plan works. That is sweet peace.

Visible vs. Invisible

We look not at the things which are seen, but at the things which are not seen: for the things which are seen are temporal; but the things which are not seen are eternal.

2 Corinthians 4:18

Consider the soil. Imagine reaching down and picking up enough to hold in your cupped-together hands. It appears inert. Oh, you might see an earthworm, but for the most part, it crumbles and stains your fingers. You don't get the sense that what we call dirt is anything but...dirt.

We compare it to a nincompoop by saying things like "dumb as dirt." Or we devalue it, saying "as cheap as dirt."

Yet, if you looked at this soil under an electron microscope, you might see a four-legged cow-looking thing with big floppy mandibles slogging through what looks like a swamp, grazing on ghoulish vegetation. All of a sudden you might see a six-legged interloper with a narwhal spear on his head run into the microscope frame and impale the cow-looking critter, sucking out its aqueous insides through the straw-spear.

Before recovering from the shock of that violence, from the other side of the microscope frame charges a twelve-legged centipede-looking attacker with massive incisors that look like scissors on his head. He lops off the cow-looking dude's head and gobbles it up into his tubelike body. The desiccated cowlike being vanishes into the marshy soil-scape, awaiting additional decomposition.

Actually, soil—I refuse to call it dirt because that has such degrading connotations—is a pulsing, thriving community of beings. Our cupped handful contains more beings than there are people on the face of the earth. In jest, I tell folks that these beings are reading books, going to school, putting on dramatic productions, and even have a microscopic football league. While that is undoubtedly an exaggeration, we do know that soil is a teeming community of beings.

Growing up in the early 1960s during the space race, I remember our culture being enamored of space and bigness. We computed the size of the sun, the distance to the next-nearest star, the size of galaxies. *Star Trek* birthed amid this fascination with the size of the universe. Of course, creationists used this newfound information to express God's magnitude in new ways and wrote praise songs with refrains like "Our God is an awesome God."

In recent years, science has become enamored with smallness rather than bigness. As our capacity to magnify increases, we find that particles we thought were the smallest are now made up of yet smaller particles. Elaine Ingham in Oregon and Pat and Dick Richardson at Texas A&M have gifted the world with a glimpse into this soil community. Now we know through work at Stanford that these microscopic beings communicate. They actually have a language and respond to each other.

They form alliances of symbiosis as well as predatory attack relationships. Nematodes, mycorrhizae, and giberrellins are only some of the most well-known players in this soil community. That the average person spends all day without even thinking about this invisible community indicates the degree of our disconnection with our ecological nest.

Colossians 1:16 tells us that Jesus created everything, both visible and invisible, and verse 17 goes on to say: "AND HE IS BEFORE ALL THINGS, AND IN HIM ALL THINGS HOLD TOGETHER" (ESV). How do all these beings know what to do, where to go? Who gives them all their job assignments? The sheer magnitude of this soil community makes even the insect world look like nothing. And we know the world has a lot of insects.

Each of us has 3 trillion bacteria inside of us. That's a huge community of beings. I like to think that our internal community and that soil community are close relatives. When I grab a carrot out of the garden and wipe it on my britches to get most of the soil off, I still ingest millions—perhaps billions—of microbes in the tiny pieces of soil still clinging as I bite off chunks. I don't have to worry about poisons and pathogens. Healthy soil is edible. I can imagine the bacteria on the carrot sliding down my esophagus and encountering the bacteria in my stomach, who gleefully welcome the newcomers: "Howdy, cousins. How goes it on the outside? I'm working my way down to the intestines now and hope to get back out pretty soon."

It's a dramatic and magnificent cycle, these visiting beings that come in and go out. God designed them, orchestrated them, wrote out job descriptions, made some like nitrogen and others like carbohydrates. Meditating on the scale of it makes your head explode. Each of our cells has three bacteria guardians. This dramatic interaction happens all over the world, all at once, every day, and has been since the beginning of time. Why don't these beings get lost or forget what they're supposed to do for the day? Most of them are pretty simpleminded. I mean, they don't have big brains. But they know enough to work together, eating, killing, birthing, decomposing, transferring, so that we can live. It all happens behind the curtain.

You and I think we're controlling the action, that we're front and center stage, getting all the attention. But our cast of stage managers who support our drama are multiplied trillions upon multiplied trillions of microscopic beings on which everyone of us completely and utterly depends. And God, as director, choreographs all of it. Awesome indeed.

According to research at the Massachusetts Institute of Technology, we're only 15 percent human. If we could take an electron microscope image of each person, we'd all look like Pigpen in the Peanuts cartoons, with a dust cloud of viruses and bacteria swirling around us. My cloud intersects with your cloud, and yours with mine. I breathe in your critters and you breathe in mine.

One breath gets recycled through an apple tree leaf and then into an earthworm and then into a red clover leaf and then into your teenager. Wow. All that we see is completely and utterly dependent on an invisible world—at least to the naked eye. And yet this invisible world gets short shrift in our daily thought process.

When is the last time you walked into a business meeting and at the end all the entrepreneurs said: "Wow, this is a great idea. In fact, I think your plan might make us all millionaires. But before we proceed at all, we must ask this question: 'What will it do to the mycelia in our town?'" Can you imagine that? How many of you reading these pages thought about earthworms this morning while taking your shower?

Did you think about how today's actions would affect earthworms? What if we didn't do anything in business or in our lives unless and until we knew it would be helpful for earthworms? If we can't even consider earthworms, how are we supposed to consider the myriad smaller critters we can't even see? And yet not one of us could live, could function, could draw breath without these beings going about their responsibilities. Doesn't it behoove us to think about their world?

New research shows that trees in Africa being grazed by herbivores ping out a phenol message to change the chemical composition of the leaves to more bitterness. It's a protective measure against grazing. Are trees sentient beings? You bet. Anything that can communicate and morph its physiology that quickly is absolutely thinking. Psalm 139:14 says life is "FEARFULLY AND WONDERFULLY MADE." Indeed.

Psalm 139 continues with its appreciation for how amazing things are and eventually ties it with the spiritual. Look how it unfolds: "MARVELLOUS ARE THY WORKS; AND THAT MY SOUL KNOWETH RIGHT WELL. MY SUBSTANCE WAS NOT HID FROM THEE, WHEN I WAS MADE IN SECRET, AND CURIOUSLY WROUGHT IN THE LOWEST PARTS OF THE EARTH. THINE EYES DID SEE MY SUBSTANCE, YET BEING UNPERFECT; AND IN THY BOOK ALL MY MEMBERS WERE WRITTEN, WHICH IN CONTINUANCE WERE FASHIONED, WHEN AS YET THERE WAS NONE OF THEM. HOW PRECIOUS ALSO ARE THY THOUGHTS UNTO ME, O GOD! HOW GREAT IS THE SUM OF THEM!" (vv. 14–17). Notice how the psalmist's thoughts regarding physical development naturally progress to God's designs on his life. That's the physical-spiritual connection that I'm trying to demonstrate throughout this book.

My brother recently returned from the Highland Maple Festival and relayed an amazing story. He was talking to a couple of elderly maple syrup gurus about sap flow consistency. For those of you who may not know, maple syrup comes from the boiled-down sap of sugar maple trees. Early in the spring, preferably during periods of cold nights and warm days, people tap maple trees by boring a hole the size of a fat ink pen into the trunk of sugar maples. The sap flows out into buckets.

The buckets are poured into evaporation pans over fire to boil off the sap, concentrating it so that about forty gallons of sap yields one gallon of syrup. These old-timers said the flow stays constant once the taps are in and the weather holds UNLESS the wind blows. If the wind blows, the sap stops running out of the tree. Now, why might that be? Here at our farm we've tapped trees for many years and observed the same phenomenon. Why would the tree quit giving sap when the wind blows?

Well, it turns out that the sap is a cleanser for the tree. You know how if you cut your finger, you want it to bleed well? If it doesn't bleed, you stand a much greater risk of getting an infection. The reason is that the bleeding helps wash impurities out of the wound. Same with the maple tree, although instead of blood, it has sap.

When the farmer bores the tap hole into the trunk, the tree sends sap to heal the wound. Sure enough, by the next spring, only an extremely observant and knowledgeable person can find the old tap scars. When the wind blows, the tree senses that a branch might break. A broken branch is a much more serious wound than a little clean tap hole in the trunk.

Therefore, the tree withholds the sap from the tap hole in case it needs to rush a bunch of sap to a broken limb somewhere. Once the wind subsides, the sap starts flowing again through the little tap hole. Sentient beings, anyone? You bet. Fearfully and wonderfully made.

The point here is that what we see around us is a tiny fraction of what's going on. Remember the much-touted human genome project? When it began, all the scientists assured us peasants that based on known genetic combinations, they would find 100,000 pairs before completing the project.

Of course, private companies projected huge profits from isolating every human problem and finally being able to manipulate these wayward genes. The budgeting, timetable, and planning were all predicated on that magic 100,000 golden number. Give or take a percent, but this was the official known quantity. As it turned out, the whole project finished way ahead of time, way under budget— it must be the first government project that ever finished under budget—and found only around 23,000 pairs.

What was the significant outcome of the project? Lots of hanky-panky going on up and down the DNA strand that we don't have a clue how to control. It ushered in a whole new sphere of scientific study: epigenetics. What we now know is that the genetic pairs respond to switches and hook up in much more complicated and intricate ways than we could have imagined. So now we're studying the switches, which appear to be far more mysterious than DNA.

This new field of epigenetics is uncovering fascinating relationships between food and these switches. In fact, food has an effect for several generations. So the junk food you eat this month could have an effect on your great-granddaughter's IQ or allergies or propensity to develop breast cancer. Talk about intricate. Talk about way over human pay grade.

The human genome project simply created more questions. Of course, the new world of nanotechnology is now the darling of the scientists. I liken modern scientists to conquistadors. They have no idea what they're dealing with, but they're going to conquer it, whatever it is—all in the name of God. Now, don't get me wrong. I'm not opposed to scientific discovery and exploration. I love this stuff.

What I despise is reckless disregard for how little we know. We create trans fats with nary a question about whether they're good for us or not. We develop a food pyramid with carbohydrates on the bottom and thirty years later we realize it created an obesity and type 2 diabetes epidemic. It should give us all pause that we would be a much healthier nation if the government had never told us how to eat.

Indeed, if we'd just eaten like our ancestors, but bathed a little more frequently, we could have had all the benefits of sanitary living without the chronic Western disease epidemic. Why do Christians think nothing of dumping Coca-Cola into their kids? High fructose corn syrup is far different from sugar, despite what the corn lobby says.

Instead of listening to the nature freaks and foodies who began warning that pesticides, chemical fertilizers, herbicides, and food un-pronounceables might be injurious, the religious right branded all these ecology evangelists as pinko commie whacko liberal cultists. But these were the folks who understood how intricate and complex this invisible world is.

A time lag exists between abuse and result. It takes a while for the compounding junk food and chemicals to wreak havoc on a populace. Too many folks assume that if something doesn't strike you down upon first encounter, then it must be fine. As a result, they discount the intricacy and the life web God created. Coming before this invisible world humbly, with awe and reverence, is far godlier than coming to it like a swarthy conquistador lopping off heads and blathering innuendos in the name of dominion for God. When is the last time a group of Christians discussed how they could instill an awe and reverence for the spiritual reality by creating an awe and reverence for the invisible world around us?

Can you imagine a youth pastor leading his charges into an examination of why Doritos damages our internal community of bacteria? I find it fascinating that sexual abstinence is front and center on youth Bible study agendas, but junk food orgies are perfectly fine.

Could we begin to wade into the spiritual universe as proudly and aggressively as we wade into the physical unknown and unseen world? The more we know, the more we know we don't know. It would behoove us to exemplify some mature stewardship, perhaps even some fear and trepidation, as we approach our physical world. I realize it's too bad that for the most part those who espouse such views have denied creation, God, and the whole spiritual universe. I get that. It's tragic.

But to ridicule those who have a much deeper respect for the complexity of life just because they don't know the Designer shows a profound immaturity on Christians' part. The world we live in is holy. The life we embrace is holy. My dad used to say, "To us, every bush is a burning bush." When we inculcate in our lives an invisible-world respect and common thoughtfulness, we create the mind-set and the patterns for appreciating that the most real world of all is one we don't even see: heaven, hell, God, Satan, angels, demons.

If we focus on the importance of this invisible physical world, and think about how to nurture it, respect it, honor it, we learn better how to do the same to the spiritually invisible world. This is not childishness and foo-foo creation worship; it is deep recognition that something bigger than we see is going on. It puts us in our place and in a right mental and spiritual relationship with something bigger than ourselves. That's a good thing.

Strength vs. Weakness

If you will diligently listen to the voice of the LORD...I
will put none of these diseases on you...I am the LORD
that heals you.

Exodus 15:26 (AKJV)

Clearly, God's plan for the Israelites in their promised land was to be
well fed, sheltered, and clothed—IF they adhered to divine instructions. Even in a fallen state, nature is supposed to operate in a regenerative way. Certainly earthquakes, floods, volcanoes, and droughts
occur, but overall the hydrologic, atmospheric, soil-building, healthful position is normal.

How many times have you seen a sick deer? How many times
have you seen a sick zebra? Certainly sick ones exist—they don't last
very long. But generally, squirrels are healthy, coyotes are strong, and
moose only die from predation. What we generally see as we study
natural ecosystems is a symbiotic choreography that functions quite
well.

The whole premise of all medical wellness traditions—as opposed
to the dominant mind-set of today's allopathic medical community—
is that the body's default position is wellness. From chiropractic to
acupuncture, the assumption is that illness or sickness indicates

aberrant conditions, that they are symptoms of imbalance or something awry, as opposed to the problem itself.

For the most part, Christians scoff at alternative medicine like acupuncture, chiropractic, osteopathy, homeopathy, or nutrition therapy.
To be sure, I'm glad we have the allopathic alternative for trauma
and specific physical repair. But most of our illnesses are a result of
things we do to ourselves. Weston A. Price traveled the world during
the early twentieth century and discovered that populations who had
not been adulterated with processed foods from Western diets had
almost no incidence of chronic illnesses.

Look at the early colonists' sketches of Native Americans around
Jamestown. Remember that Spain outlawed growing quinoa after
conquering the Incas because the conquistadors thought the grain
with the funny name was responsible for the remarkable physique
of these native peoples. The Israelites were promised to not have the
diseases of surrounding civilizations if they adhered to the sanitation
and crop rotation requirements of God's plan.

The Christian community paints the wellness-organic movement
with a broad brush that starts dubious and ends hostile. Let's go back
a bit and see why we think this way.

My brother Art was a missionary with New Tribes Mission in Indo-
nesia for fifteen years. In vivid detail he explains the daily terror these
indigenous people live under, fearful of offending the rice god or
the rain god. If a bird happens to fly by from a certain direction, it's
an omen. Every bird's flight and every animal's call portends good
or ill. It's a life fraught with fear and inhibition. Rather than simply
realizing God's magnificent design, some of which we understand
and some of which we don't, these folks arrogate to spirits the most
mundane occurrences of life.

We know now that the bubonic plague was carried by fleas on
rodents. Burgeoning trade between London and Paris added fuel to
the fire. Add to that a mini–ice age that pushed people indoors more,

and the plague grew rapidly, decimating Europe. With open sewers and a diabolical lack of hygiene, Europe succumbed to a disease that killed a quarter of the population. At the time, people developed all sorts of spiritual explanations for the epidemic. They put hex signs on their houses and created a folklore surrounding good luck and bad luck.

Interestingly, this plague developed alongside a new era of global trade. Innovative ship-building technology made larger and safer vessels, which in turn enabled greater trade. The plague did not hit the Orient. A bit of isolation can be healthful—ecosystems don't generally encourage outside influences. Most operate within self-reliant communities. The frog doesn't go too far from the pond. Some do, but most are born, live, and die in the same locale. As globalism escalates in our modern world, I wonder what unintended consequences it will create.

In the mid-1800s Louis Pasteur peered through a microscope and saw a world of physical beings. These were not spirits; they were creatures. He did not yet know, like we do today, that they actually communicate and respond to each other. A contemporary of his named Antoine Beauchamp saw the same things. Interestingly, the two men had quite different perspectives on their new knowledge.

Pasteur developed the germ theory and proposed ways to kill these critters. He saw nature as fundamentally flawed and in need of human intervention and fixing. It was not unlike the conclusion drawn by the Austrian chemist Justus von Liebig, who in 1837 concluded that all of life is just a rearrangement of nitrogen, potassium, and phosphorous. This supported a mechanical view of life, that rather than being animate, life was fundamentally inanimate.

Beauchamp, however, looking at the same bacteria through the same microscopes, came to a very different conclusion from Pasteur's. He decided these new critters they were seeing under the microscope were all part of a terrain in which either wellness or sickness could thrive. He advanced the terrain theory as an alternative to Pasteur's germ theory. Generally, the populace liked the germ theory because it fit better with the notion that these devilish beings were going around making people sick. It fit well with a victim mentality, that "the devil made me sick."

Indeed, the theological portion of Pasteur's germ theory is more powerful than most people think.

Of course, we love to believe what fits with our worldview, and it was no different in that day. It was a good thing, therefore, to destroy these germs, to kill them, and thereby kill the devil's attacks on humanity. A righteous fervor propelled this idea forward. It even fit well with the "I'm not responsible" notion: "I'm not responsible for my disease; Satan through these germs is responsible. Let's knock him out."

Beauchamp had a much harder idea to sell. If these germs, most of which were actually helpful, simply changed winners and losers based on terrain, then the question to ask was this: "How do we create a terrain in which the good bugs beat the bad bugs?" He went far afield in answering this question, even looking into sleep deprivation, hygiene (imagine that, in a time when doctors were still arguing over whether it was necessary to boil surgical instruments between amputations), and food quality.

His quest for wellness-inducing terrain occupied the rest of his life. Folklore has it that Pasteur, on his deathbed, recanted and screamed: "Beauchamp was right! It is all about the terrain!" And then he died. We'll never know the definitive on this, but suffice it to say that if it's terrain, then I'm responsible. If it's germ theory, then all I have to do is figure out a concoction to kill the bad guy.

We see this same tension in our own lives, don't we? We know Satan walks about as "A ROARING LION...SEEKING WHOM HE MAY DEVOUR" (1 Peter 5:8). At the same time, we are to take "THE WHOLE ARMOUR OF GOD, THAT YE MAY BE ABLE TO WITHSTAND IN THE EVIL DAY" (Ephesians 6:13). Even with that tension, however, we spend most of our time developing models of family, study, and life that create immunity to Satan's attacks, rather than assuming we can just destroy Satan's attacks, or stop them from occurring. That's an important distinction: destroy the attacks, or create a spiritual immunity to them.

We instruct our children that it's far wiser to stay in spiritually healthful terrains than to wander into spiritually unhealthy terrains. It's much easier to withstand temptation if we're among people and in situations where immorality, for example, is harder to do. "Don't put yourself in a compromised position," parents instruct their children. "Don't hang out with the wrong crowd" is wise counsel.

Realize that the world was industrializing at the time of Pasteur and Beauchamp. Urban expansion, the rise of the factory, and the industrial revolution all combined to create a new set of sickness issues in plants, people, and animals. For a more in-depth analysis of this, please read my book *Folks, This Ain't Normal*. I'll simply summarize that as people crammed together in cities, without refrigeration, indoor plumbing, and stainless steel, it set up a perfect storm for problems.

From smoke-clogged homes to manure-clogged streets to brewery-waste-fed milk cows, the recipe for disease could not have been better. As a result, tuberculosis, whooping cough, undulant fever, and smallpox all proliferated. Similarly, farms industrialized before plastic water pipes, wood chippers, cheap concrete, and electric fence were widely available. This created a perfect environment for hog cholera, brucellosis in cows, and Marek's disease in poultry.

Running with Pasteur's germ theory, vaccines came to the rescue. Drugs proliferated. DDT came along by World War II. All of these things promised a golden age of disease-free living. The Christian community bought into these developments just like their earlier counterparts bought into pasteurization—praising dominion and human creativity, we were going to vanquish the devil's diseases. The promise of these new fixes seemed so much more dramatic than herbal medicines, nomadic and pastoral farming, acupuncture, or any Eastern "heal thyself" practices.

The fact is that all of these diseases we brought on ourselves by not adhering to nature's patterns. Animals—even pigs—don't stay in the same slop hole all the time. Birds don't stay in confinement buildings. Cows don't eat distillers' grains. Refuse should be taken outside the community, not dumped in open sewers in which children might play. Flies and rodents were everywhere.

Poop clogged the streets. Around 1900 many urban newspapers began running paranoid editorials about the cities imploding in a mountain of horse poop. People tracked it into bakeries, into the theater, into the barbershop, into the butcher shop. Churches reeked of poop on everyone's shoes. To say things were unsanitary would be the understatement of the century.

In the midst of that time came the Mayo Clinic, staking its reputation on the healing qualities of milk from pastured cows— raw milk. Not pasteurized. Why was the milk bad in those days? Because farmers were feeding the cows distillers' grains from brewery wastes, not refrigerating the milk, and not cleaning out their dairy parlors. It was a toxic concoction of nature's protocol violated by human thoughtlessness. The industrialization of living and farming ran ahead of infrastructure like indoor plumbing, refrigeration, stainless steel, and electricity.

The point here is that raw milk from grazing cows doesn't need to be fixed with pasteurization. It's not broken. In fact, nature is not broken. It doesn't need to be fixed. Nature's default position is actually wellness, not sickness.

Christians like to do good. Eradicating these debilitating diseases seems like a good thing. But why did they proliferate? Was it a fairy-like devil walking around sprinkling indiscriminate bad-bug dust on certain areas? I say no. It was in fact negligent management, partly due to an infrastructure inadequate to handle urbanization, partly due to ignorance, and partly due to a philosophical prejudice against fixes predicated on humility rather than hubris. Milk-borne pathogens could be prevented by humbly returning to cows eating grass and milk pails being judiciously and vigorously scrubbed with hot soapy water. In hindsight, it seems like such a simple fix, but in the context of the day, lacking bacterial understanding and infrastructure, it was easier just to boil the milk. After all, if food and life were fundamentally mechanical, what difference did it make whether the milk was heated or not? It still looked the same.

But they didn't consult the 3 trillion bacteria inhabiting the human gut. And for this internal community, pasteurization completely altered the nutritive viability of the milk. Milk was assumed to be pathogenic and needing a remedy—pasteurization. That was a way to exercise dominion and solve problems.

Actually, all of these maladies could and have been remedied with proper nutrition, sanitation, and infrastructure. The problems of the time were not the problem. The pathogenicity simply resulted from imbalance or improper procedure. But this period did entrench in the minds of many that nature is fundamentally flawed and requires human innovation to fix it. In actuality, inappropriate human actions created problems that should have never occurred in the first place.

For Christians to make jokes about Rachel Carson and the definitive understanding that DDT created infertile frogs, three-legged salamanders, and a dead zone the size of New Jersey in the Gulf of Mexico is simply unconscionable in light of our creation stewardship mandate. The earth is the Lord's, not ours. If we took care of our employers' physical interests the way we take care of God's physical interests, we'd be fired and probably put in jail.

Today we continue down the same path. We went from DDT, organophosphates, and chemical fertilizer to concentrated animal feeding operations, sub-therapeutic antibiotics, and monosodium glutamate. As my dad used to say, it's the same boat crossing the same river.

We Christians have this smug idea that God is proud of whatever we're capable of doing. As if God smiles down on our accomplishments with a self-satisfied appreciation that we figured something out. Rather than being an ultimately perfect designer and demanding obedient holy adherence to a set of protocols He set in motion at the beginning of time, we view God as a doting cheerleader thankful that we've come so far.

It's like we Christians get brownie points with God for our cleverness. Folks who wouldn't dare abide a works-oriented salvation revel in a human-centric intervention strategy to God's creation. While God does expect us to interact with His now fallen creation, such activity is still bounded by immutable design.

We invent things that destroy the surrounding nature for a hundred years, create toxic waste sites, radioactive zones, and feel great that we've expressed our dominion so beautifully. Instead, we should be repenting in sackcloth and ashes.

I've asked countless people age fifty or older: "Did you ever hear the phrase 'food allergy' when you were growing up?" I have yet to get a "yes." It was nonexistent until a very short while ago. How about *campylobacter, listeria, E. coli, salmonella?* Nobody had even heard of these things as recently as the 1960s.

Back in the early 1990s when government food inspectors tried to shut down our outdoor backyard poultry-processing shed, our chickens measured 133 colony-forming units of bacteria per milliliter to the second permutation (I have no idea what I just said, but that's how they measure it), and the federal-approved supermarket birds averaged 3,600. We were 2,500 percent cleaner. We have the answer to these squiggly Latin words that people now use as if they are supposed to be part of the lexicon.

They're not supposed to be part of our lexicon. They are symptoms of God's creation crying out, "Enough! Enough abuse! Enough disrespect!" They are not the problem; they are physical manifestations of an abuse of the wellness doctrine that's unprecedented in human history. I really believe God has a desire, a plan, for everything. He has it figured out. It's not broken—unless we break it.

Look at American food consumption. You can overlay the type 2 diabetes epidemic and the obesity epidemic right on top of the government's dietary guidelines: the food pyramid. Remember that thing? It put carbohydrates on the bottom, but did not differentiate Pop-Tarts and Froot Loops from fresh-sprouted rye bread. If the government had never told us what to eat, we would today be a much healthier society.

Even worms will not eat most of the stuff from the center aisles of the supermarket. Try feeding Cheerios and Twizzlers to earthworms. They won't eat the stuff. Why should we? Is our body not the "TEMPLE OF THE HOLY GHOST" (1 Corinthians 6:19)?

I had a fascinating conversation with a youth pastor at the Catalyst conference in Atlanta a couple of years ago. The event organizers had invited me to do a presentation about some of these things. After the speech, this grossly obese youth pastor came up to me and asked: "I just love eating at McDonald's. Do I have a spiritual problem?"

I looked at him and asked him a question in return: "If you had a young buck in your youth group come to you and tell you he enjoyed screwing several of the gals in the group, then asked if he had a spiritual problem, what would you say?"

The young man began crying, big tears rolling down his cheeks: "Thank you, sir. I have some work to do on me," he said, and walked away. You see, dear friend, if we could hear ourselves talk about anything spiritually oriented the way we talk about physical or creation-oriented things, we'd be devastated with grief. We'd be flogging ourselves with repentance.

Following God's design, as outlined in nature, is the first place to innovate, not the last. It's amazing to me how many people turn to alternative medicine, diets, education, or farming only after they've exhausted their time, emotion, and money on the conventional thinking. We're like the woman with an issue of blood who "HAD SUFFERED MANY THINGS OF MANY PHYSICIANS, AND HAD SPENT ALL THAT SHE HAD, AND WAS NOTHING BETTERED, BUT RATHER GREW WORSE" (Mark 5:26). She touched the hem of Jesus' garment, and she was immediately healed.

You see, dear friend, if Satan can make God's people think that the antidote to most maladies is found through embracing the world's way, conventional thinking, and humanistic innovation, he can keep God's people enslaved to a debilitating system. He can keep Christians addicted to pharmaceuticals, sickness, soil erosion. I've encountered Christians who simply can't believe that credentialed expert scientific information can be wrong.

Answering these folks always leads me back to the resurrection. To me, this is the most poignant political statement in all of Scripture. Remember that on the third day, Jesus rose from the tomb. Angels, lightning, earthquakes—the Roman secret service (my paraphrase) all "BECAME AS DEAD MEN" (Matthew 28:4). Later, they came to and ran into the city to tell their superiors what had happened:

> NOW WHEN THEY WERE GOING, BEHOLD, SOME OF THE WATCH [THOSE ELITE SOLDIERS] CAME INTO THE CITY, AND SHOWED TO THE CHIEF PRIESTS ALL THE THINGS THAT WERE DONE. AND WHEN THEY WERE ASSEMBLED WITH THE ELDERS, AND HAD TAKEN COUNSEL, THEY GAVE LARGE MONEY TO THE SOLDIERS, SAYING, "SAY YOU, HIS DISCIPLES CAME BY NIGHT, AND STOLE HIM AWAY WHILE WE SLEPT." AND IF THIS COME TO THE GOVERNOR'S EARS, WE WILL PERSUADE HIM, AND SECURE YOU [THE GOVERNOR WOULD NOT HAVE LIKED THE NOTION THAT HIS SECRET SERVICE WAS SLEEPING ON THE JOB]. SO THEY TOOK THE MONEY, AND DID AS THEY WERE TAUGHT: AND THIS SAYING IS COMMONLY REPORTED AMONG THE JEWS UNTIL THIS DAY. (Matthew 28:11–15 AKJV)

That has to be the most profound cover-up in all human history. These crack, perhaps hand-picked Roman soldiers saw the resurrection of Jesus, God incarnate, complete with lightning, angels, and power. These guys, trained to take on any situation with courage and intrepidity, fell down like dead men. Think of what they just witnessed. It wasn't one; it was all of them. Nobody would have thought them crackpots if they told their story. They would have been the most believable, credible witnesses possible. They would have been the darlings of morning TV news shows. They'd have made banner headlines in the *New York Times*.

And yet they sold out for a handful of money. Dear people, if the elite Roman guard who witnessed Jesus' resurrection could be silenced with money, then anything, regardless of truth, can be silenced with money. I do not understand why conservative Christians who routinely fight against society's agenda on right to life, gay marriage, higher taxes, and bigger government somehow assume that society's agenda is benevolent regarding farming, food, and medicine. That's called intellectual schizophrenia.

It's immature thinking at best and diabolically inconsistent at worst. The problem is we Christians do not trust God's plan. We don't. Oh, we trust it when it comes to matters of spirituality. But we think God's plan is broken—along with mainstream scientists of our day—when it comes to physical things. The result is that we Christians marching off to sanctity-of-life rallies send our kids off to college to get a good enough education to go work for a multinational corporation dedicated to adulterating God's creation.

I would suggest that a God-honoring farm is one that shows strength rather than weakness. It's one that has no veterinary bills. It's one that has healthy plants and animals. It's one that produces food that develops healthier people. This is not a health-and-wealth message. It is ultimately a humility-and-dependency message. God's designs work.

Animals move. Cows eat forage, not dead cows. Soil wants biomass, not chemical fertilizer. Our internal digestive biota desire pronounceable things, not foreign man-made concoctions. Our food should be simple ingredients, not long man-made ingredients. Our aquifers should be building, not depleting. These are God's design, and when we follow them, they lead us to strength, not weakness.

If we do indeed serve an awesome God, people who encounter us, who walk on our farms, should be astounded at the health and strength they see. When they mention the object lesson, we can point them to the source of it all, the Ultimate Strength, the Perfect Designer.

Participation vs. Abandonment

I am the true vine, and my Father is the vinedresser. Every branch in me that does not bear fruit he takes away, and every branch that does bear fruit he prunes, that it may bear more fruit.

John 15:1–2 (ESV)

Excluding a few exceptions, the history of civilization is one of environmental depredation and degradation. From Easter Island to the Sahara, once bountiful places become less so when touched by the hand of man—generally.

Add to that the romanticism of iconic nature writers like Audubon, Leopold, Thoreau, and Muir, and you have perfect justification for the radical environmentalist's abandonment mentality. The crux of this idea is that in a state untouched by human hands, nature is perfect. Since man's hand usually means rape, pillage, and exploitation, the safest thing to do is to abandon nature. After all, nature is too sacred to be desecrated by human breath.

I can definitely appreciate this mentality. The United States now has some seven hundred riparian dead zones. Soil loss is still breathlessly high. Aquifers in irrigated areas are dropping dramatically. Desertification is on the rise. Is humankind's only integrity position toward nature to leave it alone?

This kind of thinking encourages many radical environmentalists to push for vacating the western ranches so they can revert to a
buffalo commons. Wilderness areas and more parks dominate the
guilt-assuagement agenda of people who care. To oppose locking up
more land in parks and wilderness areas is equivalent to screaming:
"I hate nature!" Indeed, we can even see this mentality in farmland
preservation efforts, where the emphasis has been on protecting
farmland without doing anything to protect farmers.

I confess that I get quite frustrated with man's historical land use
and abuse trajectory. I look in the mirror and see this large brain and
opposing thumbs on my hands and wonder if my inherent interaction with nature is to be the most efficacious pillager and rapist. I
repent for all the pillaging my ancestors have done.

Or is it just possible that I've been blessed with this big brain
and opposing thumbs to bring redemptive capacity to the earth as
healer? As land masseur? If that's the case, I need to figure out how
to participate with nature in a way that yields ultimate healing and
resiliency.

While nature provides the pattern and the principle, God expects
us to use our big brains and the innovation they enable through our
opposing thumbs to participate with creation as caretaker, nurturer,
and steward. Abraham became a wealthy man with his flocks and
herds, even though after his break with Lot he stayed on the poorer
ground. Isaac dug wells, and that is presented as a good thing. The
Kenites received God's commendation for leaving their land fertile
with lush pastures.

Jesus uses the shepherd many times to show this interaction.
From building a fold to damming up a creek for still water so the
sheep would drink to fighting off predators and creating safe pastures. "YOU PREPARE A TABLE BEFORE ME IN THE PRESENCE OF MY
ENEMIES" refers to predators, holes, and snakes where the sheep
were going to graze—Psalm 23:5 (NKJV). Cisterns are man-made
water reservoirs, and their fullness became a benchmark of God's
blessing or punishment.

Listen to this language describing a land under God's judgment:

THE STREAMS THEREOF SHALL BE TURNED INTO PITCH [OIL?], AND THE DUST THEREOF INTO BRIMSTONE, AND THE LAND THEREOF SHALL BECOME BURNING PITCH. IT SHALL NOT BE QUENCHED NIGHT NOR DAY; THE SMOKE SHALL GO UP FOREVER: FROM GENERATION TO GENERATION IT SHALL LIE WASTE; NONE SHALL PASS THROUGH IT FOR EVER AND EVER. BUT THE CORMORANT [PELICAN] AND THE BITTERN SHALL POSSESS IT: THE OWL ALSO AND THE RAVEN SHALL DWELL IN IT: AND HE SHALL STRETCH OUT UPON IT THE LINE OF CONFUSION, AND THE STONES OF EMPTINESS.

THEY SHALL CALL THE NOBLES THEREOF TO THE KINGDOM, BUT NONE SHALL BE THERE, AND ALL HER PRINCES SHALL BE NOTHING. AND THORNS SHALL COME UP IN HER PALACES, NETTLES AND BRAMBLES IN THE FORTRESSES THEREOF: AND IT SHALL BE AN HABITATION OF DRAGONS, AND A COURT FOR OWLS. THE WILD BEASTS OF THE DESERT SHALL ALSO MEET WITH THE WILD BEASTS OF THE ISLAND, AND THE SATYR SHALL CRY TO HIS FELLOW; THE SCREECH OWL ALSO SHALL REST THERE, AND FIND FOR HERSELF A PLACE OF REST. THERE SHALL THE GREAT OWL MAKE HER NEST, AND LAY, AND HATCH, AND GATHER UNDER HER SHADOW: THERE SHALL THE VULTURES ALSO BE GATHERED, EVERY ONE WITH HER MATE. (Isaiah 34:9–15)

This desolate wildness is a picture of God's judgment. It's not positive. This land devoid of rock walls and human presence is what something looks like when God punishes a place. Contrast this with the next chapter, which describes what a place looks like where God is in charge:

IN THE WILDERNESS SHALL WATERS BREAK OUT, AND STREAMS IN THE DESERT. AND THE PARCHED GROUND SHALL BECOME A POOL, AND THE THIRSTY LAND SPRINGS OF WATER: IN THE HABITATION OF DRAGONS, WHERE EACH LAY, SHALL BE GRASS WITH REEDS AND RUSHES. AND AN HIGHWAY SHALL BE THERE, AND A WAY, AND IT SHALL BE CALLED THE

WAY OF HOLINESS; THE UNCLEAN SHALL NOT PASS OVER IT; BUT IT SHALL BE FOR THOSE: THE WAYFARING MEN, THOUGH FOOLS, SHALL NOT ERR THEREIN.

NO LION SHALL BE THERE, NOR ANY RAVENOUS BEAST SHALL GO UP THEREON, IT SHALL NOT BE FOUND THERE; THE REDEEMED SHALL WALK THERE: AND THE RANSOMED OF THE LORD SHALL RETURN, AND COME TO ZION WITH SONGS AND EVERLASTING JOY UPON THEIR HEADS: THEY SHALL OBTAIN JOY AND GLADNESS, AND SORROW AND SIGHING SHALL FLEE AWAY. (Isaiah 35:6–10)

God loves humans. He delights in seeing land occupied. He delights in seeing people working in and on His creation. Realize that the land healing described here is not miraculous divine intervention; it is the result of good people coming into the land, working with it, building ponds and pastures. Planting grasses, taming the wildness, and ultimately creating a secure, safe, productive place to live.

Jesus uses many interactive principles like digging around a tree and dunging it to make it more productive, pruning a vineyard, and grafting in the Gentiles. You don't have to read much Scripture to realize God wants us extremely participatory in His creation. That includes, by the way, Noah's long-term building project and Jacob's speckled and spotted sheep. These patriarchs did not sit idly in nature excluding themselves from it. They made it more productive.

After Adam and Eve were driven from the garden, the earth changed. After the deluge, it changed even more. Earning a living by the "SWEAT OF THY FACE" (Genesis 3:19) does not indicate a lifetime of communion like some guru on top of a mountain. It indicates instead an active role in stewarding creation. Perhaps the most important goal of stewardship is to leave possessions more valuable than they were in the beginning. How do we add value to God's earth?

Very simply, we make it more efficient at collecting solar energy to grow more biomass. More biomass grows more carbon, which builds soil, feeds people, and produces more oxygen. The basic cycles and forces of ecology are not that complicated. The problem is that man's temptation has been to exploit for short-term gain rather than to utilize for long-term remediation.

I've encountered numerous Christians who scoff at this whole earth remediation notion because it's all going to burn up someday anyway, according to most biblical interpretations. This is the same mentality that fostered the notion: "EAT, DRINK, AND BE MERRY" (Luke 12:19). The whole tenor of Christ's imperative is to "OCCUPY TILL I COME" (Luke 19:13). The whole point of earth stewardship is to show our faithfulness and to draw people to God by the sheer power and force of righteous expression in a physical, visceral way.

Okay, enough of the academic. What does this look like? Let's take an example.

Where I live in Virginia's Shenandoah Valley, deep alpha soils producing massive trees and eight-foot-tall, thick grasses prior to European settlement have been reduced by several feet. Literally three to five feet of topsoil have eroded, creating turbidity in the Chesapeake Bay. The trees here now are too thick, diseased, crooked, and weedy. Massive soil erosion reveals limestone rock outcroppings deforming the hillsides. Many if not most acres are a shadow of what they were when the Europeans arrived. Something else is also gone: beavers. In today's world it's hard for us to imagine the scope of beaver activity.

Beavers extended over all of North America and literally changed landscapes. Their dams slowed the flow of rivers, creating places where otherwise fast-flowing water would drop its silt and form terraces. Over time, these deposits actually turned rivers and helped them meander rather than run in a straight line. Meandering rivers run slower, which reduces erosive energy. They also hold much more water than straight rivers, which ameliorates flooding damage. Increased capacity means a river can carry more water without breaching its banks.

Europeans poured into the Valley by the early 1700s, killing out the beavers, plowing up the grasses, and cutting down the trees. This dramatically altered landscape could not hold water. Soil organic matter, which holds four times its weight in water (one pound holds four pounds of water), burned out due to tillage. This depletion reduced the soil's ability to soak in and retain rain, which encouraged surface runoff. The silt did not collect in beaver dams, but instead flowed straight down the faster-flowing rivers. As rivers breached the defunct beaver dams, their velocity increased, cutting into the banks and incising into the landscape, lowering the water table.

The whole ecology deteriorated dramatically. Soil societies in Virginia during the late 1700s and early 1800s were huge. Thomas Jefferson, James Madison, John Taylor, and Thomas Massie—all wealthy plantation owners—wrote many letters to each other about the desperate need to create fertility. They continually looked for "virgin land" to turn into plowed ground, and would dispatch slaves to these areas to cut and burn in order to bring more fertile land into production.

By 1870, the Valley gave way to new fertile lands in the Midwest to exploit. The transcontinental railroad opened up grain transportation opportunities so the crop no longer needed to be grown where it would be fed. The Valley became an orchard region and then a pastoral area again, with relatively few acres devoted to tillage. Unfortunately, rather than mimicking the grazing patterns of the buffalo, farmers used their own negligent approach, which was continuous grazing. This further insulted the land and kept it from healing. In deference to these farmers, however, fencing was exorbitantly expensive in those days, hampering efforts at rotational grazing.

The discovery of petroleum created cheap energy for the first time in human history. By 1900, the world's virgin lands were gone: America, Australia, and New Zealand were all fully settled. The dust bowl era lurked just ahead. Feeding the burgeoning and urbanizing world population scared world leaders to death. How would civilization survive?

I view the discovery of cheap energy as a divine bonanza bestowed at a critical time in human history. If that petroleum and the machinery it powered had been strategically leveraged to build ponds in the foothills and valleys around our Shenandoah Valley, today we would have nearly re-created Eden and we would be flood-proof and drought-proof. We would look like the God-productive land described in the Isaiah passage. How so?

On our farm, we've built numerous ponds in these foothills and now have a five-mile grid of plastic pipe delivering gravity-fed water over the entire farm. We use it to water livestock and to irrigate during dry times. These ponds gradually empty during the summer and then fill back up during the winter. Every time we get a few thousand dollars, we build another pond. These ponds keep springs and aquifers full, maintaining a hydrated landscape. Done on a larger scale, of course, evaporation helps cloud formation and evens out seasonal rainfall.

If the petroleum and machinery devoted to tillage for the last century had been invested in hydration projects instead, we would have built soil instead of depleted it and built dramatic forgiveness into the landscape. While nature lovers enjoy hiking on beautiful days, every day is not like that. Winds, droughts, floods, heat, and cold are part of the fallen planet. Yes, the earth is under the curse of sin just like everything else. What is the remedy for our spiritual curse? Repentance. That's disturbing. But it's the precursor to a new heart.

If you're going to grow vegetables in the backyard, you don't just throw the seeds over your shoulder and find beets and carrots growing. No, you're going to have to get a spade and shovel and do some disturbance. To move from lawn to productive garden requires short-term disturbance in order to create a freshened ecology of succession.

That's why fire historically was the most common freshener. It rejuvenated land by weeding out brush and brambles. It converted biomass into minerals for both soil and animals. Unlike Bambi, real wildlife actually was attracted to burns because mineral-rich charcoal is a tonic. Native Americans often lit fires to attract wildlife. Disturbance is part of nature's cycle. Volcanoes and storms cause major disturbances to move land around.

Unlike the haphazard kind of disturbance from natural phenomena, however, human disturbance can be planned and focused. This is the beauty of permaculture as opposed to the radical environmental abandonment agenda. Permaculture assumes that strategic human manipulation can actually make the earth far more productive than it was in its static state. I like that. I think it's not only foolish but misdirected faith to assume that however the earth's terrain fell during its formation is necessarily the best it can be.

We don't have the beavers anymore, although what they did represented a major disturbance on the earth. We don't have unowned land with millions of bison, wolves, and passenger pigeons. But we have pigs, electric fences, cattle, and poultry.

In July 2012 our area suffered a derecho (pronounced de-RAY-cho). It's a windstorm with straight winds up to ninety miles per hour. It knocked out power for days, killed twenty-two people, and devastated the area. Farmers relying on pumped water for their livestock suffered enormously trying to keep their animals alive. On our farm, our network of gravity-fed water pipes never even knew there was a storm. Water kept flowing down out of the hills. I've always said the day gravity fails, I'm out of here.

The fact that as a culture we used this bonanza of cheap petroleum energy NOT to remediate, but to plow more and create a food system that transports the average morsel fifteen hundred miles from field to fork, indicated a universal disregard for God's gift. I don't believe using petroleum is wrong, any more than using any God-given resource is wrong. What is wrong is using it like a drunken sailor and not leveraging it for multi-generational landscape resiliency. Or using it toward inappropriate ends.

God's mandate to me is to extend His redemptive capacity into the landscape. My farm should show forth a redemptive capacity that attracts people to ask: "What's going on here? How does this land stay green and fertile even in rough times?" The physically obvious provides a springboard for the spiritually obscure because I can then answer: "The land's health is exemplifying a redemptive capacity that we've brought to it through our farming protocols. Just like we do that to heal the land, God wants us to be fruitful and healthy by being redeemed from sin."

Back in the 1980s we traded thirty acres of forest for three miles of all-weather road in order to get access to our mountain acreage. The project took three months, and during that time we were in a serious drought. When the logging crew arrived at the top, they looked down and saw our farm green compared to the surrounding areas. The crew chief stopped in the yard on his way out that day and asked me how we were green.

Of course, I broke out in a big smile and said emphatically: "We're redeeming the earth!" His quizzical expression belied both interest and incredulity. I explained our mob stocking herbivorous solar conversion lignified carbon sequestration fertilization. I told him about multi-speciation, hydration, carbon building. It was all part of a carefully choreographed participatory interaction with this farm God wanted us to steward. What a wonderful launchpad to explain the claims of Christ on the landscape of a person's heart.

Have you ever heard the phrase *worn-out farm*? That must break the heart of God. What He made good and regenerative has been ravaged by people He made in His image—clever, observant, calculating. To deplete the land is like throwing your spiritual heart away. The whole idea of repentance is to agree with God that His way is the right way. The result is spiritual productivity.

My whole mandate as a steward of God's creation is to extend my big brain and opposing thumbs into the environment to caress it into more conversion of solar energy into biomass than it's capable of in a natural state. That's true dominion exercise. I think too often Christians use dominion as a license to pillage and rape as fast as possible. That's a complete adulteration of the dominion mandate. The dominion mandate is to exercise our gifts to build functionality and greater productivity long-term.

What if God had decided not to participate with us? What if He had decided we were too special to send His Son? Solomon tells us in Proverbs that just like a father chastens the son he loves, so God chastens His children. That's disturbing. But it's the start-point for progress.

I call this disturbance ecological exercise. Just as a person needs to exercise physically and spiritually, the land needs exercise, too. Disturbance can morph into abuse if it's too long or too aggressive. The problem is that Christians generally have not identified proper participation or disturbance.

Abusive parents are certainly disturbing. Cults are disturbing. How do we know if disturbance is correct? I would suggest it's by the fruit. "BUT THE FRUIT OF THE SPIRIT IS LOVE, JOY, PEACE, LONG-SUFFERING, GENTLENESS, GOODNESS, FAITH, MEEKNESS, TEMPERANCE: AGAINST SUCH THERE IS NO LAW" (Galatians 5:22–23).

Contrast a diversified garden with tilling square miles to plant a mono-crop that ultimately creates a dead zone the size of New Jersey in the Gulf of Mexico. That's quite a different disturbance outcome than building ponds to eliminate flooding and drought. Disturbing the landscape with electric fencing to populate it with livestock in species-enhancing expression and habitat is a very different disturbance than building a confinement house that bathes the animals with fecal particulate and fills lagoons to overflow into rivers at the next hurricane, like a massive toilet flush.

As Christians, the impropriety of the abandonment mentality is easy to see. It's the basis of tree-hugger jokes. But at the other extreme, dominion does not justify abuse. While Christians say "Amen!" to my admonition for participation, they get a deer-in-the-headlights look when I balance that with boundaries to dominion.

Dominion is not an open-ended license any more than freedom in Christ gives us license to do things that make our brother stumble.

This whole topic is why I tell folks who come to our farm for tours: "I have the uncanny ability to irritate both the conservative and the liberal. I don't just make some people angry; I'm so good I can make everyone angry."

To the Christian drunk on dominion, I would admonish that disturbance must be tempered with righteousness. One of the reasons the radical environmentalists generally disagree with Christians is that they don't see Christians putting any sacred benchmarks around their disturbance. Christians exhibit an arrogant "Since I can, I will" mentality, as if whatever we do is sanctioned and blessed by God.

We would never extend that into social sins like drinking, sex, stealing, or lying. Yet when we do the equivalent toward the environment, we assume anything is fair game. Again, we're brain damaged to compartmentalize, to segregate our lives into secular and sacred, or into physical and spiritual. That's not the way God operates. He operates in one all-encompassing realm: "DO ALL TO THE GLORY OF GOD" (1 Corinthians 10:31). That pretty much covers everything.

If Christians would restrain themselves from evil disturbance and limit themselves only to righteous disturbance that honors God's design, we would offer a positive alternative to the abandonment folks. Because I spend a fair amount of time with the abandonment folks, I can say with absolute certainty that they are desperate for Christians with restraints on dominion. They don't trust Christians at all. Look at what's been done in the name of religion, from the Crusades to the conquistadors to Native American annihilation. "Manifest destiny" we learned in our history classes, likened to the Israelites' dominion of Canaan. Let me tell you a secret: English colonists did not have an Abrahamic covenant. What if the disturbance called European conquest of North America had preserved indigenous cultures, with all their wisdom and vitality? Perhaps the United States would be much smaller, would walk with less swagger, and these Protestant settlers could have shown a way to disturb an area while respecting native peoples.

Our treatment of nature and of the indigenous peoples opened us up for "GOOD [TO] BE EVIL SPOKEN OF" (Romans 14:16). I realize I've gone off into some politically charged territory, but I think as we struggle—and it is a struggle—to align our lives with the thinking characterized by "What Would Jesus Do?" we sell the whole struggle short if we make it a narrow list of lifestyle dos and don'ts. Are any of us fully consistent? No. But could we try more?

Thankfully, commercial farming can be done in an ecologically enhancing way. It's just as wrong for the Christian to disturb limitlessly as for the environmentalist to abandon limitlessly as the only answer to ecological integrity.

I would be remiss in this discussion if I didn't turn the participatory principle on the food system. Our modern techno-sophisticated culture has absolutely abandoned domestic culinary arts. An integrity food system requires that people using it be informed through participation. When people abdicate kitchen and home-centricity in food preparation, processing, packaging, and preserving, they withdraw accountability. The more people are ignorant about an issue, the easier it is for unscrupulous participants to succeed. Isn't it amazing that Christians generally get more vituperative over unscrupulous bankers than unscrupulous food providers?

When we're more interested in dysfunctional Hollywood celebrity culture or the Little League program than we are about what is going to become flesh of our flesh and bone of our bone, we voluntarily place ourselves into the corporate food agenda. That agenda is decidedly nutrient deficient, price inappropriate, and anti-community based. It promotes centralization, customer ignorance, and a mechanical view toward life.

Things that the religious right would abhor if they were promoted by churches are embraced warmly in the food system. While preachers rail against bringing junk into our homes via TV, the Internet, and pornographic literature, few bat an eye at a home stashed with high fructose corn syrup, potato chips, and Pop-Tarts. Indeed, some even suggest that the cheaper we eat, the more money we'll have to put in the offering plate. And to top it off, they denigrate anyone who would suggest part of caring for children is caring about what they eat.

Every Israelite festival centered on food. When it came time for Jesus to create a visceral reminder of His first and second comings, He chose bread and wine. In that day and culture, these were as common as French fries and Coke in modern America. Would He have chosen French fries and Coke if they had been available? I don't think so.

In that day, prior to refrigeration, bread indicated fragility. Unlike most dead bread consumed in modern America, mold grew on that bread. If you didn't eat it in a day, tomorrow it was covered in mold and tasted bad. In the famous Lord's Prayer, Jesus asks for daily bread—not weekly or monthly. Not somebody else's bread. Why? Because God wants daily participation. He doesn't want us to abandon Him any more than He wants to abandon us.

As much as He desires to interact with us, He wants us to interact with Him. We take a vacation from God to our own peril; we leave His relationship to our own detriment. Bread is a reminder of how fragile and moment-by-moment our relationship is with God. He wants us to think about Him continuously, to never let our spiritual bread get moldy, but eat it every day.

The wine, in that day without refrigeration, represented perhaps the most stable food available. Wine didn't go bad like perishable things. Yes, it represented His blood like the bread represented His flesh, but being stable, it expressed the staying power of His blood and our relationship with Him. Just like the bread expressed fragility, wine expressed powerful longevity. So it is with our relationship with God: It is both fragile and powerful. It's moment by moment, but also everlasting.

The elements were both common in that day. They were not exotic, expensive items. This demonstrates a "whosoever will" mentality (see John 3:16). God does not want to limit participation to ethnicity, education, or economic superiority. I suggest that when we get in our kitchens to prepare, process, preserve, and package food, we enter a sacred creative process that parallels our participation in the spiritual walk God desires. Why must we routinely downplay the visceral part of God's beckoning participation and elevate the cerebral and spiritual part? I suggest they are not competitive, but rather symbiotic in kind and nature.

When we pick up Kentucky Fried Chicken for the church potluck, we're participating in a system that expresses physically the very principles we abhor spiritually. That confuses not only our children, but our neighbors and friends we're trying to evangelize. Few things can express our devotion and interest in our children more than carefully scrutinizing the food that comes into our homes. When children see parents caring enough to put only high-quality food on the table, they see a visceral representation of God, who cares about our spiritual welfare and desperately wants us to discern what we feed our minds and spirits.

The foodscape wellness and demeanor should exhibit the same principles as our spiritual terrain. To say that we should care about one and not the other, or that God cares about one and not the other, is to abandon the very kind of consistency that should mark the walk of the believer. Otherwise, we appear like a bunch of scofflaws to others, and rightly so.

Here's the question: "How can I participate in food and farming in a way that exhibits the righteously transformative power of spiritual participation?" As beautiful and spiritually productive as we are from participating in Christ, does our participation in our physical nest yield the same beauty and productivity? I think wrestling with that question is what "WORK OUT YOUR OWN SALVATION WITH FEAR AND TREMBLING" (Philippians 2:12) means. It's not just a walk in the park.

It's a continuous seeking. It's opening ourselves to the challenge of others' ideas—yes, even those environmental liberal commie pinkos. It's desperately asking for the answer Francis Schaeffer routinely asked: "How shall we then live?"

Abundance vs. Scarcity

I am come that they might have life, and that they might
have it more abundantly.

John 10:10

One of the most distinguishing characteristics of the Christian life
and experience is its overarching sense of abundance. Abundant
grace, abundant eternal life, a mansion in glory. Not a cottage. Not a
bungalow. A mansion—many mansions.

And yet, in actual practice, many Christians and even more outside the faith view the Christian life as primarily ascetic and a life of
scarcity. I find it fascinating that whenever we think of Jesus not even
having a house or a place to lay His head, we don't think about Him
as impoverished. We see Him jousting with Pharisees, raising Laza-
rus from the dead, making fine wine at weddings, picking wheat on
the Sabbath. Our mental pictures of His existence do not conjure up
modern images of today's homeless, but rather a vibrant, happy, even
exuberant but laser-focused personification of perfect righteousness.

I think Jesus had a great sense of humor. God certainly does—
look at how weird I am. Trust me, God has a sense of humor. Solomon said, "A MERRY HEART DOETH GOOD LIKE A MEDICINE" (Proverbs

17:22). Jesus was not deprived like we consider it today; rather, He was focused on His mission and didn't get too bogged down in the trappings most of us call life. He was above that; we are not. He never married or had children. He made thousands of meals out of a boy's lunch bag. He was above and beyond the physical; we are not.

But even in our physical, fallen state, God wants to remind us that He has our best interests at heart. He doesn't give us stones for bread or snakes for fish. He likes us to call him Daddy and have a similar relationship.

He gave the Israelites a clearly marked area, promising to protect them within those boundaries. And then He said to multiply, occupy, and populate the land. Clearly He envisioned an earth that humankind could coax more and more production from. Otherwise, a defined piece of land with increasing population would be a recipe for scarcity and eventual starvation.

We live in a time when most people are obsessed with scarcity. Attend any environmental sciences class in any university in the world, and at least half of the course will be devoted to scarcity. We're running out of energy, money, minerals, food, water, species, air. In the 1970s many radical environmentalists predicted that we'd be out of oil by the 1980s. Most people agree that oil is not still being made—hence the term *fossil fuel*. Regardless of how much we have, whether it's little or much, we should use it judiciously. Just because these predictions overstated the case does not mean we should blow through the oil as fast as we can.

The libertarians spew epithets at the environmentalists who would dare slow down resource use and depletion. One prominent libertarian, making fun of the prominent Earth First! environmental organization, says of course he's interested in earth first: use it up and then go on to the planets. What kind of mentality is that? It's unbridled hubris and nonsense, that's what it is. It's poppycock. That's why I say I'm a libertarian environmentalist. Rod Dreher calls it *Crunchy Cons* (as in granola conservatives) in his fabulous book by that title. We live in a hockey stick time. Graphs that look like hockey sticks don't continue. They never have and they never will—at least this side of eternity.

This is what drives reasonable people into apoplexy when nations measure their success in terms of gross domestic product (GDP) and Wall Street assumes perpetual growth is sustainable. Who wants to grow the number of jails? Who wants to grow autism or cancer? Who wants to grow multiflora rose or mad cow disease? Who wants to grow deserts? Who wants to grow polluted water or smog? You see, lots of things shouldn't grow. How about sin: Should that grow?

We love to bag people, agendas, and movements. One of the most sobering verses to me is when Jesus says, "THE CHILDREN OF THIS WORLD ARE IN THEIR GENERATION WISER THAN THE CHILDREN OF LIGHT" (Luke 16:8). That should chill the heart of any Christian. What does it mean? It means that in social and political affairs, in connecting data points to track trends, more often than not the non-Christians are more astute, more clever, more with it than are God's people. It means that in the name of religion, and in the name of Christianity, we do some really stupid things. We did the Crusades and have yet to apologize enough for that. We ran a slave trade and justified it by saying we were exposing Africans to the gospel that they wouldn't have heard in their native land.

We abused and slaughtered Native Americans, disrespecting their knowledge of ecology, herbs, and long-term land care—not that all of them were good stewards by any means. But they had some good knowledge that would have served Protestant settlers well. We launched the Woman's Christian Temperance Union that culminated in Prohibition, destroying small businesses and self-reliant energy production (farm-based alcohol). This set the precedent for the culture that the government has the right to tell us what we may and may not eat, and created the mental justification and legal gymnastics to launch the current drug war. A government that can tell you not to drink can prohibit raw milk. In the name of protecting you, it can demand that you vaccinate your kids or give a certain orthodox drug regimen to your autistic child.

I warn my Christian friends to be extremely careful about what they become righteously indignant about. When we demand salvation by legislation, the law of unintended consequences kicks in. Often, we can't see it through our blinded self-righteousness, but the children of this world can see through it like the emperor's new clothes. Since when is it the government's prerogative to decide what our kids can eat, see, or buy? When we ask for additional governmental intrusion in one area, it creates precedent and encouragement for intrusion in other areas.

It's no more Christian to laugh and poke fun at environmentalists who want to protect God's gifts than it is to join the big business crowd that thinks every oil well represents progress. And just because I don't think every oil well is an assault on the earth, neither do I think putting as many as we can wherever we can and extracting oil as fast as we can is a signpost of successful dominion.

Scarcity is not God's desire. Consider Leviticus 26:5: "AND YOUR THRESHING SHALL REACH UNTO THE VINTAGE, AND THE VINTAGE SHALL REACH UNTO THE SOWING TIME: AND YE SHALL EAT YOUR BREAD TO THE FULL, AND DWELL IN YOUR LAND SAFELY." How's that for a picture of abundance?

Are you ready for another? "AND THE LORD THY GOD WILL MAKE THEE PLENTEOUS IN EVERY WORK OF THINE HAND, IN THE FRUIT OF THY BODY, AND IN THE FRUIT OF THY CATTLE, AND IN THE FRUIT OF THY LAND, FOR GOOD" (Deuteronomy 30:9).

Doesn't this sound extremely similar to spiritual promises of plenty? "I AM COME THAT THEY MIGHT HAVE LIFE, AND THAT THEY MIGHT HAVE IT MORE ABUNDANTLY" (John 10:10). How about this one out of the Epistles: "AND GOD IS ABLE TO MAKE ALL GRACE ABOUND TOWARD YOU; THAT YE, ALWAYS HAVING ALL SUFFICIENCY

IN ALL THINGS, MAY ABOUND TO EVERY GOOD WORK" (2 Corinthians 9:8). One more: "FOR SO AN ENTRANCE SHALL BE MINISTERED TO YOU ABUNDANTLY INTO THE EVERLASTING KINGDOM OF OUR LORD AND SAVIOR JESUS CHRIST" (2 Peter 1:11 AKJV).

Believe it or not, as industrial food and farming deplete mineral, soil, water, and energy resources at unprecedented rates, ecological farming is building those reserves. New technologies and new land care actually create abundance out of scarcity. Israel leads the world in greening an arid region and being able to steward water more aggressively. The poultry waterers we use on our farm came from Israel. Drip irrigation technology started in Israel. Landscape hydration is a biblical type of blessing and stewardship. So how do we hydrate the landscape?

We can start by harvesting roof water from our church buildings and houses. Installing cisterns to collect this rainwater keeps it from being a storm problem downstream, reduces public works infrastructure, maintenance, and costs. As we use it in our houses, first to shower and then to re-use in our toilets, we reduce demand for public works infrastructure, maintenance, and costs to deliver it. Our dependence and reliance on government services drops in both directions, coming and going. It helps our neighbors by not extracting from them or dumping excess on them.

As we use that water both in the house and to water our gardens and flower beds, it gradually seeps into the soil and then into aquifers. This maintains base flow, springs, and creeks so rivers remain healthy. Instead of the buildings and grounds committee at the church buying fertilizer for the lawn, how about installing a cistern to make the whole facility water independent and publicize the amount of water in the reservoir to help everyone understand ecological dependency and carrying capacity?

As I've already discussed, farms need to be building ponds instead of seeking crop insurance. The best crop insurance you can have is a resilient hydration plan. Conservatives lobby for these renamed government subsidies called crop insurance as if this is the only way to steward a farm's assets. It's absolutely the wrong way to do that. If we pull violence-driven charity and protection off the table—and if you don't think government programs are violence based, just try not paying your taxes one year and see who gets violent—then farmers are forced to start implementing more resilient, abundance-based principles.

We've already established the need for a carbon-centric model. This is looking at the same issue from an abundance standpoint rather than a pattern standpoint. It doesn't matter whether the earth is heating up or cooling down. It doesn't matter whether changes are man caused, volcano caused, God caused, or Gaia caused. Abundance grows out of participating with a carbon-centric scheme.

The overriding mind-set in our modern American culture is that the earth is a reluctant partner that must be coerced into production. I don't want to get too graphic here with the sexual metaphor, but I view the earth as a lover ready to be caressed. And just like a lover responds to affectionate and appropriate touch with abundant reciprocity, the earth responds the same way. The whole picture is one of beautiful reciprocity.

Why do we love God? "WE LOVE HIM, BECAUSE HE FIRST LOVED US" (1 John 4:19). Why does someone have a lush vineyard? Because he planted a vine, dug around it, dunged it, and loved it. Why do we have fat, slick cattle? Because we loved the soil with compost, built ponds to ensure hydration for enough grass to keep the cows well fed even in lean times, selected the best stock for rebreeding, and loved the relationship of herbivores and perennials.

The average industrial farmer does not consider himself compensated for loving the land, the plants, the animals. He considers his compensation wrestled from cantankerous, reluctant partners. His cleverness and manipulative management teased production out of the land. Can you see the difference in mentality? One is themed toward a loving partner; the other is themed toward coercion. That is a striking difference in outlook.

This theme plays out at farm conferences, and it's actually quite profound. At sustainable agriculture conferences, most of the workshops are positive how-tos. I almost never hear much discussion about sickness and disease. The overriding desire is how to work with nature as a benevolent friend. This is completely opposite of the theme at industrial agriculture conferences—the kind put on by mainstream agribusiness. Nearly all the discussions center around diseases and sicknesses. The overriding desire is how to beat nature, how to win, as if nature is the enemy that must be subjugated like a military conquest. If you don't believe me, just attend a couple of these and you'll see it firsthand. Or simply get the agendas and you'll see that I'm right.

Industrial food advocates routinely invoke the clarion call "We must feed the world" to justify its pillaging of God's resources. The world is producing way more food than it needs. But the industry knows that when people are fearful, they'll swallow almost any solution.

Let's try another take on this abundance vs. scarcity idea. Many people tell me a local-centric system can never work because people need to eat in the wintertime and lots of places can't grow things in the winter. The default position, therefore, is to abandon local food and embrace an unrestrained global and long-distance, segregated system. A system based on the fact that Minneapolis, Minnesota, is a place of scarcity in the wintertime. Minnesotans buy tender imported lettuce, mostly water, from down south, swiping their credit cards in the supermarket transaction with nothing on their minds except getting home to the sit-coms.

Why not take all that time and energy used to transport the lettuce and instead turn it into plastic solariums on the side of houses? Everyone grows their own lettuce in the wintertime using high-tech thermal mass and thermocouple-activated fans to hold temperatures at the right place. Solar energy converts directly to food, on-site, with enough left over to passively heat the house.

May I be so bold as to suggest that such a system honors God because it brings true, rejuvenated abundance proximate to our lives, with our involvement, creating an integrated object lesson of provision in the midst of Minnesota winters. You see, we're not lazy. We're just busy doing the wrong things. An abundance-based system rather than a "We can't do it here" mentality suddenly creates an object lesson for the Christian to show just how boundless God's blessings are.

Now, imagine that solarium in Minneapolis filled with spinach, chard, lettuce, beets, and carrots (cold-tolerant veggies to be sure) when your environmentalist neighbor comes over for a visit. Your atheist neighbor.

"Hey, I see green all over the side of your house. What's going on there?" she asks.

"Let me show you," you respond hospitably. "Here, step into my solarium. See, we've got lettuce and beets and spinach—there's extra. Here, let's get a bag and you can take some home. Really, I'm not kidding. See those five chickens in the corner? They eat our kitchen scraps and lay eggs. Remind me to give you some on your way out. The compost they make fertilizes these bins where the veggies grow. And all the oxygen generated by the veggies keeps the house so air-fertile we only have to take half as many breaths as we used to."

Okay, okay, that last phrase was over the top. I got carried away, but you see the drift of the conversation.

"Well, I'll be, this is amazing. What made you come up with this?" the neighbor asks, completely awed and on board.

"I've been thinking about abundance. God is so abundant in grace and provision. I thought that by putting this little solarium in to help His creation along here when it's struggling, I could enjoy watching just how abundant God really is." At this point, of course, the neighbor is wide eyed, not sure whether to hug, run, laugh, or agree. At any rate, isn't this a wonderful introduction to God's abundant grace and provision?

Dear Christian brothers and sisters, I guarantee you that if every one of us would embrace this as an imperative, and not dismiss it as some sort of greenie weenie commie tree-hugger foolishness, we'd have conversations we never dreamed of with people we can't imagine. You see, I think the way to the heart is through the visceral walk of life.

God sends His creation as a token of His patterns and abundance. He uses our hands and feet, really, physically, to do His work and will. We aren't supposed to be cloistered in some obscure place unseen and segregated. No, He wants us out and about, in and around, entering and welcoming.

By using our intellect and mechanical prowess to make winter bloom and deserts blossom through season extension, hydration, carbon-cycling, and integrated systems, we create an object lesson of His abundant provision in a spiritual life that is dead, cold, dry, and hopeless.

We have rooftops to grow on, patios, containers, backyards, interstate medians, parks, front yards. Goodness, Michael Ableman in Vancouver is placing farms on defunct multi-acre stadium parking lots using shipping boxes and spent mushroom compost. Drip irrigation and community labor round out these urban ghetto farms, which ultimately reduce crime and gang activity by inspiring young people with the majesty and mystery of growing food.

Life begets life. That's the way it works. I want you to think of the earth not as an enemy to be subdued, but as a lover to be courted. In this romance, we don't want its essence to change. Its beauty and functionality—what we're drawn to—are innate. What we do is add some compliments here, some direction there, and it responds more bountifully than we can imagine.

It doesn't want or need poisons. It doesn't mind giving up some minerals and resources, but those should be extracted with the greatest appreciation of their irreplaceable value and leveraged to the greatest strategic advantage. The idea is not to wear it out, to pillage and extract, but to instill more productivity without destroying. The bottom line of stewardship is that one becomes four. That barrenness becomes fruitful.

The idea that we would wear out a farm, or wear out a landscape, is utterly and completely foreign to God's design and God's desire. As His hands and feet, we coax. We massage. We create more than we found. That is the essence of stewardship. If creating more causes harm, ugliness, wounds, then it's not God's creating. As we bring abundance into being, we get to show just how marvelous God's provision is. That's an awesome assignment.

Freedom vs. Bondage

If the Son therefore shall make you free, ye shall be free
indeed.

John 8:36

Liberty and freedom themes permeate God's promises to His
people. Blessings including freedom from famine, freedom from
drought, freedom from pestilence defined God's promises to Israelites who lived obediently in Canaan. God's faithfulness manifested
itself in a visceral protection not only from bondage of neighboring conquerors but also from daily bondage to starvation, nakedness,
and homelessness.

Interestingly, the Levitical laws defined a way of life that liberated
the Israelites from the diseases and heartaches routinely affecting
neighboring cultures. While a casual reading may give the percep-
tion that these regulations regarding land, livestock, and food were
burdensome, they actually liberated the society from heartache.

Consider the prohibition against cutting fruit trees as they entered
the promised land. While on the surface that may appear to be burdensome, it actually provided sustained sustenance to the people.
Jesus says, "MY YOKE IS EASY, AND MY BURDEN IS LIGHT" (Matthew

11:30), even though a disciple's life entails self-sacrifice, and "HE THAT LOSETH HIS LIFE FOR MY SAKE SHALL FIND IT" (Matthew 10:39). Short-term hardship is the cost of long-term fulfillment.

A long-term Beulah land awaits those who conform to God's rules, the most important of which is to accept the sacrificial atonement of the Messiah. Believers who understand what freedom in Christ means realize that it is not freedom to satisfy our fleshly lusts. Rather, our freedom liberates us from the power of Satan, the stranglehold of lusts, and the emotional devastation of hate.

So what kind of farm and food system illustrates this type of freedom rather than bondage? Of course, biblical Egypt is a type of bondage, sin, and the unrighteousness of the world system. What kind of farm illustrates Canaan rather than Egypt?

I had a fascinating radio interview with a couple of guys hosting a farm show in Nebraska. Most of my media interviews are kind. Since media folks are generally liberal tree huggers, they tend to like my feely-meely warm and fuzzy pigness of pigs farming ideas. Interviewers love to hear me wax eloquent about the pigness of pigs, compost, pastured livestock, local food systems, and multi-species farming. Those are calling-card themes and they resonate positively with most media hosts.

But not with these guys in Nebraska. Oh no. They were loaded for bear. In fact, they ambushed me and made me struggle for a while. They asked me: "What does it mean for a chicken to express its chickenness?"

I had my stock answer that always thrilled the hosts: "It means they can run around outside, get exercise, eat grass, and scratch in the dirt."

Without batting an eye (actually, this was radio so I don't know if they batted an eye), the hosts responded: "Wouldn't the best way to ensure the chickenness of the chicken be to protect her from predators, rain, and rough weather? We think when a chicken can be killed by a hawk or die of pneumonia in a cold rain, that's denying the chicken her abilities because if she's not secure, if she dies, she doesn't have much chickenness to express."

This may sound funny, but these mouthpieces for factory farming and industrial food systems were dead serious. They thought they had me on the ropes and were going in for the knockout. I had never had hosts who dared to take umbrage with my pastured chicken nirvana. I had never had media people mount a serious argument that chickens free to run around and find bugs demeaned them more than locking them in a tiny wire cell where they had less room than a sheet of notebook paper for their whole lives.

In that moment, I realized I was dealing with industrial pros. This wasn't a sympathizer like National Public Radio; this was the big industrial farm leagues with Tyson and Monsanto. Suddenly it occurred to me that these guys viewed security, or lack of risk, as the highest expression of individuality.

These conservative heartland talk show hosts surely voted Republican, wanted smaller and less intrusive government, and embraced personal freedom. They were certainly not socialists, liberals, or bureaucracy lovers. In any other context they would laud freedom, with its inherent risks, as superior to straitjacket security. To follow their line of thinking, the best expression of the Tomness of Tom, for example, would only be possible if Tom lived in a protective cocoon where failure, disease, and physical assault could never occur.

But what ultimately defines a person's individuality? Our customized glory, if you will? Our distinctiveness? Is it not how we act out our gifts and talents? Is it not the freedom to fail? The risk of self-actualization? Would Lewis and Clark be revered as heroes of America's past had they adhered to the notion that to fully express their distinctiveness would require a no-risk, secure existence? How about Charles Lindbergh? How about Dwight D. Eisenhower? How about John Glenn and the other astronauts?

Freedom requires risk. You cannot eliminate risk and maintain freedom. If we let our children climb trees, that's freedom with risk. Would you rather be prohibited from climbing a tree? I found it fascinating that these conservative talk show hosts who normally lauded American freedom and liberty projected quite a different view toward poultry. Up until the day one of my pastured chickens gets attacked by a hawk, she lives a life that honors her legs, her beak, her lungs, her life. Is it risky having her out there in the field? Yes.

I can assure you that these conservative industrial farm defenders, in nearly any other context, would applaud freedom through risk. I'll bet they even wanted to own guns and choose their own doctors. Talk about risky. But when it came to domestic livestock, they defined freedom in terms of no choice. Interestingly, they did not perceive any risk from chickens being locked in their supposedly secure cages.

Their unspoken assumption was that a concentrated animal feeding operation was secure. That it was risk free. But that is absolutely not the case. Our pastured chickens don't get high-pathogen *salmonella* or avian influenza. As far as I know, based on every sample and every study to date, pastured poultry is immune to these industrial-strain diseases. I'm concentrating here on high-path strains, not the old-style strains that have been with us forever. That is not a small distinction. It's a similar distinction to the one we see when we measure the nutritional differences between an egg from a pastured chicken and one locked up in a secure factory farm.

The differences are profound. I put this comparison in my book *Folks, This Ain't Normal*, and I'm going to put it in here again. *Mother Earth News* spearheaded a study comparing twelve pastured egg producers with the USDA standard nutritional egg profile. Here are some of the results from our farm:

	USDA	POLYFACE FARM
Vitamin E	0.97 mg	7.37 mg
Vitamin A	487 IU	763 IU
Beta-carotene	10 mcg	76.2 mcg
Folate	47 mcg	1,200 mcg
Omega-3s	0.033 g	0.71 g
Cholesterol	423 mg	292 mg
Saturated Fat	3.1 g	2.31g

You don't have to be a registered dietician to appreciate the astronomical differences between these two columns. And yes, the folate is the real deal, not a misprint. By the way, that's a critical fatty acid for pregnant moms, just in case you wondered. Now, how much do you want to settle for those cheap, anemic, pale, industrial super-market eggs?

I would suggest that the pastured model frees up the chicken—and the egg—to be all they can be. To be physiologically perfected, to express their glory in fullness. To deny the birds the freedom to run around on pasture—and the risk of being picked off by a predator—is to deny the person who eats the egg a full nutritional package. Must we, as eaters, be bounded by chicken security and devitalized nutrition? What about our freedom, as humans, to build our bodies with the most nutritious options possible?

This is truly a fascinating discussion because it exposes the hypocrisy of the industrial food movement, which is fundamentally about control. But in pursuing control, they actually create a system of bondage. To what? To pharmaceuticals. To energy to pour the concrete and run the fans and haul manure. To lawyers to protect them from nuisance and pollution suits as a result of their toxic fac-tory houses and their externalized damages. To lobbyists who must pass Right to Farm laws to protect their obnoxious stink and pol-lution from nauseated and distraught neighbors. To more lobbyists who convince legislators it should be illegal for anyone to take pic-tures of these despicable factory houses with the intent to expose the filth and abuse contained therein.

Drive up to any factory chicken house and you'll be met with No Trespassing signs. Walk up to any industrial processing facility and you'll encounter a guardhouse with security. It'll even have a razor-wire fence around it. The assumption is that this frees the industrial-ists to act on their own instincts and pursue their mission of feeding the world. But in reality, these fences, guards, and signs signify a bondage, an inability to be transparent and honest about what goes on there.

On our farm, we have a 24/7/365 open-door policy for anyone to come from anywhere in the world at any time to see anything unannounced. Do you know how liberating it is to not live in fear that someone will see something reprehensible? That we'll need a bevy of attorneys to protect us from a wronged neighbor? That our animals have such great immune systems that we don't worry about a red-winged blackbird bringing in a disease and wiping out our livelihood?

The average factory chicken farmer lives in abject fear that a Canada goose will poop on his farm and infest his million-bird flock with a disease. Such a thought never crosses my mind. The average factory chicken farmer worries every day about some visitor bringing a disease onto his farm, carried in the creases of a leather work shoe. He dutifully buys toxic footbaths and even installs showers so visitors can shower in and shower out. He tries to lock out every mouse, every fly, every barn swallow from his facilities, desperate to provide security for his fragile birds with compromised fecal-particulate-covered respiratory tracts. Immune systems, he's told by the university and industry poultry scientists, are always ready to snap.

At our farm, we welcome guests with open arms. They don't have to walk through sheep dip, shower in and shower out, and don hazardous material suits to visit their food. We're free from the fear, the toxins, the fragility. Instead, we revel in robust immune systems and drug-free birds. Unlike our industrial counterparts, we're not in bondage to the pharmaceutical cartel. We're not beholden to industry shills who blather their paranoia to the lapdog media and duplicitous public. *Protection, safety,* and *security* are their buzzwords. The result is suffocating bondage on our farms and in our food system.

Let's shift gears to another animal for a moment and look at freedom that comes through letting herbivores be herbivores. We know that herbivores aren't supposed to eat grain and they certainly aren't supposed to eat carrion. Farmers still routinely feed both. In fact, the government subsidizes the practice. Grain feeding herbivores requires a plethora of dependency on machinery, energy, seeds, storage buildings, and distribution systems.

In order for that steer to eat grain, we have to be like the Little Red Hen. Preparing the soil, planting the seed, eliminating weeds, harvesting the crop, storing the crop, and getting the crop to the feed bin. And remember, if we don't get timely rain on the seed, it won't sprout. At the other end of the cycle, if we get untimely rain late in the season, we can't harvest.

Now juxtapose that with a grass-based cattle operation. First of all, the grass is a perennial so it doesn't have to be planted every season. The perennial has a totally different energy flow than an annual. Rather than storing its energy in the seeds (barley, wheat, corn), it stores energy in the roots. That means the perennial offers more soil fertility; it actually builds soil more effectively than annuals.

Here's the big kicker: the cattle self-harvest the crop. We don't have to run a combine over it, haul it to an elevator or storage bin, dry it down, and then haul it to the animals. Instead, the animals graze it, take out a few nutrients, and poop most of it right back out on the ground to increase fertility and grow yet more grass. Gordon Hazard, icon of Mississippi graziers, boasted that he could run three thousand steers with nothing more than a Toyota pickup truck and if times got tough, he could do it without the truck.

Some people complain that cows are inefficient in their conversion of sunlight via biomass into nutrition for humans. Well, duh, their inefficiency is what makes them such tremendous fertility builders. If they extracted all the goodies from the forage and didn't excrete most of it, the soil's fertility would diminish. Their inefficiency is the soil's gain. It's an overall asset for the ecology.

Come to think of it, taking the time to establish meaningful relationships is not very efficient. I mean, you have to invest in somebody who might bite you in a couple of years. You have to slow down, take time to talk, to listen, to care, to learn. But, dear heart, it's the very inefficiency of establishing the relationship that makes our overall lives better. Our life soil, our emotional soil, the fertility of our minds, grows when we embrace the inefficiency of relationship building. The cow is not supposed to be the most efficient thing on the planet; she's arguably the most efficacious soil builder, and that's valuable enough.

When we let the cow be the cow, in all her simple glory, she doesn't enslave us to expensive infrastructure. That's our doing, not hers. The average farm in America requires $4 worth of buildings and equipment to generate $1 in annual gross sales. At our farm, the ratio is 50 cents to $1. That's an 800 percent difference in capital costs. Note that I'm not putting the land into this equation at all. Heavy capitalization costs enslave farmers to the equipment dealer, the banker, the mortgage company. A liberated farmer doesn't spend much time on bended knee in front of lending institutions. These expensive burdens take the spring out of the farmer's step.

How about chemicals? The modern conventional farmer is in terrible bondage to what my dad used to call a serious drug addiction. I'm not talking about pharmaceuticals; I'm talking about chemical fertilizers, pesticides, herbicides, insecticides, grubicides, parasiticides—the whole toxic soup from the devil's pantry. Having drunk the chemical companies' Kool-Aid, farmers see themselves on a treadmill, needing more toxicity, more potency, and unable to afford it. To help the situation, technology dangles a tantalizing carrot: buy GPS packages to meter out chemicals in a customized site application and reduce costs. It all sounds great, until you realize that the calibrations and software are all designed by the industry.

They have glitches, and they break. And they're expensive. More costs. More bondage. Folks, the chemical merry-go-round is a vicious circle. Chemical fertilizers destroy soil by making the biota cannibalize. Herbicides create super weeds. Genetically modified organisms (GMOs) are wreaking havoc in the nation's croplands by creating mutated super weeds that must be controlled by machete-wielding hand laborers. Isn't it fascinating that the techno-industrial Holy Grail of promise ultimately creates field conditions that must be hand-weeded before the $300,000 combines can harvest the crop?

On our farm, we haven't bought a bag of chemical fertilizer

since we bought the place in 1961. We use no herbicides, no pesticides. We follow the cows with free-roaming chickens (yes, those risky, insecure birds) in the eggmobiles to provide parasite and grub control. Rather than spending money on toxins, we simply gather thousands of dollars' worth of eggs as a by-product of the pasture sanitation system.

Our fertility increases due to copious amounts of compost that we make not with expensive heavy compost-turning machines, but with pigs. Incentivizing them in the winter-generated anaerobic cattle bedding pack with fermented corn, we get all that turning and aerating done without starting a machine, buying a machine, or operating a machine. It's glorious and truly liberating.

I'm freed from getting a pesticide applicator's license, attending the classes, and paying the fees. I'm freed from wearing the protective clothing required to apply such toxins. My children are free to eat anything I apply to the soil. I'm liberated from the fear that one of my children or grandchildren will fall into a manure pit or drink a bottle of atrazine. I've never heard of someone being killed by a compost spill. I'm freed from the fears and worries clouding the mind of the average farmer. This truly is an easy yoke, a light burden.

The problem with all this expensive infrastructure, application, and input is that it enslaves us emotionally. Our toys—what we buy and what we play with—confine our thinking, or what world-class water guru Darren Doherty calls "the climate of the mind." We absolutely become beholden to our infrastructure. How do you abandon a building or a machine on which you're still making payments? If it was a bad buy, the wrong investment, unprofitable, or no longer emotionally rewarding, we have to keep using it.

When a son or daughter attends a grass farming conference and comes home to the confinement dairy all excited about letting the cows graze rather than growing corn to fill the silo to feed the cows to haul the manure out to the fields, it's a huge threat to Dad and Grandpa, who have spent their lives pouring concrete, bending rebar, and negotiating borrowed money. You don't just walk away from such things. Even if you're not economically beholden, you're emotionally beholden. The result is a young generation that feels trapped. And what do we want to do when we feel trapped? Flee. And that, dear folks, is exactly what's happening on thousands of farms across the country.

Young people are not returning to farms. That fact is not the result of freedom; it's the natural result of bondage. This bondage poses as security. It's marketed as security. The pharmaceuticals, the confinement buildings, the concrete, the GPS guidance systems, the chemicals, the genetically modified organisms: it's all sold in the name of security. Farm kids don't want to be stuck on a place that's actually a massive drug, chemical, infrastructure addiction, a treadmill with no end in sight. This is not a picture of liberty, of freedom. It's a picture of bondage, drudgery, and dead ends. If our farms are supposed to express freedom and liberty's exhilarating emotions, we're obviously far off the mark.

On our farm, an excellent example of liberating infrastructure is the pastured poultry shelter. These simple ten feet by twelve feet by two feet high floorless boxes house seventy-five broilers apiece and we move them, by hand, every morning across the pasture to another spot. They're cheap, simple, and portable. That means we can get in and get out of the business enterprise easily. If we decide to downsize or upscale, we can finance both retraction and addition with self-generated cash flow. That offers flexibility.

The ability to get in and out of enterprises is a signature trait of freedom-oriented models. If it's hard to get in or hard to get out, the model is rigid and confining. Flexibility requires fluidity. If I want to grow a chicken for one of the large poultry integrators, the first thing I have to do is build a $400,000 confinement house. Never mind that I've never raised chickens. Never mind that I don't even know if I like chickens. Never mind that I have no idea if the company holding the contract is trustworthy. Before dipping my toe in the water, before testing the model, before doing anything, I have to build that massive stationary structure.

Does that sound like freedom to you? Amazingly, the poultry company can change the contract and/or refuse to guarantee a single chicken coming to this massively leveraged facility. Routinely the poultry industry cancels contracts, leaving a wake of desperate, suicidal farmers behind. Does that sound liberating to you? If you read the testimonials of these farmers, it's apparent quickly that they are modern serfs in an economic and business system that smacks of colonialism. How Christians can sign these contracts or eat the chickens that come from such diabolical schemes is beyond me.

A liberated farm, then, should be one that's free from the bondage of chemical companies, suffocating capricious industrial contracts, pharmaceuticals, and capital-intensive single-use infrastructure. A liberated farm should concentrate on perennials, on-farm composting systems, diversified production, functional immune systems, and multiple-use portable lightweight economical infrastructure.

Finally, this discussion about liberty and bondage would not be complete without looking at marketing. Have you ever heard a farmer lament, "The middle man makes all the profits"? Of course you have. A permutation on this theme is: "The farmer is the only business who buys retail and sells wholesale." Said another way, farmers are price takers rather than price makers.

At the whim of commodity prices, farmers consistently find themselves in bondage to a wildly fluctuating, unpredictable pricing structure. Sometimes it makes sense and other times it doesn't. Because farmers are on the tail end of the pricing whip, they feel the jerk worst whenever supply and demand are out of whack. Farmers feel like they're riding a roller coaster, and feel about as much in control as you do on a roller coaster.

The bondage of price contracts and production quotas that have one goal—to drive the farmer's portion down—is quite real out here in farm country. The boom and bust cycle haunts the farmer like the four horsemen of the apocalypse. The farmer has no idea when price disaster will strike. This year prices might be great, only to collapse next year.

Twenty years ago our first farm apprentice, Tai Lopez, talked us into renting a nearby farm. We developed it for grazing with electric fence and water lines. Purchasing sixty steers at the livestock auction barn in the spring, we planned to sell them through the same venue in the fall. This was a classic commodity-based summer grazing scheme, buying the animals when the grass grew enough to graze and removing them when it stopped growing.

We made about $150 apiece on those steers and considered the scheme a great success. How hard could this be? Easy-peasy. Buy in the spring, sell in the fall. Walk away rich. Show me the money.

The next year we repeated the scheme. All looked well until we got ready to sell them and the price collapsed. Even though they had gained on average 250 pounds apiece over the summer, they sold for exactly the same price per animal that we'd paid for them. Sad day.

Fortunately, we had already begun direct marketing to customers in the area and realized the advantage of being a price maker instead of a price taker. Selling retail gave us a huge gross margin advantage and locked in our prices to the more stable retail rate. After the commodity steer fiasco, I decided that I didn't want to even dabble in that game. From then on, I committed myself to always selling retail.

Ultimately liberating ourselves once and for all from the wholesale commodity market incentivized us to pursue additional customers. We could have adopted a victim mentality and walked around in depression for a year. But we turned the experience into a catalyst to seek enough new customers to buy the beef the rental farm produced. It took us a year or two to build the business to that point, but it was certainly worth it.

Direct marketing liberates us from the bondage of the commodity market. Rather than having only one buyer, we have thousands. That spreads resiliency to our sales that could never occur if we had only one outlet. Believe it or not, most farmers sell to only one outlet.

Sometimes they have a choice, but most of the time they don't. Often what they produce is under contract long before harvest.

If I could admonish the Christian community to do one thing that would encourage more market-freed farms, it would be to patronize local direct market farms. These come in all shapes and sizes. Some do roadside stands. Some sell at farmers' markets. Some offer community supported agriculture (CSA) schemes wherein the customer buys a share of the farm's produce. On our farm, we have an on-farm store and we deliver to our own metropolitan buying clubs (MBCs). Whatever you choose, put attention on finding and buying from these local integrity farms.

Many of these farms are literally half a dozen customers away from tipping over to enough sales to go full-time. I'm a full-time farm advocate. Why should farmers have to work at some other job in order to maintain their farm addiction? If someone wants to farm as a life calling, a career choice, we can patronize that farmer directly and help the enterprise become profitable. We can help free that farmer, who has already demonstrated a liberated savvy by wanting to sell retail, from the bondage of low income and that town commute. In doing so, in a small way we liberate ourselves from depending on nameless faceless corporate mega-food entities and free up our communities to be food secure in their own rite.

Historically, societies unable to feed themselves eventually perished. The more a community feeds itself from the bounty of its own proximate resources, the more vibrant and stable that community is. Such proactive patronage sets up a visceral example of liberation that I would suggest makes a great case for illustrating liberty in Christ. If the food and farming system we develop with our patronage exemplifies bondage and a burden-based depressing system, where is the object lesson of our lives enjoying spiritual freedom? Our Christian existence is not relegated to cerebral academic catechism discussions. It is supposed to be a vibrant out-showing of spiritual truth. Let's make it that way.

Integration vs. Segregation

Whether therefore you eat, or drink, or whatever you do,
do all to the glory of God.

1 Corinthians 10:31 (AKJV)

I know *segregation* is a strong word, but I use it on purpose in order
to capture the degree of separation in America's current food and
farming system. I could use the word *disconnection* instead, but it
doesn't have the negative connotations engendered by the word
segregation.

Perhaps the most segregated thinking of our day rears its ugly
head toward the farm sector specifically, and the food sector generally. What happened to the Jeffersonian intellectual agrarian? It's
been replaced by a nearly universal notion that smart, white, creative
people don't get their hands dirty. While this applies more egregiously to farming, I see it in virtually all of the trades—plumbers,
electricians, masons, carpenters, mechanics, welders. You name it,
smart white kids aren't supposed to do those things.

I think the upwardly mobile religious right community swallowed
this idea hook, line, and sinker a long time ago. Parents at prestigious
parochial Christian schools don't encourage their little ones to grow

tomatoes or carrots in the backyard. No. The backyard is for soccer goals and lacrosse rackets. Chores? What chores? The kids are glued to their video games. How do you build garden beds with wires hanging out of your ears? Birds, what birds? I can't hear any birds; the only birds I know about are "angry birds."

We deal with this prejudice with our farm interns. Many young people, some even with master's degrees, suddenly realize they want to do something with food and farming. In consternation, parents call me wondering about this farming thing, as if their kids just decided to rob a bank or deal drugs. "I spent all this money on a college education to help them get ahead," they lament, "and now they're squandering this. Help!"

Well, they won't get help from me to dissuade their progeny from doing something as noble and sacred as touching creation. Most Christian colleges don't have agriculture programs. They don't even have environmental studies programs. Who cares about the environment? It's going to burn anyway. Only liberal democrat commie pinkos talk environmental gibberish. Give me a break.

I see it routinely when I get asked to speak at conferences. I'm supposed to come cheap because, after all, I'm just a farmer. If you're smart and capable, you become a doctor, engineer, lawyer, computer technician—anything white collar. For goodness' sake, don't wear a blue collar. That makes your mother and me a failure and our friends will wonder about our family.

So I ask the question: "What are our homes, families, and lands for?" Does God care? Are they just pit stops between life out there somewhere: the office, the school, the church building, the recreation/ entertainment center? Is our daily life a floating island segregated from the activities God desires? What does an integrated physical life look like that exemplifies an integrated spiritual life?

How about kitchen chickens, just to start the discussion? For the definitive treatise on this, I urge you to read Pat Foreman's delightful *City Chicks* book, which has firmly ensconced her as the foremost chicken whisperer of modern times. She and I are huge proponents

of urban and backyard laying chickens. They are certainly as emotionally enjoyable as a dog or cat, but unlike the dog or cat, they can
lay eggs you can enjoy for breakfast.

And they can live on kitchen scraps. Instead of throwing kitchen
scraps down the disposal (now, there's an immoral device if ever
there was one) or into the garbage to go to the landfill, feed them to
the chickens. They will turn them into wonderful eggs that are far
more nutritious for your family than those fecal salmonella eggs in
the supermarket. Not only do you keep your kitchen-generated biomass out of the waste stream (an ultimate waste), but you integrate
your life into something as creative and awesome as chickens.

I find it fascinating that Christian families who desire to give
more to missions or other worthy causes have no problem spending hundreds of dollars on pet food and vet care. Then they balk at
having a couple of chickens, which represent such a simple way to
save money and eat better. Goodness, you can get rid of the gerbil
and aquarium, the snake and lizard, and put in a couple of kitchen
chickens. They'll entertain you far more and allow you to integrate
your life with physical food so you'll have a sense of the joy and
effort you derive from integrating your life with spiritual food.

Just like Jesus and the Old Testament prophets used farming
lessons as the basis for parables and instruction, you'll surely learn
things about spiritual truth from the chickens. Chickens, like dogs,
exhibit unconditional love. They don't care if you've had a bad hair
day or if you're angry with your spouse. The animals love you anyway and go on about their business as if life is a seamless picnic.

We segregate companion animals from farm animals, as if farm
animals are somehow dirty, smelly, and below our status. Companion animals like dogs, cats, gerbils, snakes, and horses are acceptable for white-collar folks because they don't denigrate our existence
with something as low as farming. Indeed, how many homeowners'
associations prohibit farming—including having a tomato plant in
your rose garden—or even solar clothes dryers (outdoor clotheslines),
because they smack of what "those people" do? For Christians

to cavort with such thinking, even for a moment, besmirches the very nature of God and our faith. Tut. Tut. Actually, we should be ashamed that we entertain such notions—even if we don't voice them.

How about integrating edible landscaping into your yardscape? It doesn't take any more effort to plant an apple tree than it does a shade tree. Again, we have this notion that an apple comes from a professional apple orchard; it's segregated from the rest of society, out there on a farm somewhere, and comes to us via a network of packinghouses, trucks, warehouses, and supermarkets. When we buy that apple in a bag at the supermarket, swiping our card that represents cash, get into our car with fuel from who knows where, and drive to our house built from material gleaned from somewhere that runs on energy from who knows where...Are you with me here?

At the end of this transaction it's easy to not eat responsibly because we see nothing, hear nothing, know nothing. We bear no responsibility for our decisions because they're out there somewhere. We don't internalize our decisions because we've externalized our living.

If we simply cerebralize our relationship with nature, we can continue in a segregated mind-set toward our sustenance. Yes, frogs and salamanders and wildflowers are cool and everyone should see them in their natural settings, touch, and appreciate them. But ultimately we can enjoy them because we've eaten something—we've taken nourishment from somewhere. I think too often we assume that nature is out there somewhere. We have to get on a jet and fly a thousand miles to some special place in order to commune with nature.

But God says it's not about place; it's about making space for Him wherever we are and in whatever we're doing. We don't have to go on a pilgrimage to a spot; we can worship and commune with God right now, wherever we are. Our spiritual sustenance and God's sufficiency is proximate; it's integrated and not segregated. Indeed, "NEITHER SHALL THEY SAY, LO HERE! OR, LO THERE! FOR, BEHOLD, THE KINGDOM OF GOD IS WITHIN YOU" (Luke 17:21). Wow!

I don't think it demeans this spiritual truth to suggest that integrating food in our physical lives encourages our appreciation of this truth. Our dependency and integration with food and farming offer a visceral object lesson that we are surrounded, indwelt, and nestled in the arms of God every moment of every day.

May I suggest that before filling our calendars with soccer, ballet, and videos, then, we carve out time to visit a farm, to build a food-integrated vision into our lives? This is one reason I'm such an advocate of local food systems. Again, I don't think it's a sin to engage in food commerce over long distances. The spice trade is well established. But the backbone of any community is a local-centric food system.

Otherwise, we lose our most consistent reminder of how dependent and nested we are in our landscape. It's easy to disrespect food when we have no appreciation or knowledge for where or how it originated. It's easy to be ungrateful when it magically appears as goods for which we exchange a credit card swipe. We take food for granted when we don't see the sweat of the brow expressed on the person growing it. Most importantly, we miss the security of being surrounded by provision and sufficiency. Any of that sound like it has spiritual overtones?

Of course it does. All of it. Just to be clear, I put food in a different category than cars and computers—even books, although it convulses my soul to admit it. From the Garden of Eden to the ever-producing fruit tree in the New Jerusalem, God's affinity for physical sustenance as an object lesson of spiritual sustenance is palpable. We can live without cars and computers. We can live without smartphones—although many people can't imagine such an existence. We can even live without books, although it wouldn't be a life worth living. Ha!

But we can't live without food; it's necessary. And I think God wants us to understand that our spiritual sustenance is just as important, just as necessary. We must not only seek and embrace it, but He wants us to know that He provides it and sustains us. He is not far off. I think when our food is far off—mentally or physically—we reduce our capacity to appreciate how close and special God is to us. Putting attention on our food knowledge is not an idol that gets in the way of our spiritual understanding; it is a door that opens into a grander understanding of God's relationship to us.

Integrating our lives with plants and animals bathes us in object lessons about responsibility, relationship, faithfulness, expectation, perseverance, diligence, and unconditional love. You don't get that from the plastic-wrapped microwavable single-service meal packet. You don't get that from video games. Most of Jesus' parables used plants, animals, and farm business settings. At the time, plenty of artisans in metalwork, pottery, carpentry, and other manufacturing skills were around. Why not use more stories from them? Because animals and plants are living mediums and they exhibit timidity and aggressiveness, boldness and fear, death and life.

The more noise in our lives, the more distractions and activity, the harder it is to hear the still small voice. We have to find a time, a quiet getaway. Even Jesus parted from the crowds to commune with His Father. If Jesus had to get away, how about us? Do we get away from life's noise to go learn about our food? To go visit a farm or take an edible wild plant seminar?

What does it tell our kids when we carve out time in our busy schedules to get away to the source of our food? How do we cultivate in ourselves and our kids a deep gratitude for God's spiritual provision? I believe one of the best ways to do that is with our meals. That means we don't just stop for a spontaneous nameless, faceless meal. Of course exceptions happen, and I'm not proposing a rigid code

that keeps us enslaved and unhappy. I like a Snickers bar occasionally, too—but it's extremely occasional. God is okay with an indul-
gence once in a while.

I like soccer and football, too. But we also visit farms. We buy
apple juice from a nearby orchard. We buy in bulk. We don't know
every story behind every morsel we get, but we try to buy with a
conscious decision, not just for convenience. Integration requires
thought and planning. Not only do you need to think about sourcing, you need to think about inventorying and preparing. Yes, that
means we plan meals in advance.

We're aware of what is in season and out of season. Do you know
what local farmers are struggling with right now? Too many tomatoes, too many apples? Can we take some slightly blemished product
off their hands (thereby showing mercy) and can it, freeze it, turn
it into salsa or applesauce? Integration means we voluntarily place
ourselves, as dependents, into the provision of our landscape. We
don't expect someone to deplete the aquifer in Colorado to grow
grain to ship with militarily purchased oil to a feedlot that pollutes
the air and water to be slaughtered by disrespected workers to be
transported via refrigerated truck belching diesel fumes across the
country to the burger joint near where we work so we can conve-
niently and thoughtlessly eat—even if such convenience gives us
time to read our Bible more.

Have I just arrogated food above Scripture? No, not at all. If convenient thoughtlessly acquired food is the only way to create time
to read my Bible, I have far more important issues. I call this letting
"YOUR GOOD BE EVIL SPOKEN OF" (Romans 14:16). A much better
approach is to bring leftovers to work. These would be leftovers from
consciously sourced food from God-honoring farms. And yes, I do
believe God honors this kind of planning and consideration on our
part. This is our diligence in bringing our lives completely under
His dominion.

At the end of Romans 13 Paul admonishes us to wake up, to put
off the works of darkness, and "PUT ON THE ARMOR OF LIGHT" (v. 12)

and "MAKE NO PROVISION FOR THE FLESH, TO FULFILL ITS LUSTS" (v. 14 NKJV). In other words, plan, prepare, provide. Get your act together. Don't be caught off guard like those who sleep and slumber and therefore need to eat fast food (again, exceptions will happen). But think about the time and your situation and get ready.

When we provision our homes with locally sourced consciously themed food, we surround ourselves with sustenance. When we lie down at night with our beloved, knowing we're provisioned well by creation's abundance, we don't need to fear a disrupting war with our supply line, a teamster's strike, or an energy crisis. Very simply, personal provisioning of our domestic larder is a visceral act of dependency and trust. Being proximate to it in our daily lives takes the edge off worry and paranoia.

Nothing we do in life is as intimate as eating—nothing. Just as with the act of marriage, God wants that intimacy to be carefully planned, carefully caressed, carefully incorporated, and absolutely enjoyed. He doesn't want us shortchanging ourselves in this object lesson. He wants revelry, festivals, communion. Gratitude grows out of that, providing a physical expression of our gratitude for the life and sustenance God grants us spiritually.

Beauty vs. Ugliness

> How beautiful on the mountains are the feet of him that brings good tidings, that publishes peace; that brings good tidings of good, that publishes salvation; that said to Zion, Your God reigns!
>
> Isaiah 52:7 (AKJV)

Perhaps nothing defines the hand of God more eloquently than when it makes something beautiful out of something ugly. This idea carries ramifications beyond just the eyes to all the senses.

Attractive things to touch, see, smell, and hear are the gift of God. In contrast, Satan's goal is to turn God's beautiful things into ugliness. The beauty of monogamous sexual intimacy becomes filthy in the mind of a child molester, pornography peddler, or sexual predator.

In the original Garden of Eden, Satan's beguilement turned Adam's daily communing with God into a fearful proposition. Adam tried to hide after eating the forbidden fruit. Imagine what a difference that created in what had been obviously a beautiful relationship. Severed by sin, humankind lost fellowship with the Creator.

Only through the redemptive plan of the Messiah could this fellowship be restored. That God could turn this hostility and alienation into a restored relationship and eventual home in Paradise speaks to profound creative power. No wonder the Scripture ascribes: "BEAUTIFUL ARE THE FEET OF THEM THAT PREACH THE GOSPEL OF PEACE, AND BRING GLAD TIDINGS OF GOOD THINGS" (Romans 10:15).

The Christian community is supposed to be attractive. Our families are supposed to be functional. Our fellowship groups are supposed to exemplify loving relationships. We're supposed to work hard, pay our bills, have loving marriages, and take care of each other. This is God's desire for us, and He spends a lot of biblical instruction telling us how to do this.

As a teen, I occasionally worked for a farmer who had a confinement turkey house for one of the big industrial brand names. To walk inside practically took my breath away, and knowing what I know now, I should have worn respiratory protection. The stench was practically overwhelming. With fifteen thousand turkeys in a house half the size of a football field, the air was a dust cloud. Large four-foot-diameter fans along the house edges tried to circulate the air, but it was a losing proposition.

The fan blades and louvers, caked with an inch of dust, looked like relics out of a forlorn hovel in a horror movie. Uninhabited, yet inhabited. You weren't sure if this was a place where life existed or the edge of its extinguishing. The dust pall covered the turkeys and your clothes, the feeders, waterers, walls, and ceiling. It was like closely following a speeding truck on a dusty dirt road. Except this dust contained more than dirt. It was primarily particles of manure.

Known as fecal particulate, this dusty air coats the respiratory tract and grates like sand paper against the tender membranes. Creating abrasions and lesions, this is the number one animal health issue created by factory farms. Think of the ugliness along these otherwise beautiful respiratory interfaces as these animals fight for survival and in such a filthy, adulterated environment. Anyone who has marveled at the handiwork of God's creative capacity to design a functioning respiratory system should be appalled that humans have designed a system that so efficiently assaults and damages these magnificent, intricate membranes.

While humans walking into these facilities can wear respiratory protection, and usually do, the animals don't. Their living and breathing space is even lower to the floor and their feet—where the dust is worst—than the taller humans who walk among them. Nothing about this system is beautiful. It's a terrible life for the turkey. It's a terrible life for the farmer. It's a terrible life for the neighbors who must endure the stench day after day after day.

When I was in 4-H as a child, I competed in poultry judging. In fact, one year I won the state championship, which means supposedly I could tell a healthy hen from a sick one, a good egg from a bad one, and a good-quality broiler carcass from a poor one better than any other 4-H'er in the state. Practices and preparation for these contests took us into industrial poultry houses. I well remember going into egg operations, those notorious battery-cage systems.

Typically, the cages were around twenty inches by thirty inches. Each contained about nine hens. For their whole life, these birds could not stretch their wings, fully extend their legs or heads—each one had less room than a sheet of notebook paper. Entirely caged—top, sides, bottom—these birds never in their lives saw sunlight, a blade of grass, or had the opportunity to scratch. The stench was practically unbearable. Many of these cages contained a dead bird in some stage of decomposition as her cellmates gradually kneaded the carcass through the mesh floor. These are dreary, dusty, unhappy places. No wonder animal welfare advocates call them concentration camps for chickens.

Folks, this is not a pretty picture. It is despicable. Have you ever seen a laying hen in a backyard or in a pastured setting? She's alert, busy, clean, and pet-able. She's not covered in fecal particulate. Why are many state governments passing laws criminalizing picture-taking at industrial farms? Because seeing the ugliness incriminates the system. When I lead a tour of our farm, I often pause for a few minutes at the laying hens, whether in the eggmobile or in the millennium feathernet, to let the aesthetics and aromatics sink in. Then I voice what every visitor is thinking: "This is just beautiful."

Everybody nods in agreement, and it's one of the most touching moments in any farm tour.

Matthew Sleeth, founder of Blessed Earth, asks a profound question: "Would Jesus be born in a factory house?" He was born in a stable. Undoubtedly this stable had several kinds of animals in it and was fairly small. Some have even suggested it may have been a bit of a cave. Or it may have been the ground floor of a house. I have no idea, but knowing the Hebrews and the times, I'm confident it was bedded with straw, fairly small, and inhabited by donkeys, sheep, goats, and perhaps a cow and some chickens. It was a quiet place. It was an inviting place. Rude, to be sure, but far different from a modern industrial animal factory.

This brings us to the question, then: What does a beautiful farm and food system look like? If the hand of the Christian is to touch the world with beautiful artistry that illustrates the creative genius of a magnificent God, what does such a farming and food system look like? Does it look like the bowels of a factory chicken house? Or does it look like something different?

Does it smell like a confinement dairy, a cattle feedlot, or a fumigated strawberry field? I suggest that a godly farm—may I say goodly farm?—should be aromatically and aesthetically sensually romantic. It should attract us, not repel us. It should beckon our senses with whimsical enticements of participation rather than assault our senses with repugnancy. It should be something we want to embrace rather than escape. Is not this the yearning of God's heart, to use His people to extend His creative beauty into the nooks and crannies of our communities?

The metaphors used to describe us as believers have a magnetic desirability. "LET YOUR LIGHT SO SHINE BEFORE MEN, THAT THEY MAY SEE YOUR GOOD WORKS, AND GLORIFY YOUR FATHER WHICH IS IN HEAVEN" (Matthew 5:16). Clearly we're supposed to be enjoyable to look at, to live with.

The apostle Paul continues the same idea:

> BE KINDLY AFFECTIONED ONE TO ANOTHER WITH BROTHERLY LOVE;
> IN HONOUR PREFERRING ONE ANOTHER; NOT SLOTHFUL IN BUSINESS;
> FERVENT IN SPIRIT; SERVING THE LORD; REJOICING IN HOPE; PATIENT
> IN TRIBULATION; CONTINUING INSTANT IN PRAYER; DISTRIBUTING
> TO THE NECESSITY OF SAINTS; GIVEN TO HOSPITALITY. BLESS THEM
> WHICH PERSECUTE YOU: BLESS, AND CURSE NOT. REJOICE WITH THEM
> THAT DO REJOICE, AND WEEP WITH THEM THAT WEEP. BE OF THE
> SAME MIND ONE TOWARD ANOTHER. MIND NOT HIGH THINGS, BUT
> CONDESCEND TO MEN OF LOW ESTATE. BE NOT WISE IN YOUR OWN
> CONCEITS. RECOMPENSE TO NO MAN EVIL FOR EVIL. PROVIDE THINGS
> HONEST IN THE SIGHT OF ALL MEN. IF IT BE POSSIBLE, AS MUCH AS
> LIETH IN YOU, LIVE PEACEABLY WITH ALL MEN.
>
> DEARLY BELOVED, AVENGE NOT YOURSELVES, BUT RATHER GIVE
> PLACE UNTO WRATH: FOR IT IS WRITTEN, VENGEANCE IS MINE; I WILL
> REPAY, SAITH THE LORD. THEREFORE IF THINE ENEMY HUNGER, FEED
> HIM; IF HE THIRST, GIVE HIM DRINK: FOR IN SO DOING THOU SHALT
> HEAP COALS OF FIRE ON HIS HEAD. BE NOT OVERCOME OF EVIL, BUT
> OVERCOME EVIL WITH GOOD. (Romans 12:10–21)

Could a better description of community-minded living, of beautiful relationships, ever be penned? Who wouldn't want to live this way? It's beautiful.

I believe fundamentally that a farm should be a place where children want to spend time. Like a beautiful painting, beautiful music, a caressing touch, a farm should capture the heart of a child and the imagination of an adult. Here are some characteristics of such a farm.

Diversity

Can you imagine a painting with only one color? Industrial farming loves mono-speciation and singularity. Corn. Soybeans. Dairy. Apples. Chickens. Impressive, yes, but beautiful, no. Variety, we say, is the spice of life. Yet industrial farming despises variety and worships sameness.

In fact, many agricultural experts now suggest that a farm should not have both animals and vegetables due to manure contamination. Even wildlife is suspect. What kind of beautiful landscapes can we have if we view wildlife as a liability rather than an asset?

A varied landscape is a beautiful—and functional—landscape. Think of how many species God created. We're still discovering new ones, even after all this time. Think about how many things can be eaten. Indeed, the modern Western diet has become more and more simplistic. If you read cooking diaries of colonial Americans like Dolly Madison or Martha Washington, you'll see all sorts of interesting foods few of us would even be able to identify today: quince and currants. The supermarket only has a couple of varieties of apples; our forebears knew the nuances of dozens of different varieties.

A single-species farm, especially if it's large scale, may appeal to hubris, but it certainly doesn't appeal to aesthetic artistry. On our farm, we have cows, pigs, chickens, turkeys, rabbits, ducks, lambs, vegetables, fruit, honeybees, forests—it's breathtaking choreography, always dancing. Synergistic, symbiotic relationships are simply more interesting than simplistic sameness.

In our modern minds, our culture has decided that single-species farms are the most efficient. Diversity requires the farmer to know more information because each species is different. You don't herd a pig the same way you herd a cow. A chicken doesn't act like a rabbit. A tomato plant is far different from a plum tree. Too often we denigrate the generalist and applaud the specialist. But nature functions best as a generalist. Where is the mono-speciated environment? Nowhere. It doesn't exist.

I was on a ranch recently in Colorado that in 1910 supported twenty-five families. Today, it supports one. The varied prairie grasses have been reduced to a few holders-on as fertility has given way to erosion. Overgrazing reduced the variety on this landscape: people, plants, animals. Now it's a boring one hundred thousand acres of simplicity.

Farms should seek to load as many different kinds of plants and animals on their acreage as possible. The more the merrier. A beautiful painting is an interesting painting. If you can see all there is to see in one cursory glance, it's not considered good art. Good farm artistry seeks to develop a complicated web of life that re-creates domestically the variety we enjoy in wild places. Why must we travel to places devoid of human touch to encounter the awesomeness of functional variety? This magnificence should be part and parcel of our domestic farmscapes, and the farmer should be the local go-to guy for an encounter with nature's intricate and varied beauty.

Pastoral

In many surveys about the kinds of landscapes people consider the most inviting, the pastoral one beats deep forest, prairies, and gardens. The most soothing to the human spirit, across cultures and climates, is the pastoral landscape. Nobody knows why, although plenty of theories exist.

Evolutionists say that as Homo sapiens began coming down out of the trees, we liked the open setting rather than dense jungle because we felt safer being able to see potential danger. History buffs think it's because it's the landscape that most approximates the foundations of civilization: domestic livestock that defined our move from hunter-gatherer to community dweller. Biblicists would say it identifies us with Abel as a shepherd, with Abraham and the whole nomadic herdsman psyche that predated tillage and grain production.

At any rate, few things capture our eyes like domestic livestock, beautiful pastures, and widely spaced trees. Perhaps an innate sense of security drives this affinity. Unlike vegetables and fruit, animals represent portable and stable nutrition. The reason domestic livestock is still the commodity of choice for most primitive cultures is because without freezers and refrigerated trucks, it's a way to have real-time nutrition.

Other food items either have to be carried or are perishable, or both. A lactating camel, water buffalo, cow, goat, or sheep offers real-time nutrition. Always fresh. Always available. If you suddenly have to move because of drought, social unrest, or economic privation, the animals can walk with you and don't have to be carried like nuts, apples, and wheat. This is one reason why families in our modern self-reliance movements gravitate toward rabbits and chickens along with their gardens and beehives. If the power goes out and you lose what's in the refrigerator, the chickens will lay eggs tomorrow and you can dress the rabbits for dinner.

Pastoral landscapes center around herbivores, perennial forages, and human caretaking. They don't happen in nature. Pastoral landscapes are not wild; they are carefully created for long-term productivity. As long as human design and energy go into them, they remain resilient because the plants are primarily perennials. Long-lived landscapes are beautiful landscapes.

Contrast that with the ugliness of a confinement animal feeding operation. Animals confined indoors, inhaling a fecal pall, medicators squirting their pharmaceuticals—it's not a pretty picture. In our hubris we exchange pastoral beauty and strength for fecal particulate, enslavement, denial of sun and exercise, and fragility.

Few sights are as beautiful as watching animals gambol in a pasture. That we as a society have traded this ballet for the rigidity of cubicles in a fecal particulate house should bring us, sorrowing, to our knees.

Odor Free

If it smells bad, it's not good farming. I'm reminded of the farm documentary in which the chicken farmer has a different take on the obnoxious smells: "Smells like money to me." We chuckle at this off-hand remark, but it's identical to passing off a chemical company dumping toxins into a creek as "smelling like money." Would we be so quick to dismiss this abuse?

What drives the odor problem? Two things. First is scale. Simply having that much production, be it tomatoes or pigs, in one spot overruns the carrying capacity of the environment in that spot. Soiling the nest happens when you have too many birds in it, period. Good farming should be mindful of its nest, its local ecology.

On our farm, pastured chickens rotate daily and in carefully controlled numbers so that the soil can metabolize their nutrients. One of my favorite stops on our farm tours is in the middle of several thousand chickens in the field. I ask my visitors: "What do you smell?" They all sniff and whiff and the answer is "Nothing—just clean, fresh air." And yet we're standing amid thousands of chickens. How can this be?

It can be because on our farm we carefully stay within carrying capacity and we're moving onto fresh ground every day, away from yesterday's toilet area. It takes a lot of discipline to do this—another biblical principle. Paul says he disciplines his body in a race:

> KNOW YOU NOT THAT THEY WHICH RUN IN A RACE RUN ALL, BUT ONE RECEIVES THE PRIZE? SO RUN, THAT YOU MAY OBTAIN. AND EVERY MAN THAT STRIVES FOR THE MASTERY IS TEMPERATE IN ALL THINGS... I THEREFORE SO RUN, NOT AS UNCERTAINLY; SO FIGHT I, NOT AS ONE THAT BEATS THE AIR: BUT I KEEP UNDER MY BODY, AND BRING IT INTO SUBJECTION: LEST THAT BY ANY MEANS, WHEN I HAVE PREACHED TO OTHERS, I MYSELF SHOULD BE A CASTAWAY. (1 Corinthians 9:24–27 AKJV)

You see, dear folks, we can't just do whatever we can do. Sometimes just because we can, we shouldn't.

Second, the odor problem stems from a lack of carbon. While this is most acutely identified with livestock, it's also true in vegetable and fruit production. Even old-school agronomists are now realizing that the key to healthy plants is healthy soil and the key to healthy soil is humus. Organic matter. Springiness and sponginess. It's created by decaying biomass—carbon.

In livestock, the problem is that manure and urine contain highly volatile fertility compounds. These valuable and precious nutrients are hard to keep—they're unstable. Isn't that just the way with everything valuable? You have to really work at it to save it, to hold on to it. So it is with these precious nutrients. Those offensive odors are these nutrients vaporizing into the atmosphere. Just as detrimental but more insidious, these nutrients diffuse in water if they get wet and can easily contaminate wells and aquifers.

Carbon to the rescue. The molecular composition of carbon makes it attract and bond with everything. That's why we have carbon water filters. Chelation therapy is essentially intravenous charcoal (doctors, humor me here) like a Roto-Rooter for your circulatory system. Carbon is cool. In a livestock operation like ours, we are fiends for any carbon source: sawdust, wood chips, leaves, straw, corn fodder, junky hay, peanut hulls. You get the picture. When you bed animals in our housing situation with enough carbon, it stabilizes the volatile nutrients, tying them down and creating an awesome fertility savings account.

During inclement weather, housing livestock and poultry is certainly important to keep these animals comfortable and productive. Although I'm a pastured livestock devotee, on our farm we house animals during the middle of winter both for their comfort and for ours. At those times, we use outrageous amounts of carbon as bedding—what I call a carbonaceous diaper—to stabilize and then eventually leverage the precious nutrients into compost.

Mountains of smelly manure are not pretty. Obviously in order to practice this carbon-centric system, farms cannot exceed the carrying capacity of the available carbon. Indeed, if farmers had been investing in carbon rather than petroleum fertilizers, not only would we have healthier soils and farms, we would have healthier forests and a vibrant market-driven, carbon-trading environment.

Offensive odors are signs of infection, and stinky farms are as sure a sign of landscape infection as a stinky wound is a sign of bodily infection. Even though we house hundreds of cattle, pigs, and chickens on our farm in the winter, you can literally picnic among them. It's that clean and enjoyable. Notice I said hundreds—this is definitely commercial scale. Even thousands of chickens. But not thousands of cattle or millions of chickens. Scale does matter.

Why do large functional churches maintain cell groups? Because beautiful relationships occur at a smaller scale. This is wisdom, and wisdom should not be confined to our religious thinking; it should permeate our food and farming systems as well. Just because we can build a structure big enough to house fifty thousand chickens does not mean we should. What's appropriate? When it starts to smell, you can be sure you've exceeded the nest's carrying capacity.

Spontaneity

This is not a slam on meticulous planners and organizers. It is rather an attempt to appreciate surprise and discovery. Knowing every single thing is boring—hence our distaste of "know-it-alls."

Who among us doesn't appreciate a sudden likable turn of events or discovery? Whether it's a wild turkey and a clutch of downy poults skittering across the road or an unanticipated gift from a friend, we're drawn to the enjoyable unexpected. Most of our planning is to protect us from the fearful unexpected; we welcome the enjoyable unexpected.

Our walk of faith is a walk of spontaneity. Discovering God's providential care and sustaining grace, daily drinking from His provisional fountain—these are the defining beauties, are they not, of our spiritual growth? He is new every day. How He leads us; how He protects us; how He teaches us—none of us know what tomorrow's lesson will be, and that makes it all the more delightful.

A farm, then, should be filled with spontaneity and discovery. Many years ago a neighbor farming friend came over to our farm late one evening to visit, and as we walked by one of the ponds, he stopped and exclaimed in reverent, hushed tones: "Listen to those spring peepers. We don't have any of them at our farm." On their farm, not a single pond graced the landscape. No place for ducks to land.

On our farm, we've built many ponds. I'm a pondaholic. I don't think a farm can have too much water. It is the fountain of life, and having plenty of water makes a beautiful landscape. You'll find these ponds tucked in ravines and valleys. But you'll find more. In my farm chore routine these ponds constantly touch me with surprises. A quiet goose or duck hiding a clutch of eggs. Dragonflies helter-skeltering. In the evening, the sudden *haarroomph* of a bullfrog just before he kersplashes into the water.

Intersecting forest, open land, and riparian areas creates the most diversified flora and fauna but also creates the most opportunity for spontaneity. Compare that to square miles of uninterrupted wheat, or corn, or an entire house crammed full of chickens. It's predict-able, similar, and routine. When you visit our farm, you'll pop around an edge of woods and there's a herd of cows. Over a knoll is the eggmobile. In the valley a pond beckons.

It's a place of surprise and freshness. Around every corner is an aha waiting to happen. The first job for children on the average industrial poultry farm is the dead walk through the fecal particu-late house—picking up dead chickens. Doesn't that sound like just the kind of place and activity your kids would love to invite their friends to enjoy? The biggest surprise might be not finding a dead chicken, but there's small chance of that.

Certainly any farm will have routine. Chores come with the territory. But a variety of work with different types of animals and plants, along with a variety in the landscape, creates beauty through unpredictability. I'm told that in large food-processing facilities the average jobs can be taught in twenty minutes. Talk about spontaneity. Compare that with artisanal cheese-making, where craft displaces routine. Now add in a pasture-based dairy herd, where the milk changes daily based on types of plants in the pasture.

Indeed, our church lawns would be far more beautiful if converted into edible landscapes. Orchards, gardens, and fish production could grace our churchyards and offer a visible reminder of God's daily customized fingerprint on our spiritual walk. Isn't that a cool picture?

From wildlife to commercial production, a stroll around our farmscapes should be filled with wonder, awe, and mystery. Growing trees on the prairie is as good as carving fields into our forests. Don't forget the ponds. They fit anywhere.

Inviting

Our farms should be places that entice people to visit. The first thing an industrial farm places at its entrance is a No Trespassing sign. They don't want visitors.

Who isn't drawn to beauty? I've always thought that our farms should be places where children should want to be. "SUFFER LITTLE CHILDREN, AND FORBID THEM NOT, TO COME UNTO ME" (Matthew 19:14), Jesus said. Everything about Him is people-friendly. "COME TO ME, ALL YOU THAT LABOR AND ARE HEAVY LADEN, AND I WILL GIVE YOU REST" (Matthew 11:28 AKJV). Everything about Christ is inviting.

Is it inviting when stench, dead carcasses, and pesticides assault our senses? No. Our farms should be places where our children praise its awesomeness to their friends. When you have abundant and varied wildlife and surprises tucked around corners, the farm is a magnetic place.

Industrial farming tries to limit exposure and limit human interaction. From signing in and signing out to showering in and showering out, what does it say about something as basic and intimate as food when we have to walk through sheep dip and don a hazardous material suit to interact with it? These are hurdles to participation rather than helps to participation.

I've even read about efforts within the industrial fraternity to criminalize farm visits to minimize contamination and disease risks.

But what does it say about our farming system if the people who are going to eat its bounty can't visit, see, touch, and connect? I suggest that good farms should be favorite congregation spots for people. Rather than being repugnant, they should be the most soothing, inviting places in the community. They should be full of life, discovery, and inspiration. They should beckon us into a deeper relationship with life and the Creator's handiwork. They should, as it were, stand on our rural landscapes with outstretched arms, accepting without judgment, showing without condescension, and growing without paranoia.

Nested

We could call this balance, but I like the word *nested* a little better because it captures the essence of production snuggled appropriately into the larger landscape. Often when you think about food and farming today, you think of dominant infrastructure.

Industrial-scale processing plants, machines, and buildings are the images we assume. Rather than nesting gently and unassumingly into the landscape, the infrastructure dominates. The massive buildings and machines become the defining feature, the most obvious landmark. Not the trees, fields, creeks, and valleys. No, it's the structures.

Not only can you smell industrial farming from miles away, but you are awed by its features, by its sheer monstrosity. When encountering these things *Acres U.S.A.* founder Charles Walters used to call "monuments to the stupidity of man," I admit to being amazed by them. I've built many small sheds and portable shelter-mobiles in my life. The magnitude of a slaughterhouse that employs five thousand people and dispatches a hundred head of bovines per hour is indeed mind numbing and breathtaking. I respect the labor, design, and organization necessary to pull off such a feat.

But this scale represents something invasive, foreign, even insulting in a landscape. Because of the human machinations and wheeler-dealer realities behind such a monolith, these giant pieces of capital infrastructure enslave communities and landscapes. Rather than being tickets to wealth (oh yes, wealth for someone, but not for the community where they're located, to be sure), they drive land and public policy as surely as a master drives a slave.

The same is true for on-farm confinement animal infrastructure. But beyond these negatives is the ugliness that such structures bring to a landscape. They naturally draw our attention as gazers to the horizon, away from the undulations and natural features of the landscape. Instead, our eyes and minds are drawn violently to these man-made megaliths. We're tempted to pound our chests in arrogant self-satisfaction, proud of our accomplishments and our ability to "take dominion."

We're admonished to "AS MUCH AS LIES IN YOU, LIVE PEACEABLY WITH ALL MEN" (Romans 12:18 AKJV). Paul said when he was in Rome he became as a Roman—he didn't want to be a social shocker. His message was shocking enough, without adding a gauche swagger or fashion statement to his sermons. The point is that nesting in the landscape speaks to the farmer's humility and contentment.

Our farm and food system should meld with grace and balance into the landscape. That doesn't mean we can't build anything; it does mean our models should be of a scale and protocol that blend into the natural features. That is where pasture-based livestock really sings. If anything is truly at one with its ecology, it's scale-appropriate pastured livestock. On our farm, we build portable shademobiles for cattle, turkeys, pigs, and lambs. Almost all the infrastructure is portable and moves with the animals.

You could never tell someone to turn right at the poultry house. Ours is here today and gone tomorrow. The seasons, the grass growth, the grazing rotation—all of these drive where the infrastructure is at any time. It's small enough to be moved. The sheds are spread out in nest-appropriate size. Rather than one huge hoop-house, for example, we have five smaller ones. Between them are fruit trees and garden terraces. This takes the stark structural edges off the landscape, softening it, greening it, and nesting it into its ecological womb.

This is not the talk of a raving earth worshipper; it's the truth of a beauty that draws people. I'm frankly not impressed by impressive facades that impress simply because they're big. But a facade that's invisible, or makes me aware of how insignificant man is and how big God is—now that's a facade I can get excited about.

Nested infrastructure exudes a theme of dependency, and that's also beautiful.

Industrial-scaled infrastructure is like a fist raised to creation, saying in effect: "I am not dependent on you. I am man-made, man-serving, man-developed. I don't need to worry about carrying capacity, the air, soil, and water flows of our area. I am greater than all these resources." May I suggest that a farm that fits in its ecology, in its neighborhood, is an object lesson of gratitude and appreciation, along with a profound dependency on something bigger than human cleverness.

Every day when I wake up and head out for chores, I'm struck by the beauty we enjoy on our farm. Based on visitors' comments, that's a shared awareness. Not one of our doors has a skull and crossbones. We want visitors to be struck not by what we've done, but rather by how we've caressed this beautiful niche of God's creation into a productive and profoundly inspiring place. God help us to be faithful in this.

Long-Term vs. Short-Term

Lay not up for yourselves treasures on earth... But lay up
for yourselves treasures in heaven.

Matthew 6:19–20 (AKJV)

One theme that Christians share with all other faith communities
is that a long-term view is superior to a short-term view. Expediency
is the hallmark of the convenient, instant-gratification world. The
gambler, the swindler, and the robber all personify this view at its
most extreme.

How many sermons exhort the flock about eternal consequences
to today's decisions? The sowing and reaping concept creates an
immediacy about getting our hearts right before God. The works
and rewards passages regarding post-salvation effort continue the
immediacy for diligence among believers. According to the *Westminster Shorter Catechism*, man's whole duty is to please God now
so we can live with Him for eternity (my paraphrase). The point is
that Christians universally embrace the notion of long-term consequences based on today's decisions. Taking a long-term view is a
bedrock principle among Christians. Interestingly, it's also a bedrock
view among environmentalists. Why do they despise exploitative

businesses? Because it sacrifices tomorrow on the altar of today's expediency.

The "eat, drink, and be merry for tomorrow we die" mentality has no place in the believer's lexicon. We represent God Almighty in this world as ambassadors, as representatives. Could we go so far as to say His plan is counting on our obedience, which can only occur if we're thinking about long-term consequences? We don't indulge our base fleshly desires because we're ascetic or hate having fun; we refrain from indulging the flesh in order to run the race of life that we may win, and not be disqualified, to paraphrase Paul's ideas in 1 Corinthians 9:23–27.

A biblical worldview demands that we think more about tomorrow than about today. That's why we choose the narrow way that leads to salvation instead of the broad gate that leads to destruction. This is the primary difference—or at least ought to be—between children and adults. Children say whatever pops into their minds. Adults think about long-term consequences before popping off or "saying it like it is." Children want instant gratification; mature adults save for a rainy day and realize things worth having are worth waiting for.

Christians know we should be laying up treasures in heaven. We know that even though building a house on sand may be quick and efficient, ultimately it's better to build it on a rock. Why do we endure hardships, burning at the stake, jeering, and derision? A crown of life awaits those who endure to the end. What preacher hasn't devoted significant pulpit time extolling eternal-focused thinking, acting, and spiritual growth? The long-term view is the litmus test by which we judge all of our actions and thoughts. And it should be.

That's part of pleasing God rather than people. If we're going to pick one to please, we pick God. Why? Because the future we don't see is far more important than what we're doing or thinking today. This is Paul's argument for the resurrection: "IF CHRIST BE NOT RISEN, THEN IS OUR PREACHING VAIN, AND YOUR FAITH IS ALSO VAIN" (1 Corinthians 15:14).

*   *   *

Okay, what does this have to do with food and farming? Realize that everything, and I mean everything, about industrial mechanical agriculture is predicated on fast shortcuts and today's expedience. The only thing that matters is to grow it faster, fatter, bigger, and cheaper because after all, we need to feed the world so who cares about anything else.

Prodigiously productive fishing and shrimp waters in the Gulf of Mexico are now completely dead to life. How many Christian farmers along the Mississippi watershed—and that's the entire heart of America's agriculture—contributed to that death with chemical runoff? Does anyone think God is happy about His creation being killed this way? How many people wearing "What Would Jesus Do?" bracelets purchase the food produced by this debilitating anti-life farming system? Hmmmm?

As I contemplate this, I find myself once again aligning with the environmentalists, who do indeed take a long-term planetary view. You can say anything you want about radical environmentalists—you can even call them commie pinkos—but I have yet to find one who thinks a bushel of corn or soybeans today is worth a dead zone tomorrow. I recently attended a conference put on by the Savory Institute (named after Allan Savory, the originator of holistic management) and heard the following exhortation: "We should not talk about externalities. They don't exist. Everything happens here, on the planet, not somewhere else. It's all internal."

Wow, what a radical thought. It almost sounds like a preacher admonishing his youth group: "Everything you say and do impacts your life. You can't say your actions don't hurt anybody, because they do affect everyone in your relationship circle."

For decades now our produce research has been on ship-ability, not on taste, texture, or nutritional density. Genetic selection is skewed toward cultivars that can withstand bouncing around in the back of a tractor-trailer for a thousand miles. Tomatoes selected for long-distance transport must be genetically similar to cardboard, not those luscious garden-grown varieties that ooze juice down to your elbows when you bite into them. Our food system has completely ignored human health and opted instead for fast growth and convenient availability. Would anybody want to argue that nutritional density, taste, and tender texture are better than cardboard shipping qualities?

Why do we Christians not think about these things? Better yet, why do we encourage these things with our food dollar? Worst of all, why does anyone who asks these questions get branded as an environmentalist whacko by conservative talk show hosts? Where is the pastor who will dare to admonish his congregation that a nutrient-deficient cardboard tomato is gambling with your health?

Can't you hear it now? "Go home, look in your refrigerator. Do you have one of those Satanic tomatoes? Throw it out! Put it in the trash bin along with the pornography I told you to throw out last week. Don't slice it, dice it, puree it. Don't look at it, touch it, or partake of it. I know it's tempting, but it represents the lust of the world and spiritual debauchery." Can you imagine?

The whole idea of pornography, which of course the Christian community universally condemns, is instant and expedient gratification of a sacred act sanctified by marriage. Where is the Christian who dares to identify the pornographic food system that revels in death-inducing, sickness-encouraging, and creation-destroying orgies of self-indulgence? Strong language? Have you walked into a confinement factory chicken house lately? How about a confinement hog factory? Just like pornography disrespects and cheapens God-given and -sanctioned specialness in sex, factory-farmed hog houses disrespect and cheapen the God-sculpted specialness of pigs.

On my bookshelf, alongside Christian books about creation, marriage, and theology, are countless tomes documenting the evils of industrial food magnates. Buying legislative favor, abusing neighbors, upsetting whole communities with trucked-in low-paid labor: the list is endless. By and large, however, the Christian community ignores this entire body of research and information because it carries the philosophical taint of liberals. "Oh, there go those liberals taking up for workers' rights, chicken rights, pig rights. Good grief, the next thing you know they'll be saying the fish in the river have rights." The elders and deacons listening to this rant then guffaw in assent because they're steeped in the doctrine that only beings that can write constitutions and convene juries have rights. That doesn't include the fish down in the creek, yadda, yadda, yadda. It's easy for me to quote these interchanges because these are my people.

But so are the folks desperate to speak for the fish. Welcome to my world.

When will marchers at sanctity-of-life walkathons realize that taking a long-term view toward a human embryo is hypocritical if not tied to sacredness of food and life in general? Please don't think I've tipped over the abyss into the animals-are-humans idea. They aren't. But that doesn't mean God takes no thought for their treatment. On the contrary, I would suggest that their treatment forms the ethical framework of consistency that ultimately builds the human sanctity-of-life imperative. How much easier would it be to promote the human sanctity notion if we embraced the animal care notion? If we don't want our actions and beliefs to ring hollow, we need to appreciate how these two threads relate.

When the good Presbyterians, Methodists, and Lutherans were letting the gullies develop on our farm for more than a century, were they taking a long-term view? While they were putting money in the offering plate for foreign missions, or paying for the new sanctuary, were they taking a long-term view? Why is it that aligning visceral stewardship with our spiritual ministries is well nigh impossible?

As if we haven't already, let's get real practical. Suppose you have a yard with some dandelions in it. Do you hoe them out or call a chemical landscape company to come and nuke them with herbicide? You know, when you ask it like that, the answer is pretty obvious. But I can assure you that in practice and thought, Christians grab the herbicide much quicker than the hoe. But let's go even beyond the hoe. Let's get downright environmental for a minute.

Dandelions have taproots. Plants have all kinds of roots. Some have spreader roots and others have taproots—the kind that go way down deep with a central leader, like a carrot. These penetrate far into the subsoil, pumping down sugars generated through photosynthesis. These sugars feed billions and billions of bacteria and microbes, who in turn dissolve minerals and bring them into the plant's roots. It's an incredibly symbiotic and beyond-comprehension process. Oh, we know a lot about this relationship, but compared to what there is to know, we're still fairly ignorant.

Dandelions, interestingly, especially attract and synthesize calcium. As a weed, their presence indicates calcium deficiency in the soil. They grow well where calcium, a major plant mineral requirement, is in short supply. Isn't it awesome that the Creator designed a plant with a long taproot to love growing in calcium-deficient places in order to remedy the calcium deficiency? In other words, the dandelion attracts and concentrates calcium in its space, slowly ameliorating the soil's calcium deficiency. As a Christian, now what is your view toward the dandelion? Is it just a weed to be exterminated, dispatched as efficiently as possible? Or could it be part of a complex and beautiful plan to bring balance and long-term health into our backyards? Wow, that kind of changes things, doesn't it?

When you realize that the native prairies contained more than forty species of plants per acre, on average, it gives you pause that we, as a culture, have turned this beautiful long-term regenerative system into a monoculture landscape of corn and soybeans. What was once a magnificent carpet of green perennials with massive hordes of bison and wolves running across it is now an eroding, degenerating monoculture of annuals, chemicals, and monstrous equipment. The conservative religious right views this as progress. Is it really?

Here are the assumptions that make it convenient to tout this change as positive:

- Annual corn is more productive than perennial prairie.
- Chemical farming is necessary to feed the world.
- Wildlife proliferation and human dominion are incompatible.
- Herbivores are interesting but inefficient.
- Plants are more productive than animals.
- Ecosystems do not need animals.

Now let's look at each of these and give a rebuttal. Before we start, I hope you Christians reading this realize that these responses are exactly what the industrial agricultural complex wants you to believe. In other words, when you embrace this line of thinking, you're casting your worldview into the same pot as the USDA and its fraternity of sub-sidized, concessionized golf buddies that supply the cheap food mar-ket. Yes, that cheap food market Christians generally patronize in order to have more money to put in the offering plate. Okay, here we go.

First, annual corn is more productive than perennial prairie. Let's assume we're in Kankakee, Illinois, where 200-bushel dryland corn is possible. At 56 pounds per bushel, that's 11,200 pounds of corn. A steer in a feedlot gains roughly 1 pound per 7 pounds of corn it eats, which means that this production represents about 1,600 pounds of weight gain per acre.

Now let's take the same acre in perennial prairie. The rule of thumb is that 100-bushel corn ground is equivalent to 400 cow-days of forage. A cow-day is what one cow will eat in a day. Our hypo-thetical and really fertile 200-bushel corn acre, therefore, will pro-duce 800 cow-days of forage. Let's assume that we graze that acre of forage with steers that average two-thirds of a cow equivalent, since they're smaller than a cow.

That would mean this acre of grass prairie would yield about 1,050 (2/3 times 800) growing steer-days. If these steers gain a leisurely 1.6 pounds per day (in good conditions, they'll gain up to 2.2 pounds per day, and we've assumed our corn grew in good conditions), that's 1,600 pounds of weight gain per acre. Do you remember that number from before? Yes, it's the same as the corn.

And the good news? Really good news? To get that gain from the prairie, we didn't plant, fertilize, chemicalize, or run high-energy-dependent equipment across it. The animals harvested and fertilized. All it took was some plastic pipe and simple electric fence. Remember that even after that corn is harvested, we have to dry it with natural gas, store it in a metal bin, transport it to a feedlot, then haul all the manure from the feedlot somewhere. Is prairie more productive? You bet.

Why would anyone think otherwise? The reason is that most farmers do not manage their grasslands well. Consequently the production is poor. I'm assuming a management plan that approximates the way herds of bison and wolves migrated across the prairies hundreds of years ago. Interestingly, based on the latest archaeological and anthropological studies, we now know that North America supported far more pounds of animals in pre-European times than it does today, even with factory animal houses, hybrid seeds, John Deere, chemicals, and petroleum. And all those farmers. Wow.

Let me quote from *The Extermination of the American Bison* written by William T. Hornaday in 1889:

> The great herd on the Arkansas [River] through which I passed... was, from my own observation, not less than 25 miles wide, and from reports of hunters and others it was about five days in passing a given point, or not less than 50 miles deep [long].
>
> From the top of Pawnee Rock I could see from 6 to 10 miles in almost every direction. This whole vast space was covered with buffalo, looking at a distance like one compact mass, the visual angle not permitting the ground to be seen. I have seen such a sight a great number of times, but never on so large a scale.

Isn't that one of the most magnificent word-pictures you've ever seen? Imagine that mass of bison, fifty miles long and twenty-five miles wide, and so thick that you couldn't see the ground between their bodies. No wonder stampedes trampled whole wagon trains and more people lived in Nebraska and Kansas five hundred years ago than live there today. We are incredibly myopic. These snippets of history help put things in perspective.

A long-term view mandates a return to this regenerative, soil-building high-production system. It is highly complex, integrated, multi-speciated, and built the fertile soils that we are mining today. We've donned the conquistador's hat, the landscape rapist's mind-set, exhibiting a profound disregard for creation.

Second, chemical farming is necessary to feed the world. Again we see the expedient short-term paradigm rearing its ugly head. Anyone who says this is either incredibly myopic, ignorant, or earning a paycheck from oil companies. Does the average person really know so little about how biomass decomposition and soil work? Unfortunately, yes.

Mining, whether mineral or oil-based, can never be a regenerative long-term solution to soil health. I know we've been practicing it a long time, but we were blessed with lots of deposits. Deep, fertile soils on which every great civilization has been built throughout history, and the loss of which destroyed every great civilization in history, were not built with petroleum and artificial fertilizers. They were built with a carefully choreographed solar energy into biomass dance.

When properly functioning, the earth is on a weight gain program. It's supposed to get fatter every day. Have you ever tried to catch a sunbeam? If I asked your four-year-old daughter to run outside and bring in a sunbeam, you'd laugh when she ran out and tried to catch one. Isn't it amazing that something as clearly energetic, real, and powerful as a sunbeam is completely uncatchable with our hands?

But God figured out how to catch a sunbeam. It's called photosynthesis. Something as nonphysical and uncatchable as a sunbeam converts into biomass that can be weighed, handled, traded, and used. Is that not the coolest thing ever?

Grass, or forage, is far more efficient at capturing these sunbeams than shrubs or trees. Think about grass. It's like an expressway. Almost no branches. Shrubs and trees are a network of branches. Things have to slow down to make those turns. If you really want to build soil, you do it with grass. But grass has a high metabolism; it grows fast and then dies. The herbivore is what prunes it back as it approaches senescence, restarting the vegetative period and fast metabolism. All the deep, rich soils of the world were created under grasslands, not forestlands. These grasslands fed herbivores. The sun-biomass-decomposition (or digestion)-regeneration cycle is a wonderful expression of the life cycle. Long-term fertility and soil development depend on this cycle.

Unfortunately, modern cultures have abandoned this pattern in favor of a short-term mining mentality. Never before have we had the technology to enable us to leverage the biomass cycle more efficiently than we can today. With modern aerobic composting methods, chippers, front-end loaders, and electric fence, a low-energy carbon-centric fertility system is within our grasp. We certainly don't need chemical fertilizers. That more than 75 percent of material filling America's landfills is biomass, the caught sunbeams God wanted converted into fertile soil, should bring us all to our knees in repentance and confession.

Third, wildlife proliferation and human dominion are incompatible. This is the old song that says intensive agriculture can't co-exist with wildlife. Again, completely untrue. Can we have an intensive farming system that encourages wildlife? Yes.

Let's start with perhaps the most fragile wildlife: honeybees. Anyone interested in food and the future is aware that colony collapse disorder is devastating the honeybee industry. Biologists view the honeybee as like the canary in the mine—as the honeybee goes, so goes civilization. In other words, if the honeybees are having a hard time, can humans be far behind? Honeybees are having a hard time. One in every four bites of food humans eat depends on a honeybee. This is serious, and surely a solution to honeybee die-off should interest us as creation stewards almost as much as starving children in Africa.

Honeybees depend on pollen to make honey. Pollen is on flowering plants—all kinds of plants. In the prairie, with an average forty species of plants per acre, pollen was available throughout the season. These plants flowered at different times. When the bison grazed along, mature plants whose flowers had already bloomed and been fertilized through pollination went into the herbivore as part of the pruning (grazing) process.

The pruned plant then immediately began a new growth cycle, which often resulted in multiple blossoms per season from the same plant. So two things happened: a large variety of blossoms per acre, and a regrowth of those blossoms throughout the year. Result? Lots of pollen in a nice, steady supply throughout the season. Happy bees, honey-filled hives, and healthy, vibrant colonies that survived the winter intact.

On our farm, we move the cattle every day to a new paddock. This results in a quilt-like pattern of mature, immature, and partially mature plants. Something is always in flower—primarily clovers, but plenty of other plants, too. That bio-mimicry supplies steady pollen all season long, resulting in happy, healthy bees. Contrast that with either a corn-soybean regimen or a continuous grazing option. This simple regimen now accounts for the runaway majority of all modern farming practice.

The mono-crop blooms at one time, for a very short period, and that's the end of it. That's true for orchard blossoms, nuts, and other things besides corn and soybeans. As a result, the number of bees necessary to pollinate the massive number of blossoms at one time is too small. Hence, an entire industry devoted to transporting tractor-trailer-loads of beehives from area to area is now assumed to be necessary for crop production. This is just business as usual.

What if farming were diversified, multi-speciated, and growing half the corn and soybeans currently grown (because we didn't need it for cows or alcohol)? Such a farmscape could support far more bees year-round, which means they wouldn't have to be transported and would be far healthier. Bees are more prone to sickness when they're confused all the time because they're constantly moved to new locations.

I submit that it is precisely an expression of the best dominion mandate when we apply our innovative capacity to farming systems that encourage and stimulate wildlife rather than deplete it. A farming system that depletes wildlife indicates a serious breach in our creativity through the dominion mandate. What better expression of human superiority than to design intensive farming systems that not only co-exist with wildlife, but help wildlife thrive? It can be done because it is being done. The world does not need one single animal factory.

Fourth, herbivores are interesting but inefficient. Yes, that's true. But it's for a purpose. The reason herbivores and land healing/soil building go hand in hand is precisely because they only metabolize about 30 percent of what they eat and drink. They excrete the rest, but my oh my, what healing elixer these excretions are.

Let's take just one kind of herbivore: cow. She eats twenty-eight pounds of forage and excretes fifty pounds of goodies. Isn't that like a perpetual motion machine? Yes, she also drinks water, which accounts for that increase in excretion, but when she rains out her back end it's full of nitrogen and other goodies.

She concentrates calcium into bone. She provides an elastic, long-lasting covering called hide, which can be turned into leather. Prior to plastic, leather was the pliable, moldable covering of choice. Her inefficiency is her beauty because she has so much left over to give back. Truly a transmutation being, literally a professional alchemist, the cow can take nutrient-deficient grass and turn it into rich manure and urine.

By pruning the biomass, she stimulates far more production than otherwise would have occurred, which ultimately converts more solar energy into vegetation and feeds the decomposition, transpiration, and carbon sequestration process. Oh, I forgot, we Christians aren't supposed to talk about carbon sequestration. That's the language of environmental whackos and tree huggers. You know, those earth muffins.

But again, the long-term view demands that we pay attention to the carbon cycle. It's real and it's supposed to work. The carbon is riding on oxygen in the form of carbon dioxide. Plants breathe in carbon dioxide, splitting off the carbon and exhaling oxygen. If we take a long-term view, we'll be interested in plant health because ultimately that affects planetary health. Dear heart, the land, the people, the oceans, the atmosphere—it's all God's stuff.

Finally, I'm going to rebut the fifth and sixth bullet points above together because they are related: plants are more productive than animals and ecosystems do not need animals. Do you know of any animal-less ecosystem? No. It doesn't exist.

Perhaps one of the best treatments on this topic is Simon Fairlie's book *Meat: A Benign Extravagance*. With the precision of a surgeon's scalpel, he dissects the animal agriculture question and proves beyond a shadow of a doubt that animals function in numerous powerfully positive ways. From salvaging food scraps to anointing the soil with manure, the role of animals is broad and eclectic.

For me, one of the best ways to look at this question is to realize that animals are necessary for soil fertility. Anyone who farms knows that manure is magic. It really is. So are earthworm castings. But earthworms really thrive when animal manure is included in the mix, along with vegetable material.

Gravity tends to pull fertility downhill. Hence fertile valleys and infertile hilltops. But wait, many times the most fertile soils are on hilltops. How could that be? Herbivores graze in the fertile valleys and then trudge up to the hilltops to chew their cuds and lounge. Why the hilltop? To watch for those nasty predators. The herbivore-grass, predator-prey relationships are foundational to moving those biomass-stored sunbeams around on the landscape. Without animals, the anti-gravitational movement would be impossible. Without the predator, it wouldn't be incentivized. Truly, this whole ecosystem is fearfully and wonderfully made.

If you take any of these components out of the system—components that the Creator designed to work together—you end up with a floundering, dysfunctional system. Furthermore, most of the earth's land is not conducive to arable cropping. Only a tiny percentage is good enough for that. Grasslands are literally the lungs of the earth, and restoring them with animals is not only necessary, but it's the most efficacious way to restore water cycles and the carbon cycle. Right now, nothing else comes close to remediating broken ecological systems as quickly or completely as restoring large herds of grazing animals through holistic, or long-term, management.

Before we leave this chapter, I need to treat one more issue regarding short-term and long-term thinking. That is farm succession. Multi-generational farms. This is surely a hot button with me these days. The average American farmer is now almost sixty years old. According to land-grant universities that keep track of farm population actuarials, in the next fifteen years about 50 percent of America's agricultural equity will change hands.

When we look at the cause, I have a simple explanation: when young people can't get in, old people can't get out. If we are going to design long-term farming systems, we need models that encourage fluidity between generations. We need systems that make it easy for young people to get in and old people to get out. A vibrant church, vibrant economic sector, or vibrant community needs a healthy balance of young and old. Young people provide the brawn and enthusiasm to get things done; old people provide the wisdom, context, and direction for that brawn and enthusiasm.

I've written extensively about this topic in my book *Fields of Farmers* so I won't repeat all the points here, but suffice it to say that protocols for maintaining multi-generational fluidity and partnerships do exist. Portable farm infrastructure, personal accountability and responsibility through fiefdoms, and value adding through direct marketing are just some of the ways we can stack additional salaries on an existing land base.

The average farm kid who wants to stay on the farm grows up coveting the neighbor's land. Why? The only way to make an additional salary for the next generation is to increase the land base. Add more cows, more trees, more grain, whatever. Farmers routinely think horizontal expansion—more of their core commodity. But I would suggest that not a single farm in the world—including my family's in Virginia—is completely filled.

All have more salaries lurking in underutilized resources. By stacking complementary enterprises on a land base and allowing their ownership and operation to be handled by young people through their own fiefdoms (doesn't everyone want a fiefdom?) can layer countless additional salaries on a piece of land. Sometimes it's not more production, but doing something additional with the current production.

For example, a cherry orchard could add a commercial kitchen to make wine, juice, and pies. A farm with a lot of trees could add a portable band sawmill, and then a planer and kiln, and then a furniture or woodworking shop. All of these things add additional salaries vertically on the land base to create long-term viable businesses.

Short-term decision making on the part of farmers routinely dumps them into the commodity, chemical, crisis camp. Businesses that make money selling farmers things they don't need love knee-jerk, quick-fix answers. Heavily leveraged farmers inherently have a harder time making good long-term decisions because all they can see is tomorrow's payment. If that's all you can see, you'll sacrifice the permanent on the altar of the immediate every single time.

Farms that exhibit a long-term view, then, are ecologically sound. That means they don't look like what the industrial fraternity espouses; they look decidedly different. They don't have factory houses, mono-species, or rooms with a skull and crossbones on them. Those are all short-term paradigms that create long-term problems. And long-term farms have multi-generations on them with a clear business plan to successional survival.

If we'll think about these principles and then funnel our food money to the ones that exhibit them, we'll enjoy participating in a Creator-honoring farm system that takes a long-term view. Yes, I believe that honors God as surely as any other long-term view honors Him.

Faith vs. Fear

Whatsoever is not of faith is sin.

Romans 14:23

How do we increase our faith? "SO THEN FAITH COMES BY HEARING, AND HEARING BY THE WORD OF GOD" (Romans 10:17 AKJV). Any believer knows that to increase faith, we must participate or exercise our faith by spending time in the Word. As we live what we call a life of faith, where we practice stepping out of our comfort zones and ministering or starting a difficult conversation, we enjoy God's intervention and caring.

Jesus promised His followers that the Holy Spirit would instruct them in the words to use and bring His sayings to remembrance when they were brought before judges and magistrates. He admonished them to not worry, or fear, these otherwise intimidating circumstances because He would support them. The parables are filled with instructions about fear:

AND WHY TAKE YOU [ANXIOUS] THOUGHT FOR RAIMENT? CONSIDER THE LILIES OF THE FIELD, HOW THEY GROW; THEY TOIL NOT, NEITHER DO THEY SPIN: AND YET I SAY TO YOU, THAT EVEN SOLOMON IN ALL

HIS GLORY WAS NOT ARRAYED LIKE ONE OF THESE. WHY, IF GOD SO CLOTHE THE GRASS OF THE FIELD, WHICH TO DAY IS, AND TO MORROW IS CAST INTO THE OVEN, SHALL HE NOT MUCH MORE CLOTHE YOU, O YOU OF LITTLE FAITH?

THEREFORE TAKE NO THOUGHT, SAYING, WHAT SHALL WE EAT? OR, WHAT SHALL WE DRINK? OR, WHEREWITHAL SHALL WE BE CLOTHED? (FOR AFTER ALL THESE THINGS DO THE GENTILES SEEK:) FOR YOUR HEAVENLY FATHER KNOWS THAT YOU HAVE NEED OF ALL THESE THINGS. BUT SEEK YOU FIRST THE KINGDOM OF GOD, AND HIS RIGHTEOUSNESS; AND ALL THESE THINGS SHALL BE ADDED TO YOU. TAKE THEREFORE NO [ANXIOUS] THOUGHT FOR THE MORROW: FOR THE MORROW SHALL TAKE THOUGHT FOR THE THINGS OF ITSELF. (Matthew 6:28–34 AKJV)

As believers, don't we find these promises comforting, especially when we look at the Old Testament stories of God's constant and over-riding provision for His people? Whether it was an ark, a ram lamb in the bushes, a cattail boat carrying Moses—the wonder and inspiration of the Old Testament is largely the story of God's interventive provision. Indeed, Hebrews 12 hearkens back to the historical record to make the case for faith by making it clear that God provides for us.

Part of developing faith is simply practicing in things God wants us to do. We can practice a soft answer to see if it turns away wrath. Well, my goodness, it works. Amazing. We can practice giving a gift to an enemy. Well, my goodness, it works. We can practice being grateful. Well, my goodness, it works. It is in practicing, participating, immersing ourselves in a life of faith that we see our fears gradually diminish.

Now let's turn this lesson over to food. Americans fear food. A lot of Christians fear food. Why? Because too many of us don't know anything about it. The official policy of the government food police at the FDA and USDA is to fear food. Why? Because industrial food is a scary thing.

Campylobacter, listeria, salmonella, E. coli, bovine spongiform encephalopathy. This is a brand-new lexicon that has only come into common use in the last couple of decades.

Likewise, I never knew anybody who had food allergies. Now we have gluten problems, leaky gut syndrome, type 2 diabetes, and a runaway obesity epidemic. We're overfed and undernourished. The USDA began telling us what to eat after World War II: hydrogenated fat, carbohydrates, margarine. Meanwhile, big food manufacturers loved that we were exiting the kitchen and giving them proxy status over our menus.

With the kitchen sufficiently demonized as a place where losers, where underachieving non-career women served, a broad food ignorance spread across the landscape. Economic wealth with rising incomes enabled the annual special meal out to morph into daily fast food and processed food service. Devoid of culinary artistry, the kitchen became simply a place to heat up TV dinners. Indeed, no society has ever had the luxury of abdicating a relationship with food this profoundly.

Gone were the nuances about taste, texture, and odor. Neat microwavable packaging with additives to stabilize, sterilize, and sanitize replaced the whole potato, the oven-cooked pot roast, and scratch baking. In food processing, chlorine became the chemical of choice as produce and meat became filthier coming from industrial farms with faster harvesting and growing techniques. Fecal contamination could be sterilized with enough chlorine, and it is used liberally today. Pink slime in ground beef, along with cheap fillers, created a whole new type of food.

Soft drinks replaced whole raw milk. Twinkies replaced fried eggs and bacon. Packaged whole meals in Styrofoam clamshells replaced domestic culinary arts. Food was no longer prepared, processed, packaged, and preserved in the home. Those domestic skills were farmed out to professional food manufacturers with laboratories, high fructose corn syrup, monosodium glutamate, and a host of unpronounceables. As American culture unleashed itself from an ecological umbilical, we became profoundly ignorant. And we began fearing the unknown.

I would argue that food more perfectly represents God's sustaining power than any other physical substance. More than money. More than clothes or housing. More than employment. Every biblical celebration uses food and feasting as its most significant centerpiece. Do you fear food, or do you know enough about it to enjoy a deep food faith? Do you know what's in season? Do you know what farmers in your area have plenty of this year or are scarce on? Do you care?

Because food is so closely linked with biblical signposts and remembrances, it would behoove us not to fear food. How do we get over our food fears? The answer is the same as acquiring spiritual faith: We practice. Yes, we practice food craft. Yes, we get in our kitchens. We get in our gardens. We visit farmers and buy directly from local purveyors. We touch it, smell it, examine it, read about it, prepare it, pickle it, slice it, dice it. We quit buying a nameless, faceless disconnected pseudo-food-like substance of dubious extraction prepared by people with dubious agendas. We embrace a physical partnership with our food.

I think how we view food and our relationship to it sets up the depth and breadth of our desire to know God's provision—really appreciate it. That's the difference between simply ingesting food-like substances until hunger is assuaged and actually partaking of a sacred provision that we know. We talk about knowing God, personally, as a way to measure spiritual growth. How about knowing food as a way to measure our appreciation of the mystery and awesomeness of God's sufficiency?

Isn't it amazing that from our pulpits we have no problem demanding that people practice and participate in hearing, seeing, and exercising their faith, but we don't exhort people to create a framework for that spiritual understanding by doing the same thing with something much easier: food. Food is not just something we ingest on a pit stop. It's sacred provision, as requested by the Lord's Prayer: "GIVE US DAY BY DAY OUR DAILY BREAD" (Luke 11:3 NKJV).

Do you know the food in your pantry? Perhaps not all of it, but at least some of it? Do you have a memory, a knowledge base, an experience with it? This creates a framework to truly understand God's providential care. When you've worked at your food, you appreciate its power and meaning. You don't take it for granted. And you don't fear it because you know where it came from, how it was produced, who grew it. It's as safe and sufficient as your spiritual faith, which grows in your life the same way.

When we patronize an opaque food system and pop munchies, it creates an unhealthy physical body. By the same token, when we quit seeking, quit seeing, and quit discovering biblical truths for ourselves and just depend on munchies from the pulpit or a "Saying of the Day," we become spiritually weak and sick. Isn't it fascinating that our churches routinely conduct youth seminars on the dangers of the Internet and websites, but we don't conduct any seminars on the dangers of soft drinks and pretzels?

Just for the record, I don't think it's a sin to drink a soft drink once in a while. Indulgences are allowed. But drinking one a day is a different story. The cumulative effect of what is now known as the modern American diet, where virtually everything is highly processed, laden with sugar, and grown from chemicalized deficient soil, is a seriously sick population. America now leads the world in the five leading chronic diseases. That's not a good place to be number one.

Make no mistake about it, the overriding view in our culture toward food is fear. It's a product of ignorance. You can't trust what you don't know. The less we know about something, the more we fear it. The less we know about God, the less faith we have in Him. I know we're to fear God, but that's a reverence, not a worry. Godly fear is healthy because it drives us to want to please Him.

If food faith (what we see) is metaphor for spiritual faith (what we don't see), then we should embrace a food system that demonstrates knowledge and participation. If the current supermarket industrial food system demonstrates one thing, it's ignorance and lack of participation. What happens when we fear food is that we ask for government protection. Fear creates insecurity, and insecurity makes us paranoid. Paranoia is a wonderful tool used by regulators to increase their power.

Conservative Christians who want less government intervention must realize that every time we patronize a food system predicated on ignorance, opaqueness, and fear, we unwittingly and subconsciously encourage fear to creep into our lives. If we can't trust our food without government intervention, can we trust education without government intervention? Can we trust doctors without government intervention? Can we trust bankers without government intervention? Can we trust deacons and elders without government intervention?

The food system that thrives on fear is not healthy for us...in many ways. Why can't we appreciate that it's as unhealthy as a pornographic website or an alcoholic binge? Why, indeed. Because we pray for our little Christian kiddos to get a good job with a well-paying company, to show they are good Americans, patriotic citizens, contributors to society. So we encourage them to apply for jobs at laboratories and food manufacturing associations that create a destructive food system. And we're proud of their achievements when they become number one Twinkie salesmen.

We're proud of them when their engineering ability designs a machine that more efficiently injects carcinogenic phenols into hot dogs. Come on, people, wake up. Would Jesus eat this stuff? Really? We'd counsel our Christian children to leave an unscrupulous accounting firm in a heartbeat if financial irregularities were suspected. "It'll taint your reputation," we admonish.

"You don't want to be party to those shenanigans," we pontificate. "Don't stay in the devil's workshop," we preach.

Well, what kind of a workshop do you think it is whose chemicals make infertile frogs and three-legged salamanders? What kind of irregularities might you find in a place that releases genetically modified organisms into the environment to practice promiscuous orgies in crops on land where a farmer doesn't want them to be? What kind of shenanigans are they when the industry and government experts tell cattle farmers to feed dead cows to cows? Are these not irregularities? Are these not shenanigans? Are these not the devil's workshop?

Since to say anything is to identify with liberal whacko environmental tree-hugger anti-capitalists who go so far as to say the military industrial complex is too big, we Christians can't speak about these things. They're taboo in our circles. These things cause divisions. They make us squirm. And after all, we really don't know enough to have faith in a more natural system. I mean, look at the government reports. Look at what the scientists at the most prestigious Fortune 500 corporations in America say.

Do you know how silly that sounds? Would you measure the credibility of any other conviction by the fact that it was endorsed by government reports or corporate white papers? Not at all. We measure things by the Word of God. We ask if it is of faith. I submit that the entire industrial mechanical food system is predicated on fear—it thrives on fearful consumers who want government to prop it up, subsidize it, insure it, protect it, justify it. And it thrives on the fear that natural biological systems, God's design for a beautiful synergy of complex relationships from bacteria to bovines, really can't work. That we can't rely on the natural pattern of seeds bearing after their kind. We have to rely on seeds that either don't bear at all or bear after unpredictable kinds. We can't rely on whole foods. We have to rely on extruded irradiated amalgamated reconstituted chlorinated adulterated food-like substances.

I submit that a God who can't be trusted to feed us His way can't be trusted to save us His way. A God whom man's cleverness must correct is a God whom theologians must correct. If Sunday school teachers believe God's agrarianism needs to be corrected, they'll soon believe the Genesis records need to be corrected.

Once we begin cavorting with fear rather than faith, we progress as surely as day follows night into a place of anemic spiritual existence.

Now that we've explored the faith and food issue, let's move into the farming arena. What does a farm of faith look like, as opposed to a farm of fear? Does a farm of faith have a refrigerator full of vaccines and pharmaceuticals, or does it rely on something else? At this point in the book, if you don't realize that's a rhetorical question, you'd better quit now and start over because you haven't been paying attention.

The average farmer wakes up every morning fearful. What is sick? How many animals died during the night? A farm of faith says this: if I follow the Creator's patterns, immunity and wellness will follow. Yes, that's simple faith. But the alternative is an expensively stocked arsenal of crutches that signify that health can't be achieved without drug companies.

How about faith in compost and biomass rather than fear that a carbon-centric system might not work so we'd better apply chemical fertilizers? How about faith that our animals' immune systems will work so we can have visitors and let them walk about freely without fear?

Goodness, I challenge you to go to any industrial farm. You'll see anti-microbial shoe dips, shower in shower out, plastic suits. Whenever we get scientists visiting our farm, they invariably remark about how seemingly nonchalant we are about bio-security. The industry is paranoid about bio-security because their animals and plants are fragile. If our farm plants and animals had as dysfunctional an immune system as that found in industrial facilities, I'd be paranoid, too. I don't blame them for being paranoid. They're wise to be paranoid. But is it faith? No, it's abject fear.

One of my favorite stories about my son Daniel growing up was when he was thirteen and took his first 4-H illustrated talk to the senior contest at Virginia Tech. The title was "Symbiosis and Synergism in the Rabbitry." He had already been raising rabbits for five years at the time and had become quite a little guru on the rabbit enterprise. As we're wont to do on our farm, rather than a mono-species rabbitry like you see in all the production books, we built a Raken house. The rabbits were in roomy wire cages suspended at eye level, and chickens roamed freely underneath.

Hence, Rabbit plus Chicken equals Raken. Get it? A deep bedding of carbon underneath provided plenty of litter to absorb rabbit urine. The chickens scratched in the litter, which mixed the urine in, which decomposed the carbon, which created a bug-growing medium, which grew bugs, which induced the chickens to scratch, with injected oxygen and mixed-in urine...you get the picture. It's kind of like the nursery rhyme "The House That Jack Built."

Of course, it wouldn't be honest to the story to neglect the fact that Daniel had an excellent communications coach. He practiced in front of the mirror like I told him and had it down cold. The only scary thing about the competition was that it would be judged by three veterinarians in the Virginia Tech School of Veterinary Science. Not only that, but after the presentation they could ask him any question they wanted. In fact, they were supposed to ask every competitor a question in order to deduce if the child actually knew anything about the topic or had just memorized something he knew little about.

We practiced some softball questions and figured we had him well prepared. After all, both Teresa and I had won state 4-H illustrated talk competitions in our teen years, so we knew what to expect. With our thirteen-year-old prodigy and his indulgent little sister in tow, we drove down to the great school of minds on the appointed day of competition. He performed flawlessly, and from our vantage point across the room, we could see the judges smiling and completely taken with his charisma. As the completely objective parent in this case, I knew he was by far the best one in the whole competition. Family was proud.

He finished and first came a softball question: "How long have you been raising rabbits?" Easy. "Five years, sir." We had coached him on proper respect. By the way, we think eight years old is about the right time in life to start a business.

Second judge threw a softball: "How do you sell your rabbits?" Easy. "I dress them and sell them directly to customers in the area, sir."

Third judge threw the hardball: "Aren't you concerned about disease with the chickens being right there next to the rabbits?" You could hear a pin drop. I caught my breath. The question was accusatory and out of character for this friendly competition where even the last-place finisher gets some kind of ribbon—not blue, but something. I think it's called the Swedish system, where there are no real losers. We had not anticipated this kind of question.

Daniel didn't bat an eye. He didn't hesitate. He didn't flinch. He looked squarely at the doctor of veterinary medicine and replied firmly: "We've learned that most pathogens don't cross-speciate, so it's not a problem." The judges literally threw back their heads and laughed and gave him first place. The room would have mutinied if they hadn't. He went on to wow them with several more anti-establishment contrarian talks over the next several years, and never got anything less than first place. Oh, don't miss the point of the story: the vets were fearful about the Raken house.

They could not believe that a place of diversity could carry its own checks and balances. A farm with enough faith in various gifts and talents, in the self-correcting and self-policing characteristics of multi-speciated relational production, sets a visible object lesson for the same functionality in a body of believers who exhibit differences. Different gifts, different talents. These are not supposed to divide and destroy a fellowship group; they are there to sharpen, correct, challenge, encourage. They are pieces of a whole that work beautifully when all the parts exhibit their distinctiveness and agree to participate.

> FOR AS WE HAVE MANY MEMBERS IN ONE BODY, AND ALL MEMBERS HAVE NOT THE SAME OFFICE: SO WE, BEING MANY, ARE ONE BODY IN CHRIST, AND EVERY ONE MEMBERS ONE OF ANOTHER. HAVING THEN GIFTS DIFFERING ACCORDING TO THE GRACE THAT IS GIVEN TO US, WHETHER PROPHECY, LET US PROPHESY ACCORDING TO THE PROPORTION OF FAITH; OR MINISTRY, LET US WAIT ON OUR MINISTERING: OR HE THAT TEACHES, ON TEACHING; OR HE THAT EXHORTS, ON EXHORTATION: HE THAT GIVES, LET HIM DO IT WITH SIMPLICITY; HE THAT RULES, WITH DILIGENCE; HE THAT SHOWS MERCY, WITH CHEERFULNESS. (Romans 12:4–8 AKJV)

Have you ever wondered why in the world God made so many different kinds of critters? Fungi, mold, bacteria, nematodes, wild animals, domestic animals, plants, fish, coral. It really is amazing, isn't it? Even Christians tend to enjoy this variety because intuitively it's overwhelmingly beautiful. We know that each of these beings (no, I'm not going squirrelly on you, but I like to use it just to honor the distinctiveness of these critters) occupies a certain niche in the environment. We also know that their specificity is far beyond a self-organizing fatalism and required a Creator to design them with horns and lips and scales and mitochondria.

In a big sense, life diversity teaches faith in differences. I think humans are prone to prejudice. We certainly love to segregate ourselves into tribes that look alike, think alike, and talk alike. I'm not sure that's wrong. What's wrong is fearing those who are not in our inner sanctum. What's wrong is not embracing people who aren't in our tribe.

When we patronize a farming system predicated on monospeciation as being the most efficient, it encourages this idea that surrounding ourselves only with people exactly like us is the most efficient. It's safe, but I don't think it gets anything done. I'm not talking about singleness of purpose. I'm talking about background, color, verbal vs. mechanical, leader vs. follower, extrovert vs. introvert kind of stuff. We fear innovation. We fear having our assumptions questioned. I know I do.

Did God really have to create such variety? I mean, really? Did we really need a wombat? A kangaroo? A possum? A skunk? Really? Part of the wonder of God is that He is a Creator on overdrive. I mean, when God say's He's going to do something, He goes after it. He doesn't piddle around. When He made the earth, it was so much more than Venus and Mars. It's incomprehensibly blessed. When He made plants, look at the variety! Animals, look at the variety! God went all out. He wants us to go all out. If you say you're going to do something, do it with gusto.

When God wants to illustrate human variety and how big He is to welcome any of these weird costumes, skin colors, and backgrounds into His arms, that's an incredible expression of whosoever will. Farmers who fear variety exhibit a small trust system. A farm of faith has lots of variety and exhibits lots of innovation. If you come away from a farm saying: "Wow, that's creative. That's a lot of cool stuff going on," then you'll know you've been to a farm that exercises faith.

May I speak briefly to church properties on this point? How about that nice kitchen downstairs? What if somebody with dreadlocks from the neighborhood urban farm asks you if he can use the kitchen to make vegetarian potpies? Vegetarian potpies? Oh my, that would push me. Ha!

But really, what would you say? Are you afraid of the kitchen being used by somebody else? That's legitimate, but be creative and embracive and figure out how with some proper oversight it could be used. I think one of the biggest travesties in our churches is refusing to leverage all that stainless steel and kitchen infrastructure around the clock to augment the local integrity food system. How about you being the one to let everyone know: "Have kitchen for local food use. Fully equipped. Let's quit patronizing industrial mechanical food and start eating sacred food." Can you imagine the conversations such a come-on would create? You'd have evangelistic and outreach opportunities you couldn't imagine.

How about church lawns? Big, spacious, expansive monocultures. Energy-guzzling shows of elitism and royalty. I'm not saying you can't have a little area for children to play, or a volleyball court, or a play set. But do we really need two acres of golf green equivalence? To fertilize with chemical fertilizer so we can use more petroleum to mow it more? Really?

How about community gardens? Section it off for people who want to use it to grow their own vegetables. You can park the mower, forget the fertilizer and weed killer, and instead spend that time conversing with the most outrageous variety of people you can imagine. I mean, the place might start looking like the characters in a Dr. Seuss book. Wouldn't that be a hoot? You'd probably get written up on the front page of the local newspaper. It'd be a big hairy different deal, wouldn't it? And that, my friends, is what Jesus would do.

Goodness, next thing you know you'd be talking to a loan shark (Zacchaeus) and a prostitute (woman at the well). You might be entertaining neighborhood brats and foreign dignitaries. Who knows what relationships might develop?

Think of the conversations. Think of the community emotional equity. Rather than bringing industrial canned food to a box in the church foyer for the food bank to distribute to "those people," we'd be participating, interacting, exercising our faith that God's humor and abundance are the coolest thing yet. Is your faith big enough to carry you through this disturbance of innovative activity? Could the elders and trustees handle it, or would this drop a couple with heart attacks? What does our faith mean? If it means that we have to segregate ourselves into an elitist structure with our industrial cans of food for the needy because deep down we fear touching them, smelling them, interacting with them, then we're running away from faith, not pushing ourselves into it.

How about putting a solarium on the side of that massive stone church building? Whack a hole in the wall of that cathedral and let the sunlight and passive solar heat in. Let the super-oxygenated air from lettuce leaves in January fill nostrils and lungs with freshness during the morning song. Goodness, if Sister Sue hyperventilates it'll be the most exciting thing to happen in a long time. Feed Big Belly Bob some salad straight out of that soil and you might get him weaned from at least one can of Dr Pepper a day. Wouldn't that be a conversion?

Okay, we've had a good time with this, and I hope I haven't gone over the edge of decorum. But for crying out loud, folks, we Christians are blessed with infrastructure, money, ability. Why don't we show physical faith to our neighbors as directly and clearly as we do with the youth group trip to Mexico to build a house for an orphanage? Before anybody jumps me on that, I'm not suggesting we stop missionary trips. But I'm quite concerned that too often we expediently show our faith at the end of a jet airplane trip because we fear being that visceral in our own neighborhoods. That's not the order in which we should express our faith.

It should be visible most apparently where we live, where we worship, where we play, where we eat, where we entertain. That's where the rubber hits the road. It's easy to be good for a week, with groups just like us, in a place far, far away. It's hard, inconvenient, and a work of significant faith exercise to exhibit it to the people who see us get out of our cars every day. Yes, that's a whole different deal.

What if your fellowship group, along with sanctity-of-life month and missions-giving month, created a farm-of-faith month? Organized field trips to farms of faith? Bought from farms of faith for the month? We have hunger lock-ins for youth groups to identify with the hungry. Do we not identify with the cancer-stricken pesticide patients? The vomiting animal factory neighbors?

Isn't it easy to be shallow? It's like the greenies saying buy a Prius and put in LED lightbulbs: shazam, now you're taking care of the earth. We love shallow; we don't like deep. But if we are going to walk a life of genuine faith, we're going to have to wrestle with these issues. I have no problem if you think I'm too out there. That's okay. But can we at least wrestle with these issues?

The whole notion that a food system can illustrate fear or faith and a farm system can illustrate fear or faith may be an entirely new concept. I get that. But could we appreciate that such illumination from a lunatic fringer could be as valuable and neat as a new evangelistic technique or a new communication technique to help you rediscover honeymoon love? Dear Christian brothers and sisters, I really believe that if the faith community could punch through this faith or fear food and farm understanding, it would be perhaps the most powerful force for eclectic good our country has seen for a long, long time.

It would sure turn the creation worshippers on their heads. They'd sit there stuttering and stammering, unable to know where to go or what to say. We'd break their stereotypes. We wouldn't fit their pigeonholes anymore. They'd be dumbfounded, and that would be a powerful work of faith. God would smile.

Inclusive vs. Exclusive

For God so loved the world, that he gave his only begotten Son, that whosoever believeth in him should not perish, but have everlasting life.

John 3:16

Christ's love is for everyone. The most well-known Scripture verse is John 3:16: "FOR GOD SO LOVED THE WORLD THAT HE GAVE HIS ONLY BEGOTTEN SON, THAT WHOEVER BELIEVES IN HIM SHOULD NOT PERISH BUT HAVE EVERLASTING LIFE" (NKJV). For all its familiarity, this verse carries significant doctrinal weight.

First, it offers the universality of God's love toward humanity. His interest is not limited to a few exceptional individuals, to one race, type, or vocation. It's all-encompassing. Second, that love expressed itself in action: a gift of unprecedented and inconceivable value— His only Son. Not one son among many, but the only one.

Third, that salvation is given on the basis of belief, not works. Of course this theme permeates all of Scripture and even became the cornerstone of Martin Luther's epiphany: "THE JUST SHALL LIVE BY HIS FAITH" (Habakkuk 2:4). What a relief that salvation carries no human price tag except belief. It doesn't require a pilgrimage. It doesn't demand material substance. It's not for sale and entails no negotiation. It's freely offered to whosoever will. If that's not inclusive, I don't know what is. You don't need a college education or to be born into a functional family. You don't need to become good or have a background of living well. Wow.

I remember well that after I accepted this initial offering at nine years old, lying in a bunk bed in a cabin at a Christian summer camp, I had real doubts as to whether God had accepted me. Was I really saved? For growing up in such a good family, I was a bad kid. Lying, stealing, bullying. But every time I had doubts, I just recited whosoever will and the peace of God's indwelling Spirit flooded over me anew. Full assurance followed that simple phrase. Whosoever included me; what a relief.

Fourth, the verse promises a division between perishing and having everlasting life. In other words, two distinct paths exist. This is not allegory and fancy psychobabble. Two destinies await. Where our faith rests sets us upon one course or the other. The notion that all roads lead to heaven is not true. The whole idea of a scale with Grandpa God placing our good deeds on one side and bad on the other to see which way it tilts is not correct.

Although God clearly stipulates how to join His family, and clearly explains how to know you're in that family, it is absolutely open to all. Democrats, Republicans, Greenies, Socialists (well, let's not get too carried away—ha!)—the whosoever will invitation offers a breadth that embraces everyone. Everyone can participate, regardless of education, background, color, socioeconomic status.

This is what it means when God says He is "NO RESPECTER OF PERSONS" (Acts 10:34). Jesus made a big point to spend time with the physically, socially, or financially unlovely. If anything defines the raw, unbridled human attitude, it's prejudice, exclusivity, elitism, and cliquishness. Goodness, look how God had to work with Paul, Peter, James, and the other apostles after His ascension to help them understand that "whosoever will" included the Gentiles.

For the Israelites, whose whole identity and history were wrapped up in exclusivity as God's chosen people, to see God extend His grace and benefits to the Gentiles struck at the core of their being. God grafted in the Gentiles, breaking down the wall of separation that had always existed. Prior to Pentecost, non-Israelites could become proselytes, but that was as close as a Gentile could get. Now suddenly all believers, whether Jew or Greek, Iranian or American, enjoyed equal heirship status in this inclusive family.

Now let's turn the corner, in the light of these wonderful truths, and look at food and farming. Can the food system or a farm system be constructed to reflect these truths? Do these truths have any ramifications for how we design our physical lives, or are they just spiritual disembodied theological expressions that end at our sensual universe? If we could build a whosoever will food system, what would it look like?

For starters, let's look at the two currently offered to us. Don't get ahead of me—I'm not calling them the one that perishes or the one that leads to everlasting life...yet. Let's just stick with the concept of whosoever will. Let's start with something simple like eggs. In the industrial model, which is of course today's orthodoxy, eggs come from hybrid chickens that have been selected for a long time to have tiny bodies and lay like crazy. Prior to industrialization, the average backyard hen weighed about six pounds and laid 150 to 170 eggs per year.

Today's commercial bird weighs as little as three pounds and lays three hundred eggs in a year. Unlike her old-fashioned cousin, however, this newfangled industrial bird has some real needs. First, she's extremely fragile. She can't handle rainstorms or frosty nights. Second, she requires exceptionally sophisticated nutrients. If she exercised or ran around, she wouldn't be able to put all her energy into simply laying eggs. Therefore, her activity must be restricted in tiny cages inside CAFOs.

To ensure maximum production in as short a time as possible, these buildings use lights in a tightly regulated regimen to simulate ever-increasing day length. All birds lay best during increasing day length (spring) and reduce production during decreasing day length (fall). But since the industry can't abide productivity ebbs and flows, it uses artificial lights in otherwise dark houses to create perpetual spring. The problem is, eventually the lights are on all day. And wonder of wonders, the industry wizards have figured out how to hit maximum light the day the hens burn out.

The artificially induced, hyper-production cycle makes the bird lay so prolifically that it extracts calcium from the skeleton in order to keep up with eggshell demands. The industry continually wrestles with brittle, thin eggshells and a corresponding skeletal breakdown in the bird. She actually cannibalizes her skeleton in order to keep up. That sure sounds like the way I'd like to live.

Standing on wire cages all their lives, these cellmates turn on each other. The industry, therefore, burns off their beaks as little chicks so they can't peck anything except the feed that comes by the cells at carefully contrived sequences. When one dies, her cellmates gradually push her decomposing body through the wire floor, probably enjoying a bit of spatial relief. Who's next?

Few things are more laying-hen expressive than sitting on a nest to lay eggs. However, these industrial specimens don't have nests. The floor of their cage slopes. Never a day in their life do they enjoy a level cage, let alone level ground. They must simply squat, right there in the open, in front of all the other birds, and drop the egg on the sloping floor, where it rolls away on a conveyor belt to the chlorine bath and eventually the supermarket egg display.

Today, about 170 of these farms produce 90 percent of the eggs Americans eat. If I want to produce eggs for the supermarket, this is the fraternity I must join. Why? Because to get in, a whole host of hurdles await. The bigger the supermarket, the higher the hurdle. A couple of years ago I had the pleasure of hosting about ten direct-report vice presidents from Sam's Club at our farm. They, along with the CEO, were on a two-day sustainability jaunt to see if they could tweak their product mix to reflect more localization and earth-friendliness.

After the farm tour, while we munched on sack lunches in our little on-farm sales building, one of them asked me how they could get Polyface products into their stores. I didn't hesitate with the answer: "Allow something smaller than a tractor-trailer to back up to your loading dock at a time other than between midnight and five a.m." That seemed a simple enough starting point for me.

They all looked at each other, smiled a bit impishly, and dismissed the idea as impossible. Period. End of discussion. Their business model could not conceive of receiving a delivery in anything less than a tractor-trailer. Gentle people, I hope you're already making the connection: This is not a whosoever will food system. It's a closely held fraternal exclusive country club where the rules are stacked against interlopers like me.

It doesn't end with the delivery truck, of course. One of the first questions when dealing with an industrial-scale market concerns product liability insurance. The farmer often needs $3 million of coverage. I wish I had kept track of how many eager-beaver entrepreneurial farmers I've met who have been stymied at accessing a market due to these outlandish insurance requirements.

Assuming the market is big enough and the opportunity pencils out to afford the insurance, then the problem is passing the exposure risk protocols for the insurance underwriter. The bosses protecting the interest of the insurance company don't want to jeopardize their profitability. As a result, they create protocols. But how do you decide on low-risk protocols? Well, you ask experts.

Let's stick with eggs for the sake of discussion. How does, for example, Traveler's Insurance decide what kind of egg farmer protocols they're willing to cover? They call in the poultry science specialists from land-grant universities like Virginia Tech and Penn State. What do those experts believe? They believe the cheaper the egg, the better. The way to produce the cheapest egg is a CAFO. Since a CAFO is inherently filthy, unsanitary, pathogen-encouraging, and anti-chickenness, they believe antibiotics must be fed to keep the birds healthy. And each bird must be vaccinated against the virulent diseases such habitats encourage.

Now, since the eggs might be covered in high-pathogenic manure, they believe all eggs must be washed in chlorine water. Chlorine is a hazardous and deadly substance. The farmer must now have a properly constructed and licensed room to contain hazardous substances. These rooms and the regulatory compliance are not cheap.

I could belabor this ad nauseam, but I hope by now you're getting the point. The commercial egg-producing fraternity is an incredibly exclusive club, and when you buy eggs from this club, it patronizes a whole mind-set, a whole system with rigid, exclusive access. These multimillion-dollar factory torture houses, with all their wire-cage innards, feed conveyors, egg conveyors, manure conveyors, and temperature-controlled ventilation systems, are not something that any normal person can build.

We haven't even talked about the financing, mortgage, energy costs, high-volume well water requirements and sophisticated manure storage, handling, and spreading equipment necessary to get this egg to the large supermarket. Such a system is hard to break into.

Several years ago, on our farm, we had extra eggs in the spring and I tried calling Kroger's. I finally gave up after being unable to talk to anything besides a robot. The local store can't make any decisions. The number the local store gives you leads to a robot that sends you around in circles all day. Gaining access is virtually impossible. The eggs lining those store shelves are the end result of a highly exclusive system, where elite players hobnob and agree to special rules.

Those rules preclude players who would dare to use a bigger-bodied or heritage-breed chicken that had such life vibrancy she didn't need vaccines or medications. Those rules disallow birds enjoying fresh pasture and scratching in the dirt. Perish the thought that the manure from said chickens would be free of high-pathogen contamination and contain only bacteria compatible with the human gut. What? Chlorine not necessary? Impossible! And the final kicker: How dare you back up to my receiving dock with a single-axle box truck? You should be shot.

Now, just for fun, let's look at the opposite model: direct-marketed pastured eggs. For the record, I'm purposely using the premium term: *pastured*. Not free roaming, cage-free, organic, free range, natural, loose-housed, humane, animal welfare–approved, or any other clever-speak co-opted by the industry. The word *pastured* indicates a truly revolutionary belief in the chickenness of the chicken. It assumes that the chicken is a bird, and as such should enjoy fresh air, sunshine, unimpeded movement, affirmative social groupings, pecking, scratching, nesting, and seasonal cycling.

The American Pastured Poultry Producers Association (APPPA) is the official trade organization for these folks—may I say the denomination? It's a small group embracing the narrow way. See, I can't help myself. I see these spiritual counterparts exhibited in real life everywhere. Why is such synchronous spiritual-physical thinking weird? I think such synchronicity injects vibrancy, deeper meaning, and realism into what otherwise is a sterile, academic examination of impractical truths.

So here we go with a pastured laying hen. As a producer, I can start with half a dozen. I started when I was ten years old with eighteen birds. If I wanted to start with the industrial model, I'd need a million-dollar investment in infrastructure before I could sell the first egg. But with the pastured model, anybody can start, anywhere, at any time, without financial, insurance, or bureaucratic permission.

The infrastructure can be scrap lumber, some poultry netting, and some scavenged sheet metal. No fans, no augers, no conveyors, no machinery. By direct marketing to my neighborhood (I started with families in our fellowship group and neighbors living on our road), I enjoy a high gross margin. Rather than half a penny per dozen, requiring me to produce lots of dozens in order to stay in business, I can net a healthy profit of a dollar a dozen.

The hens enjoy individual nest boxes bedded with straw that they can move around as they nestle in. Hand-gathering can be performed by anyone older than four years old—that's really close to whosoever will. No self-respecting four-year-old wants to go into an industrial house where the fecal particulate covers clothing and tender mucous membranes and where the stench is strong enough to permeate skin.

If the business is enjoyable and successful, retained profits can finance expansion. All expansion can occur organically, as the market expands, in little steps. First a dozen hens, then 50, then 100, then 500, then 1,000. This simulates the way things grow in nature—little by little without overrunning skills and finances. This is a model that invites any and all to participate.

With portable infrastructure to shelter and control the birds, as opposed to a stationary single-use capital-intensive CAFO, we can divorce the farming enterprise from landownership. Since the most expensive part of farming is buying land, if we can farm without owning land, an agricultural vocation becomes possible. Since pastured poultry, by definition, uses portable infrastructure, it can be moved from place to place. Whether that's on land that's owned, or between a couple of places that are unowned, it offers easy access—a way in. That's whosoever will farming.

To take this one step further, imagine the domestic, backyard flock. More and more urban areas are granting permission for backyard poultry, and this signals a wonderful step toward whosoever will food systems. Perhaps no one has done more to encourage this movement than previously mentioned Pat Foreman, official chicken whisperer and author of *City Chicks*. She lectures widely, always using a real-life bird as her prop. Wherever she is and whatever the venue, from *Mother Earth News* fairs to state legislatures, her local companion is named Oprah Henfree.

Pat estimates that if roughly one in three households in America had a few chickens to eat their kitchen scraps and those of their neighbors, it would completely displace the entire factory commercial egg system. Many people look at me dubiously when I start talking about local and transparent food systems as if it's some winsome fantasy that could never work in the real world. Let me tell you, an egg production model centered around kitchen-scrap, ultimate-recycler chickens is ultimately far more secure, transparent, and nutrient dense than one dependent on a handful of opaque, mechanical, stinky egg factories. And which model exemplifies the whosoever will idea the best? Hmmmm?

Although we've concentrated our analysis on only one food item—eggs—in this discussion, we could do the same thing for any other food item.

The food police told us our farm's open-air chicken-processing shed was unsanitary and producing an adulterated product. They said if one fly landed on a chicken carcass during processing it created an adulterated product. They said the open air was inherently unsanitary. I'm not making this up. Oh, they weren't wearing gas masks or respirators. As far as I could tell, they were breathing the same air I was breathing. That unsanitary air.

All of this food policing, of course, has created a crisis in the integrity food and farming movement. Fortunately, we now have the Farm-to-Consumer Legal Defense Fund (FTCLDF), modeled after the Home School Legal Defense Association (HSLDA) started by Michael Farris in the early 1990s. At that time, parents faced truancy violation, and state Child Protective Services agencies would actually take homeschooled children away from the family and put them in foster care where they could be institutionalized according to educational orthodoxy. Today, we have the same thing going on in the integrity food and farming world.

The legal staff at FTCLDF offers real-time counsel to farmers facing a plethora of bureaucratic actions against food heretics like me. Anyone who values food freedom needs to join this wonderful organization. My goal is that it will become as powerful as the National Rife Association (NRA). When Americans become as militant about protecting food choice as they are about gun choice, we'll have a healthier country and a decidedly more inclusive food system.

I can feel the positive vibes coming back through these pages as I rant about gun rights, homeschooling rights, and food rights. Thank you. But when have you heard a sermon decrying police action against a farmer simply because he wanted to sell raw milk? Of course you haven't, because raw milk advocates are aligned with foodies, foodies are environmentalists, and environmentalists are pagan pinko commie liberals. Don't worry, I have the lingo down pat.

Where is the railing from our pulpits against the elitism of such a system? It can't be because the head elder is probably a health inspector who thinks he's God's gift to food safety by making sure the ignorant parishioners can acquire only food based on his orthodoxy. When will we understand that the best way to deal with hunger is to create a whosoever will food system? You can't have a food system that starves start-ups and denies access to the most nutrient-dense, body-healing foods while at the same time actually helping hungry people. So how many people bring food to the hunger relief drive that was actually purchased from an exclusive factory system?

If you're going to help a hungry family, take them some eggs from a whosoever will agricultural system. Don't go buy eggs from an exclusive club; get them from the whosoever will farms.

Why doesn't the Christian community crusade as much about the elite exclusivity of the food and farming model as we do about immigration reform, pornography, big government, high taxes, and those anti-American environmentalist whackos? I believe that if the entire Christian community embraced a whosoever will food and farming system, it would so alter the country's fabric that it's hard to imagine what the ripple effect would be in all these other issues.

To unleash the purchasing power of the entire 34 percent of Americans who claim faith-based living on the minuscule whosoever will (I call it integrity) food system would not only bolster the good guys; it would cripple the bad guys. And that would be a legacy worth leaving.

*   *   *

Finally, this discussion would not be complete without attaching the whosoever will concept to food access. We've dealt with life as a farmer. Now let's look at life as a *consumer*. And yes, I don't like that word, but until something better comes along, it's as expressive as I currently know. Realize that I'm a consumer, too, because I don't grow everything I eat. Most of it, to be sure, but not all of it.

A whosoever will food system is one that's easy to enter from both ends: as a producer and as a consumer. The harder it is to participate, the more exclusive it is. Could we agree that a vibrant local fellowship group includes people from all walks of life, backgrounds, even ethnicity and race? If we're really offering an inclusive salvation experience, our local bodies of believers should reflect the diversity inherent in God's grace.

With that in mind, is it not a proper ministry of the church to encourage a whosoever will food mentality? I mean cooking classes, food-centric gatherings from canning parties to collaborative bone broth teams? Why is that worldly? I think it's one of the most reverent, sacred things we could do. Perhaps akin to searching for a lost sheep, or sowing seeds, or catching fish, or pruning grapevines—any of Jesus' parables come to mind?

Too often the Christian community of middle-class, socially upward yearning Hollywood infatuates encourages sterile microwave single-portion industrial food. After all, this way we can spend more time sharing the gospel. We can spend more time watching our financial portfolio, which is the essence of godly stewardship. We have more time for ministry. Why bog down your life with a garden in the backyard, or a chicken, or perhaps a beehive on the roof? Why cook? Why eat family meals, together, without the TV and smartphones? Why, indeed?

Because food, and communal meals, is perhaps the most visceral object lesson of God's bridge to humanity. An inclusive,

participatory interest in bodily nourishment bespeaks the same phi-
losophy toward spiritual nourishment. If the faith community would
unleash its members, its lands, its monies, its political clout on the
current industrial exclusive food system, it would scream whosoever
will reality to a world scratching its head over John 3:16.

Imagine if the whole faith community demanded that a city
allow a single mom in an inner-city apartment to make nutrient-
dense quiche and soups for other families in her complex. Perhaps
she would grow the ingredients in a vacant lot nearby. Or perhaps
the fellowship group would funnel integrity food to her—grown by
a pastured and beyond organic farmer in the area. When the food
police, zoning administrators, building inspectors, and whatever
other elitists come knocking on her door telling her she can't do
that, the whole faith community surrounds her apartment, joining
hands and chanting: "Whosoever will."

What good are civil rights if they can't be expressed in commerce,
in access to business, in physically participating in the marketplace
and servicing the needs of our community? Let's quit this shallow
focus group discussion, writing white papers describing our angst at
poverty and hunger. Let's put our faith into action, our beliefs into
real physical change.

If we can't touch, see, or taste our freedom, what good is it?

A lady from Texas told me recently she had to pay a fine to her
homeowners association for growing two tomato plants in her flower
bed. You see, the association had a prohibition on farming. After all,
you can't defile an upper-crust community with what dark-skinned
illiterates do—grow food. No, that would never do. Roses are not
farming. Tomatoes are farming. Tsk-tsk.

From food regulations to patents on genetically modified organisms, perhaps the overarching theme of the industrial mechanistic food and farming orthodoxy is to exclude competition, exclude
paradigm-questioning innovation, and burn the heretics. How
dare someone let his poultry commiserate with red-winged black-
birds? How dare someone feed her children raw milk? How dare

someone plant tomatoes in a flower bed? How dare someone cook in her kitchen and sell the food to her neighbors? How dare someone homeschool? How dare someone defy the cobblers' guild? How dare someone carve on a cadaver? How dare someone believe in salvation by grace alone—no baptism, no sacrament, no indulgences, no cathedrals necessary? How dare, indeed?

If we would apply a litmus test of inclusive vs. exclusive to the food and farming system like we do access to God's grace, it would paint a fundamentally different food system than the one patronized by most Christians. That's the takeaway challenge. Does it matter? Does God care?

Neighborly vs. Antagonistic

And as you would that men should do to you, do you also
to them likewise.

Luke 6:31 (AKJV)

Boundaries are arbitrary. Whether they define a nation, tribe, fief-dom, or personal real estate, they transcend topography, geography, climate, and vegetation. We're all neighbors to someone, and we're admonished in the Golden Rule: "ALL THINGS WHATEVER YOU WOULD THAT MEN SHOULD DO TO YOU, DO YOU EVEN SO TO THEM: FOR THIS IS THE LAW AND THE PROPHETS" (Matthew 7:12 AKJV).

Of course, Jesus clearly teaches that neighborliness flows from the heart rather than being bounded by location proximity. The most famous biblical passage describing neighborliness is the parable of the good Samaritan in Luke chapter 10. The encounter between the Samaritan and the Jew occurred on a well-traveled road. A public road encourages anonymity.

Indeed, this whole parable starts off with thieves attacking the Jewish traveler. They certainly used the impersonal location to their benefit. After all, it wasn't like attacking the man in his house, where friends and family would come to his assistance. They chose a place that was vulnerable due to its inherent lack of neighbors.

The parable is familiar, of course. After the Jewish priest and then the Jewish Levite passed the bleeding and broken man without helping, the Samaritan stopped and went far above what anyone would consider minimal assistance. He bound the man's wounds, took him to a convalescent center, and paid for the rehabilitation. This parable sets such a high bar for neighborliness that we've all failed to reach it at one time or another.

But Jesus' idea is clear: don't hurt your neighbor, and if your neighbor needs something, help him if you can.

The northern boundary of our farm runs across a gentle south-facing slope. About a third of the slope is uphill from the boundary fence, and we own the bottom two-thirds of the slope. Consistent with any landscape undulation, this slope ends in a narrow valley that is marshy and includes a seasonal stream. The stream usually dries up in late June and begins running again when early fall rains bring moisture back to the area.

When our family came to the farm in 1961, this gentle slope was scarred by two massive gullies. Lest anyone think gullies can only occur on steep slopes, let me assure you that this slope is too gentle to offer sleigh riding in the snow. You could never slide on a sled—it's too gentle.

But many years ago, someone decided to plow up the perennial grasses on that slope in order to plant grain. When rain hits vegetation, the drops shatter into a mist before hitting the soil surface. When the soil is covered with biomass, whether it's mulch or living vegetation, it's protected from taking the full brunt of pummeling raindrops. Diffusing onto the soil surface, the water mists into the aggregates and tunnels created by earthworms and roots. This holds the soil particles in place and enables the soil to sponge up as much moisture as possible.

But when the covering is inverted and the bare soil is naked before the raindrops, the pummeling water pounds the fragile soil particles, loosening them from root hairs and aggregates. Because the moisture does not mist onto the soil surface, it doesn't soak in as well. When the rain can't soak in as well, it pools and quickly looks for a downhill path, forming little rivulets across the soil. The combination of nakedness and surface runoff begins gouging channels across the soil. Picking up speed and soil particles in these channels, the water runs brown with soil; erosion now assaults the land with an aggressive, ugly hand.

A gully always starts at the bottom of the slope because that's where the water's volume and velocity do the most damage first. At the top of the hill, the barely perceptible water channels start fairly gently. But as they enlarge going down the slope, they carve horrible gouges in the fragile soil. The gully grows first at the bottom of the slope and then gradually eats away uphill.

Often a stair-step actually forms at the head of the gully where the erosion actually digs down into the subsoil. That stair-step, if left to itself, will gradually work its way all the way up to the top of the hill. Gullies always grow from the downhill end to the uphill end. Once that stair-step forms, it's a relentless progression uphill until it gets close enough to the ridge that not enough water can be collected in a channel to do any damage. In an active gully, that is extremely close to the top because the edge of that stair-step is fragile. It breaks off easily once the topsoil and vegetation are gone.

When I see a gully, I see horrible scars and wounds on the earth's body. They are a direct assault on the health and vigor of the soil. When Dad and Mom purchased our farm in 1961, it was a gullied nightmare. The boundary fence on this gentle slope I've described runs perpendicular to these two large gullies. As a young boy, I watched our neighbor put tree stumps, old rolls of wire, and other debris against the boundary fence on his upper side. He was trying to keep our gully from growing uphill onto his land.

At the boundary, the gullies were roughly ten feet deep and twenty feet across from the top edges. Of course, these top edges formed their own stair-steps, sloughing off over time as the gully grew deeper and deeper. Gully formation and growth is a terrible disease. Once started, it can't be stopped unless something dams the water coursing down to the bottom of it. Barring that intervention, it will deepen until it hits bedrock.

Because our land is on the lower side of the slope, the gullies started on our side. We can trace our farm's owners back to the original land grant during colonial times. These were all good Protestant farmers. They attended church services regularly and donated money to missions. They defended their families from hostile forces and paid their bills like good businesspeople. But in moments of meditation, as I look at those massive scars and my neighbor's efforts to contain their relentless uphill progression, I wonder how those good people could be that hostile to their neighbors.

In the context of their day, I'm sure the previous farmers described hostile Indians, hostile British (twice), hostile Mexicans, hostile Spaniards, hostile Germans, hostile Japanese, hostile Koreans, and hostile Russian Communists. But did they stop to look at their own hostility to the neighbor? I'm constantly amazed at how easy it is to join corporate battles, to sign up for the big tribal or national campaign. Meanwhile, back at the ranch, we have a gully eating up the hill and gobbling up the neighbor's land. We're great Americans to go punch somebody else in the nose who's dared cross our boundary, but back home, on our own property, we're punching the good neighbor in the nose for no reason other than that he's uphill.

It makes me want to weep in repentance for what these previous owners did to the uphill neighbor by plowing, denuding, and baring the soil to erosion. Erosion doesn't happen on its own. The uphill farmer didn't deserve to have his land eaten away by the neighbor's negligence and shortsightedness—cash today for raping the land and who cares about tomorrow?

Some of my earliest childhood memories include working with Dad to put barricades into these gullies to arrest the erosion. He hated erosion. I remember picking up big rocks and tossing them into the gully. This created a porous dam that allowed the runoff to go through, but slowed it down enough to make it drop sediment on the uphill side. Sure enough, in just a couple of years, we had a nice silt terrace above this stone barricade.

Then we began putting debris in the gully. Bottles and discarded farm machinery, tree stumps, and even half-rotted logs all helped slow the water. Eventually we hired a track loader and dump truck to dig the sediment that had accumulated down in the marshy valley, haul it back up the hill, and fill in the gullies. That created a nice pond in the valley and completely remediated the gullies. Today, you'd never know those gullies existed. Now the neighbor's soil is building on his side of the boundary. Neighborliness takes effort; it's hard to be kind.

Erosion, in my view, steals from God. The soil is His, not mine. But as if that weren't bad enough, erosion steals from my neighbor and my community. It impoverishes everyone. A food and farm system that encourages erosion is a direct assault on our neighbors and a direct assault on God's equity. Christians routinely lament an erosion of morality, but then patronize food that erodes the earth. How can we possibly steward morality if we can't even steward our dinner plate?

We Christians extol the virtue of charity toward those less fortunate, but often help them with food that exemplifies greed and avarice. Is it any wonder the earth-stewardship community calls us hypocrites and won't listen to our message of healing and hope? They say: "What healing and hope? If it's more destruction of what's visible, why should we consider what's invisible?"

Let's step away from erosion and look at some other areas. Consider pesticide drift from aerial spraying. Thousands of neighbors whose land adjoins industrial farms receive unwanted chemical applications on their children, their wives, and their property.

If you wanted to spray paint your house blue but couldn't control the spray unit well enough to keep it on your house and it also painted some of my house blue, how would I view you as a neighbor? I can imagine the conversation that would ensue when I saw one wall of my house painted blue:

Me, laughing: "Hey, neighbor Jim, the missus and I've been desperately wanting to paint that side of our house blue for a long time. I
sure didn't know it would be so easy."

Neighbor Jim, responding good-naturedly: "Well, the spray wand
kind of went crazy in my hand. I didn't know it would fly around like
that. Before I could get it under control, it made one streak from corner to corner on your wall."

Me: "Ha! Wouldn't that be hilarious? One blue streak arcing
across our wall. Blue on brick—that goes pretty well, doesn't it? I'm
not sure whether the missus would have preferred that or this."

Neighbor Jim: "I wondered about that. It did look kind of cool,
like a rainbow without any of the other colors. Come to think of it, it
didn't look like much of a rainbow. I figured it would be better to go
ahead and fix things right away, knowing how particular you are about
things. After all, that brick just didn't stand out like the blue paint did."

Me: "Couldn't agree more, Jim. I can't wait for the missus to get
home and see the new paint job on the one side of the house. It'll be
a big help when we tell our friends where we live. 'Just come to the
brick house with one side painted blue.' It'll be easy now."

Neighbor Jim: "So glad you like it. I wasn't sure how you'd take it since
I didn't ask permission or anything, but I know you take a pretty neighborly approach to everything. I do, too. You know the old saying 'What's
mine is mine and what's yours is mine.' What're neighbors for, anyway?"

Me: "Oh, here comes the missus now. She always complains
about my lack of creativity in being able to surprise her with gifts.
Boy howdy, do I have one for her today. I can't wait."

Neighbor Jim: "Glad to be of assistance. If she wants the rest of
the brick done, just let me know. This here contraption works really
great once you get the hang of it. And Lowe's has plenty of paint."

Me: "Thanks, Jim. I just might need to take you up on that offer.
Here she comes now. Hi, dear. Boy have I got a surprise for you!"

Enough. Would this conversation ever happen? Of course not,
unless both men were playing Hollywood buffoons in a slapstick

comedy movie. Not a person reading this could imagine this conversation, and yet this is exactly what chemical companies expect us to say when their poisons accidentally cover our children in neurotoxins and hormone-interrupters.

Should Christians be boycotting a food system that takes such a cavalier attitude toward running roughshod over neighbors? Many Christians laugh off such things as the paranoia of fools and earth muffins. If our fellowship group collects food for the needy, doesn't it behoove us to collect food that doesn't depend on neighbor-assaulting techniques?

Folks, a food system that pollutes the neighbor's land, buildings, and people is not a neighbor-friendly system and therefore not a biblical system. Let's call it what it is: wrong.

I find it fascinating that groups who do live nativity scenes never portray the manger in a Tyson chicken house or Smithfield hog factory. No, it's always a straw-filled manger with nicely bedded animals. A cow, a couple of sheep, and maybe a few chickens round out the placid scene. It looks inviting, really, the nativity basking in multi-speciated and small-scaled peacefulness. Such a wonderful place to be born.

What farming systems would you want your Messiah born into? The nativity? Yes. That's okay. It was crude and I don't want to take away the rudeness of it, which is part and parcel of the Servant-King's messianic message. I get that. But in all our efforts to modernize the story, to put it in today's context, can anyone imagine the virgin birth and shepherd-worship occurring in a battery-caged laying hen house?

Really? Yet the very people standing still and erect to present this timeless Christmas message to their community probably dined on food grown or raised in conditions they—and the Messiah—would find abhorrent. Have you ever walked through a factory house? Have you ever worked in full respirator gear and a hazardous material suit spraying poisons on your food?

I remember the last time I drove through Southern California, where massive beef feedlots dot the landscape. The stench practically took my breath away, and that was from a couple of miles' distance. You could see the pall of fecal particulate, like a giant dust cloud, hanging over the facilities from several miles away.

These are all part of the externalized costs mentioned by proponents of integrity food. From superfund sites to the seven hundred riparian dead zones in the United States, the toxins tainting God's creation make Him weep, along with the iconic Indian whose tear-streak in the 1970s came to symbolize the environmental movement. Of course it was an Indian, not a Christian.

Wouldn't it have been wonderful if that iconic symbol had been a pastor or priest? Perhaps a Baptist farmer? Perhaps a Puritan? Anybody reading the Judeo-Christian writings? Of course not; it had to be a Native American. Not to take anything away from the natives, but wouldn't it have been cool if that tear could have been shed by a Christian? How would that change our gospel narrative?

I suggest it would have given us a leg up in preaching our spiritual obligations toward God by demonstrating them through our physical obligations toward God. When people see that we're serious about God's commands like being neighborly, they're far more receptive when we say we need to be serious about spiritual repentance and believing what is right. That we in the Christian community have been nonchalant about connecting these divine threads should drive us to fix our broken thinking without delay.

To be sure, few people defend private property rights as vehemently as I do. But property right freedom does not extend to spilling over onto the neighbor's, or to depriving the neighbor of equity and enjoyment in his property. When my farming practices stink up the neighborhood or pollute the community groundwater, that is not okay. The hog farms in North Carolina, the massive confinement dairies in Illinois and Idaho, the toxic vegetable operations in California and Florida—all of these destroy neighbors' lives.

From cancer to nausea to diminished property values, the fallout from toxic farms is far reaching and well documented. The shenanigans engaged in by these businesses, their buddies in the government regulatory structure, and the bankers epitomize anti-neighbor attitudes and actions. When these operators say, "It smells like money," I have no problem with their wanting to live in a cesspool. But if you can't keep your cesspool to yourself, it's not neighborly.

Has anyone gotten poisoned from a compost pile? From pastured chickens? From an organic diversified produce operation? No. The reason is that these systems work in an inherently forgiving, natural template that by definition localizes its activities. Both in scale and technique, protocols used by people who don't depend on poisons to remediate improper production models protect neighbors from spillover.

Is it any wonder that a farming system as neighbor-assaultive as modern conventional agriculture would create a food-violence atmosphere? Not too long ago, people were always glad to eat. Eating was a communal affair without drama and paranoia. But today, everyone fears their food. Church potlucks have turned into gluten-free, food-allergy espionage fests. If you invite someone over to dinner, the first question is about food allergies.

Can you imagine Abraham entertaining the angels under the Oaks of Mamre and asking if it was okay to serve Sarah's regular wheat bread? Really? Food allergies are a modern outgrowth of a food system that assaults creation. The principle of reaping and sowing is as true in creation care as it is in our own personal lives.

If we sow destruction to the earth, it will destroy us. Farming systems that assault neighbors create food systems that pit one person against another and make it more and more difficult to practice hospitality. Anyone old enough to remember the 1970s knows that at that time, the phrase "food allergy" was not even in our cultural lexicon.

Neither were things like MRSA, C. diff., campylobacter, listeria, or high-path E. coli in the lexicon. Mad cow didn't exist. Many Scriptures use food metaphors to describe spiritual sustenance; I'd say God intended food to be our friend, not our enemy. Food should be a friendly neighbor in our lives. Farms should be friendly neighbors in our landscapes.

Is it any wonder that our Christian culture is suffering a crisis of divine communion and fellowship when we're suffering acutely from food neighborliness? I would suggest that the level of our neighborliness in food creates a physical benchmark for how we trust in God. If food assaults us, food that He provides, which He created for our benefit, which He said was "good" in the Genesis record, then how can we trust Him to be beneficial to us at all times?

Consider how some large seed and chemical companies act. Instead of compensating neighbors for damages like anyone else caught in trespass, they sue violated farmers for not paying royalties for the privilege of breeding services from alien life-forms. Not only is such an attitude un-biblical; it's not even civilized. Barbarians have more regard for their neighbors' stuff than Monsanto. What Christian could possibly invest in, buy from, or work in such an evil business?

It creates mistrust and ignorance. Ultimately, it creates a food system that is fundamentally toxic to the populace—to the food's neighbors. A food system that is antagonistic to people necessarily develops into a diet antagonistic to our bodies. The two go hand in glove.

Razor wire and guard gates surround food-processing companies. That's not neighbor-friendly. Compare that attitude to how you view someone coming into your kitchen. We're not talking about enemies; we're talking about friends. Just curious seekers. Have you tried to look into an industrial chicken-processing facility? Goodness, the industry is lobbying more states to pass laws criminalizing taking pictures on farms or in processing facilities that are subsequently used to disparage the organization by publicizing its atrocities.

Anybody can come to our farm anytime to see anything from anywhere unannounced. Compare that to the neighborliness exhibited by the industry that constantly hides behind a cloak of secrecy and security details. The kind of food that comes out of such a model is inherently vicious toward the people who eat it.

A Golden Rule food system is open and embracing toward people. It's neighborly. If that one standard were applied to our farmscape on a broad scale, it would fundamentally change the way Americans eat... for the better.

Relational vs. Separational

I have called you friends; for all things that I have heard
of my Father I have made known unto you.

John 15:15

Certainly no one would argue that the premier biblical theme is
about relationship—God establishing His creation in a familial
bond: how we as humans enter into a relationship with God; how
He makes a pathway through the Messiah for us to access such a
relationship; how we are supposed to illustrate that relationship in
His church and with the brethren.

What is the number one evangelistic tool according to Jesus, the
defining object lesson of His flock? "BY THIS SHALL ALL MEN KNOW
THAT YOU ARE MY DISCIPLES, IF YOU HAVE LOVE ONE TO ANOTHER"
(John 13:35 AKJV). *Love* is not a thought; it is an action verb. It is not
a thing, but an expression. You can't love in a vacuum; love demands
an object. It demands a relationship.

"NOT FORSAKING THE ASSEMBLING OF OURSELVES TOGETHER"
(Hebrews 10:25) shows God's desire for horizontal relationships.
Indeed, the early church "CONTINU[ED] DAILY WITH ONE ACCORD
IN THE TEMPLE, AND BREAKING BREAD FROM HOUSE TO HOUSE,

DID EAT THEIR MEAT WITH GLADNESS AND SINGLENESS OF HEART"
(Acts 2:46). The Epistles focus heavily on interpersonal relationships: husband-wife, child-parent, church leadership–parishioners,
neighbor-neighbor. To be sure, it admonishes separation from the
world, from unruly brethren, and from Satan's agenda.

But separation is the result of relational failure. God's desire is
"NOT WILLING THAT ANY SHOULD PERISH, BUT THAT ALL SHOULD
COME TO REPENTANCE" (2 Peter 3:9). His desire is to establish a
relationship with all of His creation. In that context, functional fellowship communities exhibit deep friendships, encouraging both
formal and informal get-togethers.

Now, while it's true we can be in love with our cars or a nice vacation package, God calls us to a higher love. He wants us to work
on relationships with people and with Him, more than relationships
with things: idols. The whole narrative of our relationship with God
carries the recurring problem of idols and misplaced allegiance.
God's desire is that we cultivate interpersonal relationships rather
than material ones. Servanthood is focused on the needs of others,
not the "LUST OF THE FLESH, AND THE LUST OF THE EYES, AND THE
PRIDE OF LIFE" (1 John 2:16).

Now let's shift gears to a farm. If we agree that God wants relationships, both vertically with Him and horizontally with others,
what does a farm that exhibits these goals look like? If you drive up
to the average industrial farm at one p.m., you'll be met with a No
Trespassing sign, perhaps a sign-in book, and certainly no people.
What you'll see are massive buildings with whirring fans and feed
augers emitting a nose-numbing stench.

You won't see a person. If you go to the average row crop farm,
again you'll be struck by the absence of people. Rows and rows
of corn or soybeans, sugar beets or wheat, extend as far as the eye
can see. If you go to the average medium-size farm, you won't see

anyone, either, because everyone is in town working at a job in order to get a paycheck to support their farm habit.

If you come to our farm at one p.m., you'll be struck by human activity. It's literally abuzz with people doing different projects and chores. They're laughing, sweating, lifting, pounding, toting, herding—a whole host of things that affirm the need for people. Our whole farm is set up to leverage people. One of the most common condemnations of our kind of farming leveled by the industrial agricultural community is that it requires more labor. That means more people.

The assumption is that people on the farm indicate civilizational backwardness. After all, sophisticated, technologically advanced cultures shouldn't have people getting blisters, encountering manure, or working in the soil. That's for brown people, dumb people, underachievers. Calloused hands simply indicate that you're too stupid to invent a robot.

But what does a personless farm illustrate to the visitor? It's not a place of laughter. It can't exhibit forgiveness or any of the other characteristics essential to creating successful relationships. It's sterile, bleak, and dead. I don't apologize a minute for having a labor-intensive farm—I applaud it! I would suggest that a people-centric farm is foundational to a relationship-expressive farm.

Essentially, our farm replaces pharmaceuticals and CAFOs with management. Because we're bubbling with people, we have a huge incentive to keep things beautiful and smelling nice. People don't like working in ugly, stinky surroundings. Visitors and customers are drawn not only to the physical environment but also constantly remark about how happy everyone is. A machine or building does not express happiness.

While I certainly know some farmers who would much rather hug their John Deere than a person, I'll take a warm body over a machine any day. I think such an attitude pleases God, who devotes His constant energy to cultivating a relationship with me. Farms brimming with people accentuate this divine desire.

So how do we cultivate farms brimming with people? First, the farmer needs a spirit toward community. The sad truth is that most farmers don't want anybody around. In fact, a lot of farmers really don't like people. That's why they're farmers. I call them hermit curmudgeons. Is this a Godly spirit? Does God want us harrumphing around scowling at visitors who invade our space? Or does He want a welcome committee attitude?

Struggling alone, this is why farmers have a higher suicide rate than any other occupation. Fiercely independent, farmers too often drive themselves and those closest to them to frustration and despair. Unable to cultivate healthy relationships, they face their trials alone. But this is how they feel they show their masculinity—this ability to face down weather, bureaucrats, markets, and machinery...and win. By themselves. Without help.

I have never been alone. I started as a child in the family. Then when Teresa and I married we lived on the farm. As our children were born, my parents were still on the farm. And today, we have four generations on the farm. I could not have done it myself. I have no desire to be self-made. Few things please me more than to affirm Teresa, my parents, our children, and now our staff and interns as critical to my success. I am completely and utterly dependent on all of them, and spend a lot of time praising, affirming, guiding, and inspiring this awesome group of people.

I can't imagine doing things alone. The greatest blessing of my life is growing old surrounded by what we call bright-eyed, bushy-tailed entrepreneurial self-starters. But I'm getting ahead of myself. The first point, then, is that farmers should have a multi-person, mutual-dependency spirit.

Second, farms must offer additional salaries. Unfortunately, most farms barely pay one wage, let alone two. How does an existing farm generate two incomes? In my book *Fields of Farmers* I go into this in much greater detail than I will here, but it hinges on multiple, complementary enterprises. Most farms are single-enterprise operations. They grow cattle or hay or fruit or vegetables. And their market is narrow: the processor, the grain elevator, the livestock auction.

The average farm is fairly one-dimensional. By definition, one-dimensional anything is not very relational. Yet if anything expresses relationships, it's nature. The complexity, synergy, and symbiosis captivate our attention for lifetimes. How can we ever discover all the relationships in the soil, let alone above the soil? As our understanding of the soil food web grows, we realize that a host of sharing, gathering, eating, and feeding goes on in the electron microscope realm.

Every handful of healthy soil contains more beings than there are people on the face of the earth. That's a pretty serious community. Now just imagine the anti-relational spirit exhibited by Justus von Liebig, the Austrian chemist who in 1837 captivated the world's attention with his discovery that all of life is just a rearrangement of nitrogen, potassium, and phosphorous. How do you think boron felt being left out of Liebig's discovery and world-changing announcement? How about iodine, molybdenum, and cobalt?

Goodness, these are just inanimate minerals he failed to recognize. How about bacteria, nematodes, mycelium, and hyphae? How about earthworms and the host of beings exchanging particles of carbohydrates and protein? He dismissed them out of hand, and spawned a mechanistic approach to life that the Western world largely continues to endorse. The entire synthetic, chemical approach to life that Liebig popularized ripped the entire relational aspect of life out of the human lexicon. Is it any wonder that evolution and abortion could be far behind?

The environmentalists rejected this mechanical notion long, long ago. Substituting compost for chemical fertilizer, the life-as-biology paradigm underscores every single gathering of the earth stewardship community. Trust me, far more relationships occur in a compost pile than in a bag of 10-10-10 chemical fertilizer. If life is foundationally about relationships, then we as Christians should be embracing a farm and food system that embraces a living relational paradigm.

Any study of nature reveals magnificent intricate relationships between plants and animals, bacteria and carbohydrates. We serve a God who not only conceived and created this relational complexity, but who also delights in our extending this pattern into our lives. And so a farm with multiple enterprises, a multi-income farm, and one that honors the soil community offers an object lesson of relational function.

The farm, then, that exemplifies relationships actually looks like a mosaic. On our farm, the chickens follow the cows. We use pigs to build compost. We have turkeys, chickens, and cows in the same field. Direct marketing to customers puts us in direct contact and relationship with the folks who eat the food we grow. We don't sever those contacts through a host of middlemen who make those who eat what we grow a nameless, faceless, faraway horde.

A people-centric, species-multiplying, multi-enterprise farm exhibits a highly complex relational structure. We respect and honor the relationships in the soil, feeding the soil only things that stimulate and augment those relationships. If we feed the soil things that destroy those relationships, we've reduced the number of relationships on the farm. If we grow only one thing, one way, with chemicals and machines rather than people, we also eliminate all those potential relationships.

I have a suggestion for the next church potluck. This comes straight from my participation in many local-food get-togethers where I do speaking engagements. To preserve the relationship from farm to fork, these folks usually label each dish with the name of the grower. If it's an heirloom tomato, often the identification card includes the name of the variety as well.

What a delight to go down a long table laden with personally prepared dishes and see each one identified as to preparer, origin, and type. Instantly it changes the meal from a nameless, faceless feeding

frenzy into a thoughtful, relational time of appreciation. Such identification encourages folks to give each other compliments. It facili-
tates conversations about growing or culinary techniques. Suddenly
breaking bread, if you will, exercises relationships rather than just
being a necessary pause in the hurried, harried, more important
busyness of life. Such tags, though simple, make the table live, rather
than the table being a reluctant pit stop on the way to life.

I'd challenge folks planning the next church potluck. How about
having food-acquaintance cards on each dish? Where did the potatoes come from? Who cooked them? What do you call this dish? Do
you know the farmer who grew the chicken? Introduce folks to him
via the card. Such attention and care indicates a relational appreciation of physical sustenance, which in turn drives the point home:
we're here to work on, cultivate, and grow interpersonal relationships
and a relationship with our Redeemer.

Now I want to drill down just a little deeper on this issue. Let's say
we have a noxious bramble like multiflora rose. This is an invasive,
non-native, highly obnoxious shrub that in the Mid-Atlantic region
has become one of the most hated plants on the landscape. Birds
spread their seeds in the fall. Opportunists, these plants sprout on
exposed soil and especially like edge areas along fence lines.

They gradually spread over the ground and can make large areas
virtually impenetrable and unusable. They love to trellis up trees
along the edge of a field, and can climb twenty feet high in a few
years. I view this plant as a scourge, part of the curse, and an embodi-
ment of the devil himself. Did I say I don't like this plant?

Most farmers in our area ride through their fields dutifully in late
summer spraying herbicide on multiflora roses to try to kill them.
Usually it doesn't kill them, but it sets them back for the season and
they sprout anew the following spring. From the seat of the tractor or
four-wheeler, the farmer hits the weed from a distance and does his
due diligence to rid his land of this pest. This is such standard operating procedure that our county, from time to time, offers cost-share
money to farmers who spray the plant.

In complete contradiction to this battle plan, all my life I've been hand-chopping them out. Several years ago I made a long-handled mattock so I could chop the base from farther away without getting my hands and arms full of stickers. These shrubs act like they're alive, extending octopus-like barbed tentacles quivering out from their base. They snag your ears, bloody your nose, and impale your skin everywhere with fishhook-like thorns. They're nasty.

To be sure, I usually wear gloves and a long shirt when battling multiflora rose. But no matter how well protected I am, I always return home bloodied and splintered. Why in the world would I do this when I could just spray it with herbicide?

First, manufacturing the herbicide is laden with danger. If you don't believe anyone has been harmed or any water has been polluted by herbicide manufacturers, we're not mentally on the same planet. The simple manufacture is a nasty, nasty process from an environmental and societal standpoint.

Second, I have to mix it at home. This is something I can't do with the children, the wife, or anybody else. This stuff is deadly and I wouldn't be exercising my responsibilities as a husband and father to expose my family to it. Does God smile on me while I'm mixing it up, getting poisoned myself, to keep my family from exposure? Can I protect and take care of my family if I poison myself?

Third, the stuff is toxic as crud out in the environment. When the industry says it breaks down, yes it breaks down, often into more deadly foundational chemicals. When the label says, "Don't enter a field where sprayed for three days," what does that mean? It means this is nasty material, deadly to plants, animals, insects, butterflies—whatever life happens to ingest or encounter it.

Fourth, it removes me from a visceral relational interaction with this demonic plant. And here is where I'd like to park for a minute. What was the result of Adam's sin? Thorns and brambles filled the earth. No longer did humankind tend a perfect utopian garden: no weeds, year-round production, perfect weather. I don't know what tending such a garden looks like. Apparently it didn't have any weeds or other noxious plants. It surely didn't have brambles and thorns. Nothing died because sin had not yet occurred. It didn't need fertilizer, irrigation, or planting. So I honestly don't know what tending that garden entailed.

But I do know that it was incredibly enjoyable and encouraged Adam to commune with God in long conversations. Wow, what an existence!

As I approach a multiflora rose, mattock in hand, it's a poignant reminder of sin. If my relationship with this physical manifestation of sin only requires me to get a few yards away and never actually physically tangle with it, I deny myself the breadth and depth of the object lesson.

The work of chopping, hacking, and sweating imprints me, indelibly and forcefully, with the results of sin. I don't curse the plant. I don't yell at it. I go at it systematically and aggressively. I look for its weaknesses. Where is the main root? Does it come out of the base to the left or right? In front or behind? Using all my collective wit and wisdom, I attack the plant with a careful game plan. I may swing the mattock high to whack over some of those pesky tendrils. Then I advance, steadily, knowing that I'm going to win.

This plant that epitomizes sin is going to be vanquished. It may be easy; it may be hard. But I'm going to calculate, analyze, ponder, then attack. The attack will be carefully controlled. With the skill that comes only after years of practice, I bring the mattock down on the base of the plant. It shudders. I smell retreat. It leans over a little, giving me better access to its vulnerable base. Now I see the main root, off to the right. I switch positions and chop as if I'm going for a home run in baseball. The root cracks but doesn't sever.

I bring the mattock back for a second swing. Hitting the damaged root, the blade severs it and the plant rolls to the side. Several smaller roots, like tendrils, hang on to the soil, but it is mortally wounded. I reposition myself and take another whack. The whole base of the plant skids away from where it grew. The entire bush lies helplessly on its side and I grin in triumph. Success! Believe it or not, I actually carry on a conversation like this when I'm doing battle with multi-flora roses.

It's a narrative of righteousness against evil. It's a running dialogue examining my own hatred of sin and dedication to holiness. How am I doing with the brambles in my life? My temper? My prejudice? My busyness? Hmmmm? I'm not saying by any means that this spiritual conversation requires dueling with multiflora roses. But I contend that the difference in bramble relationship between the herbicide and the mattock is poignant.

Dear folks, we must work at sin. We don't just prance around it with human cleverness of dubious consequences. We must know sin. We must understand it in order to attack it. We must plan, seek strength, become skillful in dealing with sin. In this extremely simple way, perhaps the most mundane task of all mundane tasks, I contend that relationship requires effort. It makes a difference in how we view life and view spiritual warfare.

Okay, you youth pastors. I have a great idea for your next youth gathering. How about getting all the young people to bring old clothes, shovels, and mattocks to a farm and do a "Bramble Extermination Day"? The farmer doesn't have to use toxic herbicides, and the young people receive a memorable, visceral object lesson about sin. They get some exercise and meaningful productivity to boot.

Compare this with going to Six Flags or participating in the Pregnancy Help Center walkathon. I never did understand walkathons. If you want to do something, how about doing something productive? How about getting sponsors who will give you a dollar for every multiflora rose you kill? How about collecting money for solarium installation on the south side of a house? Digging fence postholes? Building compost piles? Planting gardens in the yards of elderly folks?

Because we have a prejudice against visceral creation healing and we aren't connected with life foundations, these kinds of activities never cross the spiritual-exercise radar. I'd say that such neglect cheapens our spiritual understanding, denies us the kinds of relationships God covets for us to develop, and keeps us living in a shallow, egocentric mentality.

I walk a lot. When I see the variety of nature while I'm walking through the field rather than riding, it's sensual. It invades my eyes, ears, nose, skin, and consciousness. In a well-managed pasture, a cornucopia of forage species—grasses, legumes, herbs, forbs—grow in beautiful synergy. Butterflies, spiders, grasshoppers, rabbits, snakes—goodness, you can't imagine all the life there.

Contrast that with walking through a chemicalized mono-crop. Plenty of scientists have documented the relative collapse of whole species in these conditions. A farmscape exhibiting more species, more varied life, will inherently demonstrate a relational theme. A system that reduces life variety and all these intricate synergies denies creation its vibrant relational message. In such a system we're all losers.

So, dear heart, why isn't it appropriate to ask, in the next fellowship meeting, what a farming and food system that encourages relationships looks like? Does it look like McDonald's? Does it look like Dow Chemical? Or does it look like vibrancy, diversity, life? I think you know the answer.

Empowering vs. Disempowering

But as many as received him, to them gave he power to
become the sons of God.

John 1:12

"I CAN DO ALL THINGS THROUGH CHRIST WHICH STRENGTHENS ME"
(Philippians 4:13 AKJV) is a truth that propels believers through adversity. This oft-quoted verse offers solace to the depressed and energy to
the weak.

Indeed, God enjoys empowering us: "BUT AS MANY AS RECEIVED
HIM, TO THEM GAVE HE POWER TO BECOME THE SONS OF GOD, EVEN TO
THEM THAT BELIEVE ON HIS NAME" (John 1:12). This is not just power,
but sonship. Paul takes this even further in the epistle to the Galatians:
"THEREFORE YOU ARE NO MORE A SLAVE BUT A SON, AND IF A SON, THEN
AN HEIR OF GOD THROUGH CHRIST" (Galatians 4:7 NKJV). Heirship, of
course, is a theme throughout the epistles to the early churches.

That God trusts us to represent Him, to speak for Him, to steward for Him speaks volumes about our standing with Him. Because
of this, we come "BOLDLY UNTO THE THRONE OF GRACE" (Hebrews
4:16) and enjoy personal appointments as a "ROYAL PRIESTHOOD"
(1 Peter 2:9). This is pretty heady talk, wouldn't you agree?

Can you imagine a corporate president using this kind of language to his staff? Talking about adopting them as sons and daughters, making them heirs, giving them unimpeded access to his office, deputizing them with the keys to the business. Wow. That's real trust. A business that exhibited such trust would be an exhilarating place to work, don't you think? It would be a place with little red tape. A place that embraced innovation and individual talents.

That's exactly what the church is supposed to look like. It's a hierarchy where the leaders are the chief servants. The leaders don't lord their authority over others, but rather encourage all the different gifts and talents to be exercised to their fullest. It's not a stoic, dead, dry bureaucracy of rigid formality, but a place of discovery, affirmation, enthusiasm, and excitement. When David danced before the Lord wearing common garments, he exemplified the kind of excitement we should exhibit in corporate worship—at least sometimes.

How many of us would be embarrassed at David's spontaneous expression? By the same token, those of us from a more charismatic background must appreciate the quiet, meditative, contemplative worship style of liturgical groups. When you look around at how differently God's people operate, you might say: "Well, clearly these Christians don't have a clue. How can the Anglicans and the Amish be right? This is madness. If God can't maintain more homogeneity among His followers, He must be either weak or, or, or—enjoy empowered self-expression?"

Ah, there's the rub. Is it possible that God, rather than wringing His hands about the different takes on perfect obedience to His demands, instead relishes and exults in His people's liberty to seek, to create, to find their own fit? To be sure, God's protocol for attaining salvation is clear, as are the fruits He's looking for: "BUT THE FRUIT OF THE SPIRIT IS LOVE, JOY, PEACE, LONGSUFFERING, GENTLENESS, GOODNESS, FAITH, MEEKNESS, TEMPERANCE: AGAINST SUCH THERE IS NO LAW" (Galatians 5:22–23).

What I'm getting at is that God empowers us in a way that encourages innovation and personal affirmation. Even under the Mosaic law, with all the social, religious, and dietary regulations, He left a lot up to the individual. In both dispensations, law and grace, God empowered His people. He did not disempower them by protocols that left them unable to express their gifts and talents.

If God micromanaged our affairs—what we would wear, how we'd cut our hair, choir robe style, or whatever, we would not be empowered; we would be disempowered. We wouldn't think on our own; we'd simply be robots marching like storm troopers to instructions whispered through earbuds. If God wanted that, He would not have given us any freedom.

I heard an attorney recently make the point that even after Adam ate the forbidden fruit in the garden, God let him defend himself. "WHERE ARE YOU?" (Genesis 3:9 NIV) was God's first question. Did God know where Adam was? Of course. But He was deferring to Adam, showing respect, and honoring him. How precious.

Second question: "WHO TOLD YOU THAT YOU WERE NAKED?" (Genesis 3:11 NIV). Third question: "HAVE YOU EATEN OF THE TREE, WHEREOF I COMMANDED YOU THAT YOU SHOULD NOT EAT?" (Genesis 3:11 AKJV). Of course, Adam tried to blame Eve, but even in turning to her, God dignified her with a question: "WHAT IS THIS THAT YOU HAVE DONE?" (Genesis 3:13 AKJV). How deferential.

Of course, Eve passed it off to the serpent. Notice that God does not ask the serpent a question. He addresses the serpent directly, immediately: "BECAUSE YOU HAVE DONE THIS, YOU ARE CURSED ABOVE ALL CATTLE, AND ABOVE EVERY BEAST OF THE FIELD; ON YOUR BELLY SHALL YOU GO, AND DUST SHALL YOU EAT ALL THE DAYS OF YOUR LIFE" (Genesis 3:14 AKJV).

Dealing with Adam and Eve, God established an "innocent until proven guilty" foundation, even though His sovereignty enabled Him to know everything without witnesses, juries, or judges. What I'm getting at here is that God wants us to express our thoughts, to be creative. He doesn't suffocate us with accusations and regulations. He loves when we fully leverage our gifts and talents.

So, what does a food and farming system that illustrates empowerment vs. disempowerment look like? I'd say it would look like the church. Lots of independent groups doing lots of different things. Individual practitioners would have a lot of latitude.

Is that what America's food system looks like? I wrote a book several years ago titled *Everything I Want to Do Is Illegal* to help people understand our farm's battles with the food and farm police. I'll just hit a few highlights here to give you the flavor.

Federal and state food inspectors showed up on our farm one day and told us we could not legally sell our chickens if we processed them in an open shed. They said the air was inherently pathogenic. They wanted bathrooms, impermeable walls, and artificial light.

Interestingly, we had just participated in a laboratory test comparing bacterial colonies on our chickens to those on the federal-inspected birds in the supermarket. Several samples of each were taken and cultured. The chlorinated federally sanctioned birds averaged 3,600 and ours averaged 133. In case you're struggling with the math, that's 2,500 percent cleaner, or 25 times in case percentages are too complicated to understand.

Now, folks, wouldn't you think that these government agents, supposedly charged with food safety, would be excited about something that much cleaner than their stuff? Not only were they not excited, they blew it off. They wanted walls. They wanted better lights. The sun wasn't good enough. They wanted bathrooms, even though my mother's house was fifty feet away and my house was fifty feet away, both of which had two bathrooms.

The suffocating rules and regulations from America's food police disempower farmers from accessing the market with better food, with cleaner food, with safer food. That is the truth. When paranoid people, ignorant about food, ask for "more government oversight" to protect them, this is the kind of insanity it encourages.

We now have a food system in which it's perfectly safe to feed your kids Twinkies, Cocoa Puffs, and Coca-Cola, but not raw milk and fresh-squeezed apple cider. It's perfectly safe to eat sterile microwavable packages of unpronounceable ingredients, but homemade food is unsafe. Velveeta that doesn't mold, rot, or desiccate is safe, while farmstead cheese that's alive enough to grow mold is unsafe.

One of the best things a farmer can do is build a pond in a wetland. That's a great permaculture concept and an extremely environmental thing to do because it creates many additional habitats rather than just one. But government agents will put you in jail if you mess with a wetland.

The plethora of regulations tyrannizing farmers and food opportunities are too numerous to imagine. Bureaucracy does not bend well to round pegs in square holes. Building inspections that outlaw greywater systems or alternative building materials make it difficult to build an environmentally friendly house. Try installing an innovative composting toilet and see how friendly the inspectors are. Workers' compensation is extremely rigid and does not recognize that a farm like ours has people doing lots of different things. It's designed for factory farms and specialized jobs. Anyone who has tried to start a bologna business in their home can attest to regulatory atrocities. If you think I'm being overly judgmental, just go ahead and try it.

I routinely receive letters from folks desperate to launch an innovative food alternative in their community only to have their dreams dashed by bureaucrats. The regulations have nothing to do with safety; they have everything to do with rigidity, orthodoxy, and market access.

What if your fellowship group could not meet in a home, but had to meet in a licensed building? I can already hear someone responding: "Surely you aren't advocating having a one-thousand-seat auditorium with no building inspection!" No, I'm not advocating that, but what if you only have twenty people? Do you need lighted Exit signs and breakaway doors?

You see, Jesus told His disciples: "FOR WHERE TWO OR THREE ARE GATHERED TOGETHER IN MY NAME, THERE AM I IN THE MIDST OF THEM" (Matthew 18:20). Do you know how empowering that is? We don't have to get ten or twelve or fifty or one thousand. God is not limited by many or few, which is the point He made to Gideon. But America's food system honors the big players and despises the little players. If you don't believe that, just try to make some quiche in your kitchen and sell it to your townhouse neighbor.

The answers to our food issues, from volume to quality, are fairly easy. But these answers for the most part can't see the light of day due to the disempowerment of the current system. That is why in my view we must go outside the system: "LET US GO FORTH THERE-FORE UNTO HIM WITHOUT THE CAMP, BEARING HIS REPROACH. FOR HERE WE HAVE NO CONTINUING CITY, BUT WE SEEK ONE TO COME" (Hebrews 13:13–14).

From raw milk to backyard-processed chickens to homemade quiche, the system's orthodoxy denies access to these heretical items. Just like the Israelites created an alternative civilization and the church is not of this world, I believe the integrity food and farm-ing system cannot be found in the current mainstream models. It's found at farmers' markets, community supported agriculture sys-tems, on-farm markets, Internet shopping carts—anything except the big supermarket players.

We had a large buyer wanting sausage, but delivered on a Sysco truck. I asked Sysco what was required and they sent me seventeen pages (fax, so I had an accurate count) of requirements. The first one was a magnet big enough to pull metal shards through twelve inches of meat on a conveyor belt. Dear folks, at our small local federal-inspected abattoir, not only do we not have a conveyor belt, but if we did indeed have a magnet like that, all the workers' belt buckles would be stuck to it because they couldn't get far enough away.

Our little processing plant doesn't have a room big enough to install such a magnet. That was just the first of seventeen pages. I called Sysco back and lamented that it would take even an industrial business a year to comply with all this, to which the lady on the phone responded: "Yes, that's the frustration of my job. Every day I get calls from customers wanting local product and I can't get it to them."

Did someone say something about disempowering? More and more, insurance is becoming the big bully in the integrity food business. Due to our litigious culture, businesses don't want to buy from a vendor unless the vendor has a large product liability policy. In order to get the policy, the food vendor (which could also be a farmer, in our case) must pass the exposure (risk) test. Guess who determines risky food? Industrial agriculturalists at our land-grant universities.

Here's how the circle goes: I have a customer who wants sausage. He wants it on a mainline distribution truck. I call the trucking company. They say I need $3 million of product liability insurance. I call my insurance company. They send out an agent who starts asking questions:

1. What is your vaccination program?
2. What is your animal health pharmaceutical protocol?
3. Does your pesticide room have a lock?
4. Who has access to that lock?
5. Where is your tractor service record?
6. Who certifies that your tractor doesn't drip any hydraulic fluid or oil?
7. If it drips, what is your hazardous substance plan?
8. Where is your written evacuation plan in case of an oil drip?
9. Where is it posted?
10. Are you a libertarian?
11. Do you believe in creation?
12. What's wrong with you?

Okay, so I took some poetic license, but you get the drift. If we don't do any of this stuff like vaccinating or pesticides, we get thrown out as a high risk. They don't have round holes for our square peg. The result is that very few clients can get served with higher-quality innovative soil-building creation stewardship food because the industrial system throws up too many roadblocks to access.

If we ran our churches this way, we couldn't meet for a service without accredited insurance, a license, a permitted building, and a certified evacuation plan. Why would such a system be repugnant to us? Because we want no impediments to fellowship and building relationships. We would say a system that binds us to cultural, governmental, and industrial protocols disempowers believers and local church autonomy. If we wanted to get constitutional about it, we could even say it disrupts the "free exercise of religion."

We want unfettered personal and corporate empowerment for our spiritual development. And when we feel society infringing on our churches, we cry foul, march in the streets, sign petitions, and demand legislative change. We consider denying full access to spiritual food tantamount to an attack on God.

Don't you see, dear heart, that a similar access denial, or severe impediments, to your choices of food is equally insulting to God? The typology of physical food to spiritual food throughout Scripture shows a close link in God's mind. From the sacraments to feeding the hungry, God uses physical food to draw parallels to spiritual truth.

Isn't it intellectually and theologically schizophrenic to militantly defend a freedom-oriented, personal-empowerment church system and then patronize a food system that is diametrically opposed to these principles? So where are you going to shop for the next church potluck? When you have the next youth group bash, where is the pizza coming from? Instead of serving industrial soft drinks, how about making your own carbonated beverages out of juice and carbonation? It's to die for—and ultimately the kind that won't kill you.

So far in this chapter, I've focused primarily on the human level. But what about animals? Does it empower pigs when they're confined in massive buildings on slatted floors in tiny pens without enough room to turn around, ever? Does it empower a chicken to be housed for a lifetime in a cage that allows less room than a sheet of notebook paper? Does it empower corn to have its DNA blasted with a cannon and foreign genetic material inserted in the helix?

The most empowering food thing we can do is to let people grow it anywhere (yes, in-house chickens and backyard gardens and bees), and let them sell it to whomever they want, and let people buy it from whomever they want without insurance companies, food police, zoning inspectors, building inspectors, or anyone else denying access.

Because it's so close to my heart, before I finish this chapter I must address empowerment of beginning farmers. Rather than get bogged down in a discussion of land prices relative to production capacity, let's just agree that the easier it is for young people to begin farming, the more empowering the system. If it's hard for people to attend our fellowship, that's not a good thing. We should make it easy, desirable, appealing for newbies to attend our fellowship, right?

Our churches are full of landowners. What's being done with your land? Do you consider it something for you to enjoy by yourself, or do you see yourself as a steward of a niche of God's creation that should be maximized in solar and resource return on God's investment? If so, how about encouraging an aspiring young person to start a farming operation on your land?

My book *Fields of Farmers* goes into great detail on how collaborative agricultural arrangements can work. Germinating good land stewards seems like as good a ministry as germinating new churches. We talk about planting churches; when are we going to talk about planting plants? The truth is that deacons, elders, and the rest own millions of underutilized acres. Meanwhile, we have thousands of frustrated young people trying to get a foothold.

Sometimes we miss the most obvious truths. Here's one: young people empower older people and older people empower young people. What is the average age of the farmers in your church group? The national average is about sixty, which is roughly twenty-five years beyond vibrant businesses. Multi-generational partnerships work in families, in churches, and in farming. A one-dimensional age creates problems, whether it's a kindergarten class or a nursing home.

The family as building block of civilization is inherently multi-age. To be stewarded best, our land needs multi-age stewards. Would it be too far out to suggest that along with the missions budget and building fund we should have a beginning farmer fund? These farmers could grow the food for the families who attend the fellowship. The youth group can go help weed the green beans or butcher chickens. Older folks in the group can use the church kitchen to teach culinary skills such as canning and fermentation.

This allows the whole group to unplug from the disempowering industrial food system, and the exclusivity of the supermarket, and the disrespect toward the animals and plants that wind up there. It would create a fellowship culture of empowerment toward the land, toward the people, and toward creation's biology.

I believe this visceral empowerment would help everyone appreciate Christ's indwelling empowerment to us. And as the food and farming relationships spawned intimate friendships, these in turn would facilitate a new spiritual empowerment in the group. Rather than sitting around treating spiritual empowerment as only a theological and academic issue, we'd achieve spiritual success by viscerally creating a food-empowerment object lesson. That's exciting.

Sun Driven vs. Earth Driven

And he is before all things, and by him all things consist.
Colossians 1:17

Would you agree that regenerative living requires that we somehow figure out how to live on real-time energy? Some might argue that it includes all resources, but let's stick with energy for now. I'm not ready to tackle whether it's wrong to mine for aluminum or copper.

I know one of the arguments against using solar panels is their heavy mineral content. The naysayers liken it to trading the devil for the witch, trading petroleum depletion for mineral depletion—what's the difference? For the record, I don't believe mining things is inherently wrong. God placed deposits around the earth for us to use. I don't know how long some of these deposits will last, but I do believe we should see how little of them we can use and not how much.

My focus here is on the principle of real time. Our walk with Christ has both a historical and a real-time component. We see this in Hebrews: "FOR WE ARE MADE PARTAKERS OF CHRIST, IF WE HOLD THE BEGINNING OF OUR CONFIDENCE STEADFAST TO THE END;

WHILE IT IS SAID, TO DAY IF YOU WILL HEAR HIS VOICE, HARDEN NOT YOUR HEARTS, AS IN THE PROVOCATION [OF THE ISRAELITE WILDER-NESS WANDERINGS]" (Hebrews 3:14–15 AKJV).

The Christian life, although founded in the finished work of the Messiah's death, burial, and resurrection, also contains an immediacy theme. From Jesus' prayer for "daily bread" to Paul's "I DIE DAILY" (1 Corinthians 15:31), our spiritual condition requires present-tense feeding and upgrading. We can't flourish forever on yesterday's Thanksgiving dinner. It might be enough to carry us for a couple of days, to be sure—and maybe it didn't make us flourish—but sooner or later our bodies need replenishment. Even a snake needs nourishment several times a year.

We can't live a spiritually vibrant life from a onetime mountaintop experience. I don't care how wonderfully touched and moved by the Spirit I may have been at a certain service or in a certain place. It won't sustain me over the long haul. I'm going to need renewal. That means daily spiritual food through meditation, prayer, feeding on the Scripture. Otherwise, I'll become spiritually depleted, mined out, if you will. You could say I need daily Son power.

I think one of the most perfect parallels between the spiritual and the physical is the closeness between Son power and sun power. I've gone into great detail already describing the beauty and intricacy of how the earth runs on solar energy.

I want to move on in this discussion, however, to contrast old, stored energy with real-time energy. Let's start by looking at fertility. Sir Albert Howard, writing in *An Agricultural Testament*, pointed out that the temptation of every civilization has been to turn nature's fertility into cash.

God gave Adam and Eve a rich, abundant garden. God gave humans an earth in which, even in a fallen state, people lived for hundreds of years. Think about the fertility required to uphold ancient civilizations: Egypt, India, Mexico, Peru. God gave the Israelites a fertile place:

THE LORD YOUR GOD BRINGS YOU INTO A GOOD LAND, A LAND OF
BROOKS OF WATER, OF FOUNTAINS AND DEPTHS THAT SPRING OUT OF
VALLEYS AND HILLS; A LAND OF WHEAT, AND BARLEY, AND VINES, AND
FIG TREES, AND POMEGRANATES; A LAND OF OIL OLIVE AND HONEY;
A LAND WHEREIN YOU SHALL EAT BREAD WITHOUT SCARCENESS, YOU
SHALL NOT LACK ANY THING IN IT; A LAND WHOSE STONES ARE IRON,
AND OUT OF WHOSE HILLS YOU MAY DIG BRASS. WHEN YOU HAVE EATEN
AND ARE FULL, THEN YOU SHALL BLESS THE LORD YOUR GOD FOR THE
GOOD LAND WHICH HE HAS GIVEN YOU. (Deuteronomy 8:7–10 AKJV)

Of course, we know what happened: fertility depletion, erosion,
famine, and drought.

I don't know that Sir Albert Howard was a religious man, but listen to his words penned in 1943:

Mother earth never attempts to farm without live stock; she always
raises mixed crops; great pains are taken to preserve the soil and to
prevent erosion; the mixed vegetable and animal wastes are converted into humus; there is no waste; the processes of growth and the
processes of decay balance one another; ample provision is made to
maintain large reserves of fertility; the greatest care is taken to store
the rainfall; both plants and animals are left to protect themselves
against disease. (*An Agricultural Testament*)

For the most part, the story of civilization is the story of resource
depletion, primarily soil and vegetation. But as I read the promises
of God to the Israelites as they enter the land of Canaan, I see a plan
for replenishment. They were to occupy, multiply, and develop, but
the source base simply expanded with them. They were to do this
on a clearly defined land area. In other words, God did not promise them more land. Obviously, if you're going to have a long-term,
thriving culture, you have to maintain a long-term, fertile ecology.
But that is not what happened.

Notice again Howard's commentary: "Agricultural research has been misused to make the farmer, not a better producer of food, but a more expert bandit. He has been taught how to profiteer at the expense of posterity—to transfer capital in the shape of soil fertility and the reserves of his livestock to his profit and loss account."

In America's history, a plea for real-time sustainability permeates all the colonial writers. Consider this from John Taylor's *Arator* written in 1818:

> Let us boldly face the fact. Our country is nearly ruined. We have certainly drawn out of the earth three fourths of the vegetable matter it contained, within reach of the plough. Vegetable matter is its only vehicle for conveying food to us. If we suck our mother to death we must die ourselves. Though she is reduced to a skeleton, let us not despair. She is indulgent, and if we return to the duties revealed by the consequences of their infraction, to be prescribed by God, and demonstrated by the same consequences to comport with our interest, she will yet yield us milk.

Moving closer to modern times, in his iconic 1943 bestseller *Plowman's Folly*, retired agricultural extension agent Ed Faulkner offered this principle: "We may be sure that unless soil really is self-sufficient, its future complete exhaustion is predictable, regardless of future farm practice in the use of fertilizers." Self-sufficient soil? Really? Today's industrial farming and food system can't imagine such a thing. The whole system depends on inputs from far-flung places and energy-intensive processing to supply soil nutrients.

The whole modern system depends on never-ending deposits of petroleum and minerals in order to survive. I don't know about you, but I'm not ready to assume that all of these nonrenewables will still be here for my grandchildren. Just like spiritually we cannot build long-term health on yesterday's deposits, we cannot build long-term physical health based on ancient deposits. We can't even build long-term muscular function on yesterday's exercise.

*   *   *

Several generations of good Lutherans and Presbyterians mined our own farm to its bones of rocks and gullies. Who cried about this? Who prayed about this? It was ongoing for generation after generation. Good church people, sitting in their pews, put money that was derived from raping their own property in the offering plate for foreign missions. Surely Howard was spot-on to call these people bandits. And yet because it happened slowly, it had no sense of urgency. It had no immediacy.

How would you like it if you spent a lifetime (you could do it in six days if you were God, but that's another issue) carving a beautiful statue only to have some rogue come along—a Bible-preaching rogue, I might add—and hammer off one side of it? Pure desecration. You'd be justifiably righteously indignant, yes you would. How do you think God feels when His sculpture, the epitome of His creative genius, is summarily hacked away, plundered, and desecrated?

Do you know what I dream about? I dream about how our farm can capture more sun. How can we convert more sun energy into biomass for energy, for feeding the soil, for the ultimate ecological cycle? Today. Right now. Our farm can't live on old deposits; it has to create new deposits. It has to create new soil, new fertility, new energy. And the only source of that is the sun. It always has been and always will be.

Fortunately, we don't have to depend on ancient deposit depletion. We can operate on a real-time sun-driven system. We've already explored in depth how biomass, decomposition, and fertility work, so I won't belabor it again here. The main nuance I want us to understand from this discussion is the relevance of sun-driven, real-time sustenance as an object lesson of daily spiritual nourishment.

I would suggest that when we eat food that comes from a production model that builds soil and runs on real-time energy, it cultivates in us a sense of daily urgency about our spiritual sustenance. Is our spiritual tank being filled today? If not, why not? If not now, when?

You see, the kick the can down the road, fix it tomorrow mentality that we see evidenced in our farm and food system is the same thing we see in our lethargic, lackadaisical view toward solving our spiritual needs. May I humbly suggest that if we put attention on a God-honoring food and farming system, it would engender a renewed sense of excitement toward spiritual renewal? Lest anyone think I'm advocating earth worship in order to facilitate God worship, I'm not.

But I'm close to that. Perhaps earth stewardship as an object lesson of our spiritual stewardship would be a less edgy way to portray the idea. What if when you sat down to a meal with your kiddos, you said something like this:

> Susie, we're eating grass-finished beef this evening because grain-finished, feedlot beef requires huge amounts of old energy that we're using up far faster than it can be replenished. The grass-finished beef came to our plate by eating today's sunlight converted to grass— today. Not a decade ago, today. It built soil and replenished all the energy it required to grow.
>
> That's how our spiritual lives must be. We can't depend on last Sunday's sermon to keep us alive, or last century's saints. Those are all great deposits, but we need to be making our own deposits. Eating this grass-finished beef is an object lesson of this great truth, that today, today, today, we build our relationship with God.

How about tomatoes? What's the permutation for them? Okay, let's try this:

> Susie, we're eating these compost-grown tomatoes this evening because the ones that grow in chemical fertilizers require huge amounts of old petroleum energy. The farmer who grew these tomatoes makes compost from plants grown with today's sun. Not sun from back centuries ago or even before Noah's flood, but current, real-time sunlight converted into plants now. This means that nature is balancing itself as we eat, and our farmer who grew these is

taking care of today's sun's energy, through plant material, to build more fertile soil.

Just like that, God wants us to build our lives on real-time Son energy—from His Son, Jesus. Not last week's sermon. Not Grandma's testimony. But today, today He wants our attention. He wants us looking Son-ward right now, not depleting old deposits of spirituality or depending on ancient revivals. Isn't it wonderful that we can interact with Him right now, today, and build spiritual understanding like these tomatoes will build bones and muscles? Cool, huh?

Why can't we talk like that in our families? Why can't we talk like that in our Sunday schools? Because talk like that sounds like a bunch of environmental whacko mumbo-jumbo commie pinko tree-hugger drivel, that's why. But wouldn't building a deep understanding of ecology's economy in real-time sun-dependency produce a sense of urgency around Son-dependency? Why must the two be a source of friction rather than synergy?

I would go one step further even to suggest that a farm and food system predicated on capturing more sun energy rather than stored earth deposits is like reaching out for more grace. I see the sun every day as an amazing gift of new wealth. I don't deserve new wealth. But God placed this sun up in the heavens to literally beam down energy. Every day, on every piece of our farm, we're showered with energy. Every time I see a sunbeam converted into vegetation, I see new wealth.

How did I come to deserve all this free energy? All this free wealth? A loving heavenly Father gave it to me, just like grace. I didn't put the sun in space. I didn't make the plants. I didn't make the seeds or the trees, or the birds or wind that carry the seeds from place to place to make sure that the earth sprouts vegetation abundantly. I didn't do any of that. I just walk out in the morning and there's that huge ball of fire in the sky, shining down buckets of energy. I don't have to gamble for this new wealth. I don't have to borrow money for it, fill out a loan application, or do anything. It's just there, showering down.

I want it used. I want it converted into biomass. Just like grace. God's grace is abundant. I don't deserve it. I don't have to work for it. It's here, every morning, every moment, to be received and leveraged into how I interact with other people, how I see the world, how I worship God. The more I can drive my farm on the sun and on real-time immediate energy, the more it manifests what a life running on real-time Son energy looks like.

My dad used to pray: "Thank You for Your grace that is ever-new." I love that phrase because it speaks to vibrancy rather than staleness. And that brings up yet another nuance of this immediacy idea: fresh food rather than old food.

Today's industrial food system loves oldness. Look at the shelf life of the average food item in the supermarket. Much of today's food research is about how to extend shelf life. Even something as fragile as milk can now last months without refrigeration through the miracle of ultra-pasteurization. That even organic brands succumb to such adulteration shows the depth of our food depravity.

Folks, if it won't rot, it won't digest. We've added stabilizers, emulsifiers, artificial flavorings, colorings, and a host of unmentionables all in the name of extending shelf life. Tomato research does not center on nutritional content. It centers on transport viability. Can the tomato withstand fifteen hundred miles rattling around in a tractor-trailer? That's the primary concern. A tomato that can withstand that must be half cardboard, and it tastes like cardboard. Ever wonder why your kids don't like vegetables?

If we fed our kids spiritual food like we feed them physical food, they'd say "Yuck" and leave our churches. Oh, maybe our spiritual food is like our physical food. Did anybody say something about losing our Christian youth? Hmmmm.

You don't want old food. How long will Cheerios last, sitting there on the supermarket aisle in that box? Squeeze Velveeta on a plate and walk away for a month. It doesn't mold, doesn't desiccate, doesn't do anything. It just sits. Question: How fast will your spiritual condition deteriorate if left by itself?

If you stopped reading your Bible every day, stopped praying every day, stopped attending fellowship opportunities regularly with others—frankly, if God got taken away from you—would it dramatically alter your life? You see, part of the long-term stability of food comes from sterility. If it's sterile, nonliving, dead, it can last a long time.

Fresh food, living food, has an immediacy about it. If you don't eat it, it goes bad and you have to throw it away. Remember, God is the one knocking on our door: "BEHOLD, I STAND AT THE DOOR, AND KNOCK: IF ANY MAN HEAR MY VOICE, AND OPEN THE DOOR, I WILL COME IN TO HIM, AND WILL SUP WITH HIM, AND HE WITH ME" (Revelation 3:20). He's wanting to eat with us, now.

Certainly I'm a big believer in storing food. Dehydration, fermenting, and canning have all been practiced for a long time. Canning is relatively modern, and some would argue has no place in integrity food culture. Freezing is modern but preserves the goodies. Look at what David's friends brought him when Absalom tried to take over the kingdom: "[THEY] BROUGHT BEDS, AND BASONS, AND EARTHEN VESSELS, AND WHEAT, AND BARLEY, AND FLOUR, AND PARCHED CORN, AND BEANS, AND LENTILES, AND PARCHED PULSE [PEAS,] AND HONEY, AND BUTTER, AND SHEEP, AND CHEESE OF KINE [COWS]" (2 Samuel 17:28–29).

What a larder! Some things like dried beans, wine, and nuts, can keep a long time. Other things are not conducive to keeping a long time. In modern days, we've taken things already cooked, meant to be eaten immediately, and formulated them with processing and packaging so they don't have to be eaten soon. When does food cease to be food?

When does going to church cease to feed? When does spiritual literature become a liability and not an asset? "BELOVED, BELIEVE NOT EVERY SPIRIT, BUT TRY THE SPIRITS WHETHER THEY ARE OF GOD: BECAUSE MANY FALSE PROPHETS ARE GONE OUT INTO THE WORLD"

(1 John 4:1). If we wanted to modernize this, we could say, "Try the TV preachers," or "Try the theologians." Why is it not acceptable to try our physical food, to see whether it is healthy for us or not?

Can you imagine an announcement at the next church potluck: "Let's try to bring food that grew in soil fertilized with compost and that has a short shelf life." Why, goodness, the garden club ladies would be in a dither over such a thing. First, most wouldn't have a clue about what the announcement meant. Second, half their pantries wouldn't qualify. Food discernment hardly exists.

How can our church people develop spiritual discernment?

By reading Scripture texts while munching on Domino's pizza? You see the disconnect? How about we source the pizza from real food in the area, then use the church kitchen (or the masonry wood-fired pizza oven that the church members built) to cook the pizza, all the while emphasizing the need to discern sourcing and cooking techniques so that they are real-time sun-driven? Then when we sit down with our text about spiritual discernment, we're sitting there munching on the visceral object lesson of the spiritual truth.

That's the way we inculcate in our spiritual lives an immediacy to our Son-driven daily walk. As we do that, we begin depositing a spiritual legacy for future generations. They won't live on it, either, but it'll sure provide spiritual equity to help them in their journey, just like fertile soil built on a sun-driven farm provides opportunity for the next-generation farmer.

Narrow Way vs. Broad Way

I am the way, the truth, and the life: no man cometh unto the father, but by me.

John 14:6

Perhaps the most familiar biblical passage, except for the Ten Commandments and the Twenty-third Psalm, is the Sermon on the Mount. Occupying three whole chapters in the Gospel according to Matthew, this synopsis of Jesus' direct words carries numerous profound truths. One of them is this: "ENTER YOU IN AT THE STRAIT [CONSTRICTED] GATE: FOR WIDE IS THE GATE, AND BROAD IS THE WAY, THAT LEADS TO DESTRUCTION, AND MANY THERE BE WHICH GO IN THEREAT: BECAUSE STRAIT [CONSTRICTED] IS THE GATE, AND NARROW IS THE WAY, WHICH LEADS TO LIFE, AND FEW THERE BE THAT FIND IT" (Matthew 7:13–14 AKJV).

While God's arms open wide for anyone to come to Him, His embrace is reserved for those who come His way. We can't purchase or work our way into God's kingdom.

A relationship with God exists through and only through the finished work of His Son, Jesus Christ. While some things are not clear in the biblical record, other things are, and this is one of them. The apostle Paul gives as succinct a definition of the gospel (good news) as is found anywhere: "FOR I DELIVERED UNTO YOU FIRST OF ALL THAT WHICH I ALSO RECEIVED, HOW THAT CHRIST DIED FOR OUR SINS ACCORDING TO THE SCRIPTURES; AND THAT HE WAS BURIED, AND THAT HE ROSE AGAIN THE THIRD DAY ACCORDING TO THE SCRIPTURES" (1 Corinthians 15:3–4).

Peter, standing before the Jewish rulers who demanded by what power he performed miracles and preached, flatly explained: "NEITHER IS THERE SALVATION IN ANY OTHER [EXCEPT JESUS]: FOR THERE IS NONE OTHER NAME UNDER HEAVEN GIVEN AMONG MEN, WHEREBY WE MUST BE SAVED" (Acts 4:12). This is the offense of the gospel, you see. It's not about a creed, a pilgrimage, a building, or a deed; those are complex and works-oriented.

God's way is simple and that's why people stumble at it. We'd rather hang all sorts of pageantry and requirements around it; anything except simple faith in the finished work of the Messiah. Of Himself, Jesus said: "I AM THE WAY, THE TRUTH, AND THE LIFE: NO MAN COMES TO THE FATHER, BUT BY ME" (John 14:6 AKJV). This is the core of every evangelistic endeavor in Christendom. It's not religion; it's relationship. It's not works; it's faith in Christ's finished work.

But what about all the other religions? What about all the other good people? Do you really mean to tell me it's this exclusive? Yes. Welcome to the principle of the narrow and the wide gates. The fact is that far more people choose to believe in something else rather than to believe in Christ. That's the way it's been since the beginning, and it will continue to be so until the end.

The Christian right, for which this concept is as commonly known as the fact that the earth is round, has no trouble with it. It's a fact of our existence. Being in the minority is part of our makeup. I don't sit here in emotional turmoil because Christians are not in the majority. And when I hear anti-Christian rhetoric or see Judeo-Christian-bashing on the news, I don't question my beliefs. That most people think I'm a crackpot for believing this way doesn't shake my faith one iota.

Goodness, Jesus was crucified. Talk about a political loser. Jesus predicted what life for Christians would be like and encouraged them not to be offended: "THEY SHALL PUT YOU OUT OF THE SYNAGOGUES: YES, THE TIME COMES, THAT WHOEVER KILLS YOU WILL THINK HE DOES GOD SERVICE. AND THESE THINGS WILL THEY DO TO YOU, BECAUSE THEY HAVE NOT KNOWN THE FATHER, NOR ME" (John 16:2–3 AKJV).

As Christians, we assume that mainstream religious thinking will be incorrect, that college professors will be wrong regarding spiritual truth. That the news media don't understand our faith. That world leaders don't have a clue about the historical centricity of the death, burial, and resurrection of Christ, or about why Arabs hate Jews, or that Revelation foretells end-game reality.

Truth is out there, but you have to dig for it. You have to find it, like lost treasure. That's the principle of the narrow way. The principle spans every facet of life. The Christian striving for philosophical and biblical consistency should assume that what "everybody says" is wrong. A contrarian view is the hallmark of a discerning person when the whole world is drunk on its own conceit.

When the bipartisan mob screamed "too big to fail" during the 2008 banking collapse, I was screaming "too big to be honest." Perhaps we could say "too big to be good." I think it grieves God's heart when His people embrace the narrow way for their spiritual salvation, but fail to see its implications everywhere. We embrace it for this narrow use, but then educate, medicate, recreate, invest, and eat like the world.

Back to the Sermon on the Mount, Jesus admonished: "YOU ARE THE LIGHT OF THE WORLD . . . LET YOUR LIGHT SO SHINE BEFORE MEN, THAT THEY MAY SEE YOUR GOOD WORKS, AND GLORIFY YOUR FATHER WHICH IS IN HEAVEN" (Matthew 5:14, 16 AKJV). Notice it is works that the world sees. The world doesn't see how you dress on Sunday, how you sing, or even hear your sermons. The world, known as the broad way, sees what we do.

Now, if our Christian distinctives are the evangelistic magnet for the world, doesn't it make sense to figure out which ones will get us the most leverage? In other words, having a certain kind of haircut probably won't make people want what we have. Dressing in a certain kind of costume won't, either. What kind of thing is everyone doing that if we did the opposite, it would make an impact?

A list could certainly include the fruit of the spirit identified succinctly in Galatians: "LOVE, JOY, PEACE, LONGSUFFERING, GENTLENESS, GOODNESS, FAITH, MEEKNESS, TEMPERANCE" (5:22–23). We've already addressed these relative to factory farming, genetically modified organisms, centralized food systems, and food control regulations. I defy anyone to defend the notion that animals denied daylight, fresh air, and even the ability to walk around exemplifies a system that expresses these attributes.

If we don't figure out how to express these attributes in our plants and animals, how are we supposed to envision them in our lives? It is not meekness or love to dope our animals with drugs. It is not joy to deny our animals the most basic expression of their lives. Few things are more gratifying than watching a group of pigs carve out lounge spots and nestle into them for a porcine repose. It's as basic to pigs as snuggling under a blanket is to humans. But the overwhelming majority of pigs in America will never enjoy this experience.

If a person is known by the company he keeps, perhaps another leverage point would be to simply go in the minority direction. Perhaps the hottest Hollywood celebrities should not be on the Christian's hero list, for example.

If everyone thinks we should meddle in the Middle East, maybe we shouldn't. I find it fascinating how we selectively apply our truth perceptions. For example, most conservative Christians laugh at anything the Environmental Protection Agency (EPA) says. Whether it's numbers or regulations or programs, it's all bunk. But if the Pentagon says something, it must be true. Of course, the same is true for the liberals, but it's switched. Anything the Pentagon says is a lie, but anything the EPA says is the gospel.

This is the great downfall of political debate. Neither side respects the other. The whole game is about choosing sides quickly and denigrating the other side. One thing I learned during my school debate experiences was that there are two ways to look at things.

I'm laying a foundation here because I think it's important to appreciate how many Christians have laughed at my positions, because every land-grant university and all the agriculture experts and the American Farm Bureau Federation—ALL agree that without factory farms, mono-speciation, and chemical fertilizer, we just couldn't feed the world. This is the standard line. "How can you disagree with all this expert opinion?" my Christian friends ask.

Of course, they think I've bought the line that big business is bad so I've joined the anti-capitalist bandwagon and become a pinko commie liberal. But if they could only hear themselves in another context, they'd realize how silly the assumption is. If they hear a statement from the EPA as a result of a study done at some scientific think tank, they immediately scoff: "Listen to those whacko environmentalists now. What a bunch of nutcases. Of course those scientists are wrong; they believe in evolution and global warming. Who in their right mind would trust them anyway? Bunch of agenda-driven pinko commie liberals. What do they know anyway? They're trying to take everybody's land."

I think it behooves us as Christians to assume that if the mobs are going one way, perhaps truth is in the other direction. That may not always be the case, but it provides some protection. So if the mobs are shopping at the supermarket, maybe that's the wrong place. If the mobs are eating at Burger King, maybe that's the wrong place. If the assumption is that factory farms and chemicals and drugs are the right thing, maybe they're the wrong thing.

Christian friends respond to my thinking like this: "Well, if what you say is really true, why doesn't everyone do it? If you really can get more production, make more profit, and build more resilience by farming your way, why doesn't everyone just flock to it? Why do they call you a bio-terrorist, Typhoid Mary, and a lunatic? Why do your good churchgoing neighbors think you're nuts?" I could turn this question on its head. How about this for a response:

"If salvation is really so simple, is really as easy as simply casting yourself in faith on the finished work of Christ, why doesn't everyone do it? Why do most people have rites, pilgrimages, worry (am I good enough), costumes, icons, and buildings? Why not just dispense with that and accept Christ? Forget the trappings and step forward in faith. God doesn't demand any of this other religiosity stuff. Why doesn't everyone buy into this?" Because we love complexity. We love to obfuscate and complicate. That's the broad way.

We humans revel in making the simple complex and confusing. So no, compost can't maintain fertility to grow crops. We need petroleum, chemical fertilizers, a distribution system, massive centralized processing factories with labyrinths of stainless steel tubes. We need hazardous materials teams in case something spills, and we need lethal-dose numbers for EPA-approved labels. That will require whole college courses, professors, and more personnel running trials and building more laboratories, preferably at taxpayer expense.

We'll need special rooms on farms to store this stuff, locked, to keep it away from those pesky, adventuresome, and curious children. We'll put a skull-and-crossbones sign on the door to mark it. And we'll need special protective clothing to apply this toxic stuff. Good; that spawns an entire hazardous material industry, from cleanup crews to clothing to writing protocols for truck wrecks and spills.

Since substantial amounts of this chemical fertilizer run off into creeks, it'll stimulate algae blooms and kill fish. Now we'll need special task forces to monitor stream health and issue government reports. We'll need boats, testing equipment, and more laboratories. Once it gets to the Gulf of Mexico, it'll put thousands of people out of business as the dead zone grows. All those shrimp boats and water excursion businesses will leave, so we'll need a homeless/helpless government program to aid them in their transition to other employment.

Okay, we'll stop there, but compare that with compost. You can eat it. It's not toxic. I've never heard of anyone getting sick from a compost spill. You don't need hazardous material handling equipment or protective clothing. It's made from materials on-site—carbon (sawdust, straw, corn stalks, tree chips), nitrogen (manure, vegetable and lawn clipping waste), water, air, and microbes (essentially ubiquitous in nature). No laboratories, no skull and crossbones.

The chemical approach appeals to our cleverness, our pride. We can look at all the big mines, big trucks, big ships, big chemical plants, big payroll, big reports, and beat on our chests like Tarzan, screaming: "Wow! Look how dominant we are. We can do anything. Nothing can stop us. Let's build this tower to heaven." I'm alluding, of course, to the Tower of Babel and the arrogance its builders exhibited before God brought the work to a screeching halt.

Why can we not grow food with the simplicity of compost, pastured livestock, integrated fruits and vegetables? Why can't the system embrace this alternative, this salvation? Well, because to do so would flip all the power, position, and prestige of the industrial food system on its head. If truth were widely adopted, all the big boys would be bucked off and the minority weirdos would be sitting in the saddle.

When it comes to food and farming, the broad way is actually quite articulately defined. You don't have to be a rocket scientist to figure out what the world's leaders, as a mob, believe. Following is their orthodoxy.

Nature Is Broken and We Have to Fix It

God's template is fundamentally flawed and human cleverness must switch it around so it works. If something is sick or diseased, wellness comes from pharmaceuticals. A sick animal is pharmaceutically disadvantaged.

In direct juxtaposition to this view, my belief is that nature's default position is wellness. If something is diseased or sick, then

I did something wrong to precipitate the problem. You see, dear heart, when we Christians ask people to repent of their sins—their faults—but then patronize a food and farming system that assumes no responsibility for breaking God's wellness template when things go awry, we Christians are guilty of theological schizophrenia. Certainly inconsistency.

When our lives are messed up, we should look in the mirror first. What did I do to become separate from God? What did I do to make my wife yell at me? What did I do to irritate my child? What did I do to alienate that friend and bring tension into the relationship? What did I do to get into this terrible financial problem? We in the religious right love to complain about our society's current victimhood mentality where nobody wants to take responsibility for their marriage, finances, health, or happiness.

But we ingest material that at its core refuses to submit to godly principles. What are some of these? They're extremely simple.

Animals Move. We live in a society in which this is considered heresy. The orthodoxy is that animals are supposed to be locked up in buildings and often in tiny prison cages. And where their manure becomes a hazardous waste instead of a soil-building blessing. And no, the answer is not biogas digesters and burning it for electricity generation or making diesel fuel.

We universally applaud efforts at zoos to create natural habitats for the animals and then think nothing of buying food—on site— from vendors who acquire their ingredients from production systems that don't give a hoot about habitat for domestic livestock.

Perennials Trump Annuals. Stay with me here. A perennial is a plant that doesn't go through its life cycle in one year. Trees, grass, asparagus—these are perennials. Annuals need to be planted every year—corn, soybeans, sugarcane, cotton, wheat, rice. Guess which ones our taxpayers subsidize? Only annuals. But in God's template, perennials rule; annuals take a backseat.

Carbon-Cycling. Until the last few decades, the world ran on solar-driven carbon cycles. Deep, fertile soils built up under herbivores, rest, and disturbance cycles. Chemical fertilizers have and always will be completely unnecessary and debilitating to the system.

Multi-Speciated. No animal-less ecology exists, and no monoculture exists. God's design is for symbiosis and synergy with complex relationships between plants and animals. Farms should be mosaics of diversity. Tell that to the factory farm.

Local-Centric. Nature customizes everything, from genetics to species to soil types. It's not a one-size-fits-all or a centralized formula. On-site information determines adaptation. Likewise, markets should be fundamentally localized rather than globally oriented. That doesn't mean you can't buy bananas in Virginia, but it does mean that if something can be grown locally, it should be. We should minimize global transport and maximize local sufficiency.

These are just a few to get you thinking, but you can see quickly how far today's orthodoxy deviates from God's simple principles. This overall view that nature is fundamentally flawed has numerous corollaries, some of which we've already addressed extensively in this book.

For example, the idea that *life is fundamentally mechanical rather than biological* skews thinking toward a repair or rework mentality rather than awe and wonder. If a pig is just a machine, or a chicken is just a machine, we have both emotional license and mental mandate to tinker with it. Cut off its beak, cut off its tail, pull out some genes here, insert some genes there, a few drugs today, some hormones tomorrow—it's all akin to fashioning a plastic widget or automobile part. "Faster, fatter, bigger, cheaper" becomes the mantra without any moral constraints. No reverence or honor toward its biological distinctiveness.

Efficiency Requires Mono-Speciation

The very notion that we can have a multi-speciated efficient farm doesn't even register in the orthodox lexicon anymore. Everything is moving, as John Ikerd, guru of sustainable agriculture economics, says, toward "specialization, simplification, routinization, and mechanization." We're seeing regulations criminalizing pigs on dairies, for example. Goodness, the Swiss built their entire farming system around pigs eating whey leftovers from cheese-making high up in the Alpine meadows.

If you grow chickens for an industrial factory outfit, you can't have any other chickens on the place—not even for your own personal consumption. You can't have them outside, in your backyard. If you have a produce operation, regulatory efforts are under way to prohibit any animals from setting foot in the vegetable patch. Ditto historically normal grazing under orchard or vineyard. Some vegetable operations are even signing affidavits that no children under five years old can visit the farm. Why? To eliminate diapers as a potential hazardous material.

Heretics like me embrace a completely different view. Not only do we believe in diversity and multi-speciation, we believe in intricate stacking arrangements. Stacking is a permaculture concept that deals with multiple enterprises occupying the same or proximate space. For example, on our farm we run cattle, egg-laying hens, broiler chickens, turkeys, and lambs across the same pasture at different times.

All of this multi-speciation does something else: it confuses pathogens. Confused pathogens are a good thing. Most pathogens are species-specific. Believe me, we want confused pathogens. All of this is far more productive per acre than single-species models.

One final benefit: no carpal tunnel syndrome. Food and farming systems that enjoy significant diversity also require many different processes. Maintenance tasks from one hour to the next involve quite different types of work. That, in turn, exercises a whole different set of muscles throughout the day. Variety truly is the spice of life. Think, however, about the kind of farm encouraged by the industrial system. It's devoid of variety and all of nature's checks and balances.

Farms should be seen as art forms. They are landscape sculptures. They should not be boring and same old, same old.

Home Kitchens Are Unnecessary

Today's orthodoxy thrives on someone else doing the cooking. The single-service packet from the supermarket has replaced the sit-down home-cooked meal as the most common food choice. Easy foodism disengages people from the process and creates a level of food illiteracy unthinkable just a few short decades ago.

Christians should be militant about this convenience food addiction. Funny how we get bent out of shape toward easy believe-ism when it comes to salvation, but we don't bat an eye at falling in lock-step with the rest of society when it comes to easy foodism. Since when could you ever get something for nothing? You can't have capsule spiritual food any more than you can have capsule physical nourishment.

Heretics like me believe home-centricity is the foundation of integrity food. We talk about the importance of attending church services but don't talk about the importance of attending communal family meals. Domestic culinary arts are the way to participate with food, just as daily devotions are the way to participate in God's desire for our lives. The parallels are profound. The adage about the family that prays together stays together is equally valid for the physical: the family that eats together stays together.

Just imagine if the Christian community rose up, en masse, against these orthodoxies? It would literally turn our civilization upside down, and I think I speak for most of us in the religious right, that we think that would be a good thing. We fret and fume about social misconduct. But what about us participating in an orthodoxy that defies, denies, and denigrates the narrow way God established for His creation?

To me it's a natural thing to assume that God has a narrow-way principle for a lot of things, and He wants us to search, to ask, to seek and knock, to find that door and go through it. He doesn't just embrace an anything-goes mentality. He has specific regimens for family, for morality, for finances, for the land and ecology. We in the Christian community should eagerly find and enjoy that template, realizing that in doing so, we create spiritual protocols that eventuate in properly understanding God's desires.

Dependence vs. Independence

I can do all things through Christ which strengtheneth me.
Philippians 4:13

Our dependence on God flows throughout Scripture both in direct admonition and in metaphor. If one thing irks God's heart, it's when people develop an independent streak and turn into rebels toward His ownership and control.

In the famous vine and branches discourse, Jesus says: "ABIDE IN ME, AND I IN YOU. AS THE BRANCH CANNOT BEAR FRUIT OF ITSELF, EXCEPT IT ABIDE IN THE VINE; NO MORE CAN YOU, EXCEPT YOU ABIDE IN ME. I AM THE VINE, YOU ARE THE BRANCHES: HE THAT STAYS IN ME, AND I IN HIM, THE SAME BRINGS FORTH MUCH FRUIT: FOR WITHOUT ME YOU CAN DO NOTHING" (John 15:4–5 AKJV). While this passage indicates a relational intimacy, it also stresses our complete and utter dependency on Him.

How about one of the most famous chapters in all Scripture?

THE LORD IS MY SHEPHERD; I SHALL NOT WANT [NEED ANYTHING].
HE MAKES ME TO LIE DOWN IN GREEN PASTURES: HE LEADS ME

BESIDE THE STILL WATERS. HE RESTORES MY SOUL: HE LEADS ME IN
THE PATHS OF RIGHTEOUSNESS FOR HIS NAME'S SAKE. YES, THOUGH I
WALK THROUGH THE VALLEY OF THE SHADOW OF DEATH, I WILL FEAR
NO EVIL: FOR YOU ARE WITH ME; YOUR ROD AND YOUR STAFF THEY
COMFORT ME. YOU PREPARE A TABLE BEFORE ME IN THE PRESENCE
OF MY ENEMIES; YOU ANOINT MY HEAD WITH OIL; MY CUP RUNS OVER.
SURELY GOODNESS AND MERCY SHALL FOLLOW ME ALL THE DAYS OF
MY LIFE; AND I WILL DWELL IN THE HOUSE OF THE LORD FOR EVER.
(Psalm 23 AKJV)

A more beautiful polemic could not be penned to express God's
care for us and our nestling into His provision. Notice how plants
and animals form the basis of this intimate dependency metaphor.
If you've never tended sheep or pruned a grapevine, the depth and
breadth of these metaphors cannot be fully appreciated. Having personal knowledge of the agrarian object lessons makes them live in
our hearts.

Permaculture advises new landowners to not do anything for one
year. Instead, they're admonished to visit the land one day per month
for a whole year. Notepad in hand, these visits provide information
about patterns and natural proclivities.

For example, during these data-gathering visits, you'll discover
where wet spots are. These are places to avoid with a road, but may
offer great pond sites. Where does the snow pile up and where is the
ground normally swept clean by the wind? Places that enjoy routine
snow buildup not only get more moisture, but also offer freeze protection for the soil. That thick blanket of snow provides insulation.
Air moves in streams, or tunnels, across the landscape. Where are
the warm tunnels? Those are places to plant frost-prone things.

One of my favorite permaculture concepts involves noting the
type of native vegetation growing on an area. If you discover a spot
impregnable with entwined wild grapevines trellising up into the

trees, that's obviously a great spot to grow domestic grapes. If you find a patch of wild blackberries, that indicates a predisposition to bramble fruit. The point is to recognize the desires of a place prior to imposing our will on it. This permaculture spirit, or attitude, promotes a dependency on the climate, topography, and resource base rather than a demeanor that lords over the ecosystem.

I deeply appreciate this permaculture dependency idea because it creates a framework for our creativity that stays within the bounds of our resource base. The Australian water genius P. A. Yeomans developed what he called steps of permanence. That list has now been modified into ten steps by another genius Aussie named Darren Doherty, who, with his wife, Lisa, founded Regrarians.

The idea is that these steps go from most permanent to least permanent. In other words, the hardest ones to change are the first ones, and the easier ones are the last ones. This list is both confining and liberating. Because it identifies boundaries, it keeps us from fretting or frittering away our time about things we cannot change. By the same token, it frees us to work on the things we can. I believe this is one of the most profound assessments of human-ecology dependencies that exist. When we implement changes, they become part of the new environmental equity. Here are the ten "rules of the game," as Darren calls them:

1. **Climate.** It is what it is. I'd be foolish to bet my farm's prosperity on growing bananas. I can't change the rainfall, average temperature, longitude, or latitude. I'm dependent on that. However, I can do things to extend the season, like cold frames or greenhouses. We can modify, but only so much.

2. **Geography.** Darren calls this "the board game." It includes topography, demography, geology. You aren't going to turn your hills into flat ground or your marshes into high country. But you can create contour lines for keylining (invented by Yeomans—*Water for Every Farm*). Ponds for water catchment can be strategically placed.

3. **Water.** This is the fuel that powers everything. Harnessing, storing, dispensing water are key. Plastic pipe lets you move water to places where current streams and springs don't flow.

4. **Access.** Roads, pathways, and lanes from ancient Roman times are still evident throughout Europe. Place these strategically for easy maintenance and to use as gutters to channel water to catchments.

5. **Forestry.** Trees change slowly, but we can accelerate change by pruning, strategic weeding, and other good silvicultural practices. How many and what kind of trees do you want long-term? Trees provide fuel, lumber, carbon, wildlife habitat, erosion control, hydrology cycling, transpiration. We depend on them.

6. **Buildings.** Portability is preferable because it's the lowest cost and most versatile. Buildings will inevitably become obsolete. Realizing that our infrastructure is dependent on things beyond our control, like the economy, technology, or the interests of future owners, pushes us toward multi-use, simple, cheaper structures that can be easily modified.

7. **Fencing.** Ditto the buildings discussion above. One of my rules of thumb is this: install only what is obvious and necessary (like fencing out streams, ponds, gardens, access lanes). Leave everything else portable. Whatever you leave up and don't move for three years can be converted to permanent. On our farm, all of our fences follow topographical lines. We have no straight fences; they're all crooked to follow the terrain. Did somebody say something about being dependent?

8. **Soils.** Soil maps give a good starting point, but all soils can be upgraded with good management. Heavy soils or light soils dictate practices. Violating those rules has done and continues to do a lot of ecological damage.

9. **Economy.** The economy may go up or down and none of us can do anything about that, but the way we market, the way we interact with consumers, ultimately dictates our success.

So yes, we can't change things on a macro scale, but we can greatly change our personal micro-economy.

10. **Energy.** We live in a petroleum-dependent time, and none of us can change the price of diesel fuel at our local stations. But we can move our farms to more solar-driven operations, whether that be actual solar panels or more leaves on plants to generate more biomass. We'll see more development in this arena, of course.

There you have it, the ten steps of permanence that define our dependence on what is, but offer lots of opportunity for innovation within those confines. What a different discussion than the one engaged in by today's industrial farmers. They live in a world of disease, commodity price roller coasters, sickness, stench, erosion, and economic fragility. To me, recognizing our dependence ultimately liberates us to responsible innovation.

You see, dear folks, we live in a time when sophisticated technocrats unilaterally sell the notion to the populace that humankind can break its dependency on an ecological umbilical. That this nest we call the earth has no control over us. That God's patterns don't exist, or if they do, they're meant to be changed however the clever human mind can conceive to change them. If we don't like the way DNA works, we'll just blast it with gene-splicing cannons to make it into our image.

Similarly, if we don't like what God says, we'll just change it to suit our times. We'll make God a woman, pull out the exclusivity of salvation through Christ, add in a few routines, explain away the miracles through higher criticism—including the resurrection. We'll just change things to suit, call it a theological upgrade.

Can we physically upgrade ourselves to *Star Trek*? We live in a time when the average person thinks we can sever this inconvenient tie to soil, air, and water, this unhandy dependency on earth's womb. And we're going to sail off into some cosmic nirvana existence free from food requirements, earthworm requirements, and soil. We don't need to think about, engage in, or consider ecology day-to-day.

In fact, we go visit nature. We're completely disconnected from it, so we visit a park, national forest, or wilderness area as if nature is out there somewhere. Folks, we are nature. We are part of it. In our condos, in our workaday world, at the soccer game, at the dining table. We are arguably the most natural part of nature. We're not disembodied from creation; we are its primary caretakers.

I wrote a book about this titled *Folks, This Ain't Normal*, detailing the numerous ways our modern techno-sophisticated existence thumbs its nose at historical civilization norms. It was written in direct response to interactions with young people who expressed far more dependency on earbuds, smartphones, and laptops than on earthworms, carbon cycles, and their own internal 3-trillion-member community of beings.

Because I am deeply committed to God's patterns, I view some innovations quite unfavorably. While scientists—and certainly some Christian ones—exult in creating a new genetically modified organism, for example, I view such a thing as tantamount to shaking your fist in the face of God. This gets to the nub, doesn't it? The Christian who creates genetically modified organisms might share the following praise at Bible study: "Today, God enabled me to do something amazing in the lab. We broke through that pesky species barrier. It'll let us feed hungry kids in Tanzania. I could almost feel the Spirit move me as I worked in my lab. His presence was over my team as we did the final test and it worked. Oh, we serve an awesome God, and I thank Him for letting me help solve world hunger and farm production problems."

Indeed, perhaps some Christians are already involved in projects seeking to pull the stress genes out of pigs. Factory farming pigs makes them stressed, so they fight each other and develop other problems. Scientists surmise that if they can get rid of that pesky porcine stress gene, then we can assault the pigness of pigs more horrifically but the pigs won't care. Dear friends, doesn't that sound just like the kind of project a Christian could get behind, could seek divine counsel for during prayer, and joyfully celebrate when successful? How dare I suggest that a Christian should not be undertaking this research.

One of my favorite—and most convicting—passages in all of Scripture comes out of 1 Samuel 15. To set the context, Israel's first king, Saul, is empowered by God to vanquish threats to the people. He wins battle after battle in decisive fashion. Eventually, Samuel, who of course is Israel's high priest who reluctantly anointed Saul to be king, dispatches Saul to destroy the Amalekites.

Samuel gives God's explicit instructions to Saul: "Now go and smite Amalek, and utterly destroy all that they have, and spare them not; but slay both man and woman, infant and suckling, ox and sheep, camel and ass" (1 Samuel 15:3). Pretty clear, wouldn't you say? These people had been a thorn in Israel's side long enough. God's mercy gave way to his perfect judgment, and He wanted these people expunged from the earth. Dear heart, you don't want to mess with God. You want to come to God on His terms, not yours.

Anyway, Saul gathers up about two hundred thousand soldiers and heads over to Amalek and God gives him a great victory. The biblical account is clear:

And Saul smote [killed] the Amalekites from Havilah until thou comest to Shur, that is over against Egypt. And he took Agag the king of the Amalekites alive, and utterly destroyed all the people with the edge of the sword. But Saul and the people spared Agag, and the best of the sheep, and of the oxen, and of the fatlings, and the lambs, and all that was good, and would not utterly destroy them: but every thing that was vile and refuse, that they destroyed utterly. (1 Samuel 15:7–9)

How could anyone not applaud Saul for exercising his intellect to admire good breeding stock when he saw it and save it for Israel's future gene pool? I mean, after all, this is simply good stewardship and taking care of creation. We're supposed to be upgrading our animals, right? That's how we express dominion over them. Goodness, Saul probably had some homeless folks in mind when he saved the best of the cattle and sheep, world hunger, helping farmers. Extremely noble ambitions.

By any reasonable person's account, Saul succeeded beautifully and deserved a "Kumbaya" togetherness gathering to celebrate God's atta-boy congratulations.

But things were not as Saul and his generals thought. While they celebrated a great victory and reveled in their conquest, God had a conversation with Samuel: "IT REPENTETH ME THAT I HAVE SET UP SAUL TO BE KING: FOR HE IS TURNED BACK FROM FOLLOWING ME, AND HATH NOT PERFORMED MY COMMANDMENTS" (1 Samuel 15:11). Wow. You mean I can be successful and do great, amazing things and God's not pleased? Yes, dear heart.

Samuel heads to the war zone to confront Saul and finally finds him at Gilgal. Saul comes out with a huge smile on his face, satisfaction in his heart, merriment in his stride, and greets Samuel: "BLESSED ARE YOU OF THE LORD! I HAVE PERFORMED THE COMMANDMENT OF THE LORD" (1 Samuel 15:13 NKJV).

Samuel responds: "WHAT MEANETH THEN THIS BLEATING OF THE SHEEP IN MINE EARS, AND THE LOWING OF THE OXEN WHICH I HEAR?" (1 Samuel 15:14).

Saul has wonderful excuses, like "The people made me do it," or "I was going to use them for sacrifices," or "It's not really that big a deal!"

Then come two of the most profound verses in all of Holy Writ:

AND SAMUEL SAID, HAS THE LORD AS GREAT DELIGHT IN BURNT OFFERINGS AND SACRIFICES, AS IN OBEYING THE VOICE OF THE LORD? BEHOLD, TO OBEY IS BETTER THAN SACRIFICE, AND TO LISTEN THAN

THE FAT OF RAMS. FOR REBELLION IS AS THE SIN OF WITCHCRAFT, AND STUBBORNNESS IS AS INIQUITY AND IDOLATRY. BECAUSE YOU HAVE REJECTED THE WORD OF THE LORD, HE HAS ALSO REJECTED YOU FROM BEING KING. (1 Samuel 15:22–23 AKJV)

Take a minute. Let that sink in.

If you're a true softhearted Christian, tears flow at this point. I see myself in Saul. Defensive. Going my own way. Best of intentions. God is not impressed, and when Samuel delivers his edict, Saul begs for a second chance. Saul suddenly does an about-face: "I HAVE SINNED: FOR I HAVE TRANSGRESSED" (1 Samuel 15:24). But it's too little, too late. God wants obedience, dependency, respect from us. Think about the most holy religious thing you can do. Partaking of communion? Being baptized? Attending church services? Preaching sermons? Going to the mission field? Giving to missions?

God goes to the most sacred part of the Jewish religious experience—the sacrifice—and says it's nothing compared to obedience. As Samuel takes Saul through his early days and his humble dependency, he tries to get the king to understand that his standing is dependent on obedience. That is the ultimate sacrifice, the ultimate act of worship.

How many accomplishment parties have actually celebrated something that God finds evil? Wow, that should sober up even a five-point Calvinist. You see, ultimately one of the biggest human tragedies is succeeding at something God sees as evil. We may think it's great. We may even have good intentions. Our friends may applaud what we've done. But the question is, does it please God?

As noble as fighting world hunger is, does my plan please God? As noble as stopping a sickness may be, does the cure please God? These are huge questions and should drive us to seek, to ask, to knock. All that to say, in my opinion, the Christian scientist exulting over his gene-splicing success is like Saul exulting over his conquest of the Amalekites. If it violates God's stewardship parameters, is it righteous or evil?

These are strong words. I don't expect every reader to come down on every side of every issue with me. But I beg the Christian community to dare to wrestle with these things.

To me, dependency on God's principles is ultimately inspiring and invigorating.

It's exciting to awaken each morning completely dependent on God's sufficiency. And He's not a landlord, a boss, who wishes us ill. He loves giving gifts and showing us how to solve our problems. All we have to do is assume a teachable spirit before the Creator of the universe and let Him shower us with answers. How cool is that?

This dependency removes from us the tension between quality and quantity. The industrial farm community is completely wrapped up in volume production. How do we produce more, more, more? It's all about bushels, pounds, and numbers. Fatter, faster, bigger, cheaper. Today's dollars. Today's profits. Meanwhile, the immunological terrain erodes; the soil erodes; the water becomes toxic; the aquifer shrinks; diseases increase; food allergies proliferate; food-borne pathogens mutate, acclimate, and inundate.

God tells Saul something profoundly simple, if I may paraphrase: "I'd rather have one day of obedience than a lifetime of sacrament performance." Friends, that is sobering. But it's also incredibly freeing, because suddenly the goal is not quantity, but quality. It's not how, but why?

Suddenly it's not about going to worship. It's about, am I worshipping in the right place? It's not about how many chickens we can produce on this farm, it's, are the chickens being raised in a way that pleases God and makes people healthy and gives the Creator a good return on His stuff? That is downright liberating.

Of course, what we've found on our farm is that when we devote ourselves to obedience, everything else takes care of itself. And of course, that's exactly the way God provides, isn't it? He doesn't reward miserly, or reluctantly: "PROVE ME NOW HEREWITH, SAYS THE LORD OF HOSTS, IF I WILL NOT OPEN YOU THE WINDOWS OF HEAVEN, AND POUR YOU OUT A BLESSING, THAT THERE SHALL NOT BE ROOM ENOUGH TO RECEIVE IT" (Malachi 3:10).

I would suggest that a farm and food system that refuses to consider the pigness of the pig, for all of its noble intentions, is actually shaking its fist in the face of God. If we refuse to acknowledge God's claims on a pig, what about His claims on me, on you, on us? God owns the pig. He cares.

My agenda needs to submit to God's desire. Period. God gives me tools like reason, experience, emotion, and His word to understand what kind of stewardship, what kind of care over His stuff would please Him. That's not whacko environmentalism; it's an object lesson of dependency on a holy, righteous owner. That's wisdom.

Forgiving vs. Fragile

And hearken Thou to the supplication of Thy servant
and of Thy people Israel when they shall pray toward this
place, and hear Thou in heaven Thy dwelling place; and
when Thou hearest, forgive.

1 Kings 8:30 (KJ21)

Nature, like life, is not always pleasant. Bumps happen. We live in
a fallen world, after all. Every day is not seventy degrees, sunshine,
and perfect—not even in San Diego.

God's forgiveness enables us to go on. Without forgiveness, a holy
God wouldn't be able to hear our cries, answer our prayers, or accept
us into His presence. Forgiveness is what gives us the ability to survive with God even though we fail time and again.

"IF WE CONFESS OUR SINS, HE IS FAITHFUL AND JUST TO FORGIVE
US OUR SINS, AND TO CLEANSE US FROM ALL UNRIGHTEOUSNESS"
(1 John 1:9). What a precious promise in light of God's holiness,
which puts Him completely out of our reach.

"THOU ART OF PURER EYES THAN TO BEHOLD EVIL, AND CANST
NOT LOOK ON INIQUITY" (Habakkuk 1:13). That puts God out of our
reach, plainly and simply. It gets worse: "IF I REGARD INIQUITY IN
MY HEART, THE LORD WILL NOT HEAR ME" (Psalm 66:18). This is

certainly the perfect storm. We're separated from God with no way to be reconciled. I call that a pretty hopeless situation.

But forgiveness breaks through all of this, and when we confess and repent, God promises to forgive and build a relationship with us. That's resilience and strength. Fortunately, our relationship with God is not fragile from one moment to the next; it's actually quite strong since He protects us from Satan's attacks. This forgiveness entitles us to armor:

WHEREFORE TAKE UNTO YOU THE WHOLE ARMOUR OF GOD, THAT YE MAY BE ABLE TO WITHSTAND IN THE EVIL DAY, AND HAVING DONE ALL, TO STAND. STAND THEREFORE, HAVING YOUR LOINS GIRT ABOUT WITH TRUTH, AND HAVING ON THE BREASTPLATE OF RIGHTEOUSNESS; AND YOUR FEET SHOD WITH THE PREPARATION OF THE GOSPEL OF PEACE; ABOVE ALL, TAKING THE SHIELD OF FAITH, WHEREWITH YE SHALL BE ABLE TO QUENCH ALL THE FIERY DARTS OF THE WICKED. AND TAKE THE HELMET OF SALVATION, AND THE SWORD OF THE SPIRIT, WHICH IS THE WORD OF GOD. (Ephesians 6:13–17)

Without forgiveness, we can't access that protective uniform. Extending to person-to-person relationships, we know that forgiveness creates wiggle room for those times when we irritate each other. A marriage without forgiveness doesn't last very long because all of us will get up on the wrong side of the bed one day. Forgiveness is the centerpiece of the Christian life because without it, the crucifixion is of no effect, a relationship between people and God is impossible, and the heavenly hope is unattainable. If a farm and food system illustrates anything spiritually, it should be forgiveness. Secularists would call this resilience. Sustainable agriculture aficionados refer to shock absorbers that can handle bumps in the road like droughts, floods, aging, price fluctuations, and disease. Weather, culture—things—are sometimes cavernous bumps. How well does our farm and food system hold up?

With that in mind, let's look at the current state of affairs and see if a forgiveness model can provide relief. *Salmonella. E. coli.* Avian influenza. *Pfiesteria. Campylobacter.* Bovine spongiform encepha-lopathy. Hoof-and-mouth disease. As recently as two decades ago, who among us had ever seen these words? Add to these a nationwide obesity epidemic, fish kills and air pollution from factory farms, and failing farmers driving their population below that of prisoners, and any thinking person must ask: "How can we turn this around?"

Our culture has not practiced forgiveness farming for a long, long time—perhaps ever. This notion is comprehensive, encompassing many aspects. A farm must be successful in many areas in order to have forgiveness, or resilience. Here are some characteristics of for-giveness farming.

Relationship Forgiveness

All businesses, including farm businesses, can only be as success-ful as their personal relationships. You can't have a thriving farm when members of the team don't communicate. It's hard to pull together when you're pulling apart. Agreeing on a common mission statement is more important than anything—even ecology. Even an ecology-minded farm can only be successful if its team members feel comfortable in their roles. That includes knowing what each other's dreams are and working together to realize them.

The beauty of ecological farming is that it creates a safer environ-ment for everyone to spend more time together. On our farm, we don't have to worry about the children finding the pesticide room and splashing around in a deadly liquid. They can splash around in some fish emulsion or guzzle some liquid seaweed without kill-ing themselves. How many industrial farmers can't wait to take their toddlers up to the confinement poultry house with them to check the fifteen thousand birds crammed beak-to-toe in a fecal pall?

Just like industrial farming compartmentalizes food produc-tion, it segments the farm team and makes myopic specialists rather than eclectic participants. With softer, quieter tools and infrastruc-ture come more opportunities to talk while working. And to let the children be intimately involved without fear that they will be gobbled up by noise, dust, or machinery.

I've never seen a child drown in a compost pile. But I've seen whole families knocked out in manure lagoons. The increased disease consequences from exposure to common farm chemicals is documented beyond question. I've never seen someone get cancer from moving chickens through a garden to debug it.

Relationship nurturing requires fellowship, and fellowship rarely happens when the working environment is noisy, stinky, dusty, or dangerous. Working with nature rather than against it turns our farm environment into one that better stimulates healthy relationships. That's forgiving.

Emotional Forgiveness

Ever notice how paranoid industrial farmers are? If you attend any conventional farm conference, nearly all the lectures and all the impromptu hallway discussions center around "things that are coming to get us." Diseases. Low prices. High costs. Imports. Bankers. Lawyers. Organic farmers. Liberals. Environmentalists. Animal welfare groups.

Industrial farmers are fixated on bad things. From soybean rust to avian influenza, their whole lexicon concentrates on things to fear. They walk around every waking minute emotionally drained. Rather than having a focused attention on success, they look around timidly, furtively, to see what goblin from "out there" may be lurking to doom their farm. Constantly complaining and never praising, they drive away their family and, finally, their joy.

A factory farmer who escapes the pathogen goblins one more day breathes a sigh of relief that he may live to stand another day. But he won't be victorious. He will only be not defeated . . . maybe. An ecological farmer once told me that he quit industrial farming when he realized that his first waking thought every morning was: *I wonder what's dead up there in the hog house today?* He couldn't hear the birds chirping. He couldn't enjoy the sunrise, or the rainbow after a thunderstorm. And his kids wanted nothing to do with the farm.

But after this epiphany, he closed down the pig concentration camp and devoted himself to pasture-based farming. Suddenly his children wanted to be involved. His thoughts turned lofty. He developed a can-do spirit. And his emotional zest returned.

The sheer mystery and majesty of heritage wisdom, contained in each cell, each mitochondria, instills in the farmer who respects and honors the pigness of the pig a daily emotional high. The satisfaction of being nature's nurturer always trumps the short-lived adrenaline high of being nature's conqueror. Such an attitude offers spiritual ascendance over physical domination, which never really happens anyway. And that's why the industrial farmer, for all the smoke and noise and horsepower, never feels in control, but always dreads being drowned by the nature he thinks he's controlling.

Ah, what emotional forgiveness awaits those who marvel at the food web's intricacies and the compost pile's miracles? Every day is a day of discoveries, satisfaction, and fulfillment as the Creator's design endorses our efforts, gently nudging us with a "WELL DONE, THOU GOOD AND FAITHFUL SERVANT" (Matthew 25:21).

Infrastructure Forgiveness

Capital-intensive, single-use infrastructure is extremely hard to retrofit when it no longer is financially or emotionally profitable. Multiple-use machines and buildings can be adapted to the next production permutation without jeopardizing the farm's viability.

As pasture-based livestock systems become more widely utilized, large confinement dairies and large feedlots will be the last to join the new paradigm. The sheer emotional and financial investment in these structures requires 24/7 throughput, even when farmers see a better way.

That is why anything you build or buy today should be multiple-use, adaptable, and as simple as possible, including the ability to be modified. That's one reason I like pole buildings. They have fairly open spans and can be outfitted easily for different kinds of animals and uses. The more concrete you pour, the less likely you are to abandon the structure if and when that production model becomes obsolete.

When infrastructure drives our decisions, it's not very forgiving. This is the problem with huge ethanol plants and factory farms. While nothing is wrong with bio-fuels or raising animals, the problem is that the scale of these facilities enslaves us emotionally and economically. In fact, we'll destroy the environment surrounding them rather than abandon them because we invested too much time and money in them to abandon them. These massive single-use facilities dominate the land-use decision making radiating out many miles. That is not forgiving.

I know a fellow who started a pastured poultry enterprise on a nearby rented piece of land. Everything went along great for two years and then the landlord decided to sell the property. No problem. The farmer found another piece of land to rent just up the road, loaded his portable shelters on a lowboy trailer, and hauled them over to the new place. Welcome to the portable farm. How many farmers can do that with the factory chicken houses?

A compost pile is far more forgiving than a manure lagoon. A handful of electric fence and a Rubbermaid water trough with cows on pasture are far more forgiving than a $200,000 combine and all the equipment that goes before it and the feedlot after it. The farmer simply cannot afford to owe his soul to some monolithic piece of infrastructure if he is to be free to adapt to tomorrow's new context. Forgiving infrastructure offers adaptability and freedom.

Landscape Forgiveness

Large-scale monocultures are an assault against nature. Period, end of discussion. Natural systems enjoy a degree of diversity, even within apparent sameness. The undergrowth beneath an arboreal forest of Douglas fir is amazingly varied. But beyond just the species, the buffering of open land, forestal, and riparian zones create checks and balances within flora and fauna.

This ecological tapestry encourages hydrological cycling, predator balance, and controlled wind patterns. Native prairie contained some forty plant species per acre. The Corn Belt obliterates those on a massive scale. Nature builds soil by gently laying carbon like mature grass, dry leaves, and needles on top of the soil and letting the earthworms plow it in. Nature does not knife in carbon or nutrients. It does not denude.

With all the money expended on soil conservation programs in the United States, we are still losing soil at an alarming and escalating rate. Some of the last figures I've seen estimate five bushels of soil for every bushel of corn. We are literally raping our landscape, rather than building forgiveness into it.

A forgiving landscape is one in which water can never build up velocity and volume at the same time. Diversion into ponds slows everything down and allows sediments to drop. It is one that supports a plethora of varied species closely intersected in a mosaic of forestal, open, and riparian environments. It is one that is clothed with vegetation and unclothed rarely. The old seven-year rotation of five years in grass with two in row crops is probably about as unclothed as any landscape can afford to be—including an organic one. The biblical seven-year rest for cropland mirrors this idea.

Every time we violate these landscape principles, we create more risk for erosion and imbalances. On our farm, we've planted forestal zones within two hundred yards of all the open land to give insect-loving birds protection and a friendly habitat. This is simply one of the practical applications when we begin trying to build forgiveness into the landscape.

Health Forgiveness

Nature sanitizes in two ways: rest and sunshine; virulent decomposition. The first is typical in a rotated pasture and grazing model. Animals move from paddock to paddock so that at least a twenty-one-day host-free period exists between visits. This breaks the pathogen cycle and keeps the bad bugs under control. Obviously, a dirt-loafing yard is not forgiving. Neither is a concrete pad nor a slatted floor with a slurry pit underneath.

In the second model, deep bedding with a 25–30:1 carbon:nitrogen ratio, with enough moisture, air, and microbes, will stimulate vibrant decomposition. This activity encourages nematodes and enough good bugs to hold the bad bugs in check. Furthermore, ensuring at least one or two thirty-day host-free cycles per year, preferably with a different species on the bedding, will create what I call pathogen dead ends.

On our farm, we move the rabbits and chickens from their houses to tall tunnel hoophouses in the winter. Pigs move into the rabbit-chicken (Raken) house for the one hundred days of deep winter. Any animal confinement facility could drastically reduce its pathogen load by vacating the premises for two months per year. But in industrial agriculture, we don't design our structures to accept a different species. And we certainly don't think about vacating...ever. And therein lies the dependency on stronger and stronger concoctions from the devil's pantry to fight the building pathogen load in these nonrested structures.

The same protections occur in orchards that graze sheep or poultry underneath. In cropland rotated to pasture. And in animals fed and treated in ways that respect their physiological distinctiveness.

For decades the USDA romanced farmers to freebie dinners in order to teach them how to feed dead cows to cows. Because it violated the most fundamental herbivoreness of herbivores, it eventually created mad cow disease. At least, that's the official belief. Cows are herbivores, and herbivores in nature do not eat dead cows, chicken manure, grain, or fermented forage. A host of regulations and government agencies now surround combating this disease that never would have occurred had we simply followed God's template. Virtually all of our diseases reflect a departure from God's patterns. Most of the research and industry built up around remediating these things never would have been necessary had we followed a forgiveness pattern from the beginning.

Weather Forgiveness

Drought, flood, cold, and heat will be with us until the end of time. Part of the farmer's ministry is creating forgiveness toward all of these anomalies to minimize their damage and maximize resiliency. That means farmers should be far more interested in building ponds to collect flood runoff and disseminate it in the drought than they are in lobbying for crop insurance and low-interest loans to protect them from crop failures.

This really came home to me during one of the many Mississippi floods when the TV news showed National Guard troops removing half a dozen pigs from atop an Iowa hog factory into a twelve-foot skiff. Unlike most viewers, I happened to know how many thousands of pigs were down below that roof, all drowned. At the time, I had about a hundred hogs in various pig pastures, scattered around the farm. If we had had a flood, I could have just herded them to high ground. And they would have known how to root and fend for themselves on some acorns and grass until we could get to them again. My goodness, I suppose our hogs could swim away.

That was like an "aha" moment, in which I realized that perhaps the single most important component of stewardship is to make the farm more capable of withstanding the vagaries nature sends. No government program can protect us from that.

And when we have a portable production model, with a higher gross margin so that we don't need the millions of units for a profit, we can salvage things easier in the crisis. Imagine a thousand-acre commodity cornfield in a drought. Not much you can do. But imagine a five-acre cornfield supplying a value-added family-scaled milling and corn bread–baking enterprise. The potential gross sales from both enterprises are identical. But the family with the smaller enterprise can go out there with five-gallon buckets and water those five acres to salvage their livelihood. This is the kind of forgiveness we need to think about.

Price Forgiveness

Industrial agriculture and its ugly cousin cheap food work together to shove product margins further south every year. The only farms showing a profit are the huge and the tiny. The huge because they can spread their overhead across more units and the small because they don't have any overhead.

Creating price forgiveness requires us to build higher quality into our products and demand compensation for that quality. My dad used to say: "You might as well do nothing for nothing as something for nothing." Why do farmers abide the annual assault against the value of what we've produced? Because we don't let ourselves think about alternatives. Including the alternative called do nothing.

One of the best ways to create price forgiveness is through some sort of specialty-differentiated product and/or direct marketing. This differentiated product can be organic, pastured, or whatever. The point is to find a niche that is under-filled, for which people are willing to pay a premium, and fill it. Producing the same old, same old for buyers who haven't had a new thought in a decade is not the way to command a better price.

The farmer only gets around ten cents of the retail dollar. Have you ever heard someone say: "The middleman makes all the profits"? When a farmer dons some of those middleman hats, he taps into that processing, marketing, distribution value chain. Those dollars are not subject to the vagaries that plague farming. The tires on the distribution truck don't blow away in a drought. A blizzard does not close down the Internet connection to customers. Nonproduction dollars are more insulated from these unique farm vagaries.

With the information network and superhighways at our disposal, many, many more farmers could begin marketing directly to their foodshed than currently practice it. I don't have the answer for every ranch in Montana located a hundred miles from a Coke machine, but I know that if every farmer who could touch his food-shed directly with his wares would do so, we couldn't even conceive of the new opportunities that would spring up for those who don't have population bases nearby.

Owning your price, and pricing to value, is the way to build for-giveness into the pricing equation.

Marketing Forgiveness

In the industrial farming sector, farmers are beholden to just a hand-ful of buyers. And that includes the organic industrial sector.

Building market forgiveness requires having a diversified portfo-lio of interest. That might include community supported agriculture (CSA), a couple of farmers' markets, on-farm sales or roadside stands, Internet sales, restaurants, and buying clubs. The greater the mix of these venues, the more stable the marketing portfolio.

Customers are portable. They will follow the market venue around. Look how they follow Walmarts when the mega-stores abandon facades and build new structures across town. You can start farming on rental land, and if you lose that piece, move to another and your customers will follow you to the new place. This builds tremendous forgiveness in the farm—to not even be tied down to a place. And it's made possible by proximity between producer and patron.

The industrial food system is wringing its hands trying to figure out how to export more to far-flung countries, most of which now show declining populations. What is a food system predicated on an ever-increasing world population supposed to do when the popula-tion flattens? Anyone who builds a business centered around their community, their neighborhood, will have access to customers and loyalty unattainable in far-flung arrangements.

A close-to-home market, within the farm's foodshed, is much

more forgiving than one controlled by capricious global cartels and international intrigue. An outsourced decision structure is a hard market taskmaster. When we own our customers, when we know our customers and they know us and respect us, we have market forgiveness.

Product Forgiveness

Faster fatter bigger cheaper is the slogan of the industrial food movement. Pushing every plant and animal to its biological limits makes everything vulnerable to being culled by nature for being unbalanced.

Pushed by sedentary confinement and starch-laden diets, animals become flabby and grow themselves into weakness. Consider how quickly dairy cows burn out in milk factories. Or how breathing in fecal particulate air creates lesions on the mucous membranes of chickens. As a result of these practices, milk must be pasteurized to kill all the pass-through pathogens from an improper production model. Chickens must go through chlorine baths to kill the heavy bacteria load on and inside the carcass.

Spinach and lettuce face routine recalls. Actually, about 90 percent of all food recalls are for leafy greens, not animal products. The nutrient devitalization and pathogen load carried into the food chain is horrendous. More and more charts showing the diminishing nutrients of today's produce and fruit compared to fifty years ago graphically illustrate the demise of food quality.

A forgiving farm enjoys animal and plant production that is not pushed to the extreme. Intuitively we all know that nothing operates most efficiently at full throttle. Is it any wonder that a food system predicated on faster, fatter, bigger, cheaper would create an ignorant, duplicitous, harried, obese citizenry? A culture's people carry in their heads and physiques the manifestation of their food system's objectives.

If America has a health crisis, perhaps it is time to identify our food crisis first. The best health care plan is product forgiveness on the plate. Researchers at Cornell proved years ago that feeding cows forage for two weeks before slaughter would practically eliminate the *E. coli* problem. But the industry vilified the study rather than adopting a new protocol.

A pasture-based livestock farm maintaining happy animals is simply not as vulnerable to pathogen attack in or on what it produces. A vegetable operation maintaining high organic matter soils creates a natural buffer against anything that would taint the produce. While the rest of the world stays awake nights wondering if their food will hurt somebody, a forgiveness farmer can sleep like a baby, assured that following God's designs encourages healthful, pathogen-free products.

Neighbor Forgiveness

Pick up any conventional farm magazine and you will find numerous articles and editorials about those nasty neighbors that don't like the smells and unsightliness emanating from farms. Ditto the animal welfare crowd that is trying to put factory farms out of business.

If we had never stooped to factory farms, the virulent edge of the animal rights movement would have never launched. In fact, the militant groups like People for the Ethical Treatment of Animals (PETA) do not represent a new spiritual state of cosmic awareness, but rather the inevitable result of extreme disconnectedness from the living world. Factory farms fuel their agenda. But rather than being constructive and encouraging good animal husbandry, they go vegan and view a cow as a cat as your aunt as your dog as your nephew. When the only living things a person encounters is a house plant or a pet cat, it kind of jaundices their view toward the natural world that lives and dies, that decomposes and springs to life in another form. Everything is eating and being eaten.

If they are to be regenerative and sustainable, our farms must be forgiving to our neighbors. That means they must be aromatically and aesthetically pleasant. And that means our workers should not walk around in hazardous material suits looking like they are walking on the moon instead of on our friendly earth. And the animals should be happy, busy, cooing, content.

A Virginia subdivision now has restricted deed covenants against "farming and other nuisances." Can you imagine? In our culture, we are actually labeling farming as a nuisance. What have we done to ourselves, that the oldest and noblest vocation on earth, the educated agrarian proletariat envisioned by Thomas Jefferson, has been reduced to nothing more than a nuisance?

This has not come as a result of ecological farming, or following God's template. It is the direct result of an anti-human, anti-God industrial food system that divorces food courtship from dinner and turns the populace into farm-haters. That is a tragedy of epic proportions. We must devote ourselves afresh to building neighbor forgiveness into our farms, to rekindle an enthusiasm for the agrarian arts. Building beautiful farmsteads with diversified species on verdant pastures with dancing animals is the way to draw in our neighbors, to reconnect, and to build forgiveness.

Forgiveness farming encompasses everything we are and do. It includes how other people see our farms as well as how we want to see our farms. It's abundantly practical. And it's totally opposite the industrial food system. Forgiveness farmers can lie down at night knowing we have not violated creation, we have not raped the earth, we have not angered our neighbors, and we have nurtured our families. In short, forgiveness farming honors God's full spectrums of how we should live on the earth and in our communities.

Patronizing forgiveness farms allows us to offer financial patronage, emotional support, and practical encouragement to a God-honoring food system. When visitors leave our farm, I always wonder: *Did they see forgiveness here?* Whatever I can do to enhance that object lesson, I pray for the strength and creativity to do it.

And Samuel said, Has the LORD as great delight in burnt offerings and sacrifices, as in obeying the voice of the LORD? Behold, to obey is better than sacrifice, and to listen than the fat of rams. For rebellion is as the sin of witchcraft, and stubbornness is as iniquity and idolatry.

1 Samuel 15:22–23a (AKJV)

If you've made it to this point, I think you'll agree that we've covered a lot of ground in these pages. I'm sure you'd say I'm a bit of a zealot, but you need to know I'm a friendly, respectful, diplomatic zealot.

I'm not a food cultist. I drink half a dozen Cokes a year. I do believe that you can be a Christian and a Tyson chicken farmer. I think you can even be a Christian and work at Monsanto. I don't think eating at McDonald's will condemn you to hell—at least not one time. Ha! Fortunately, God's grace transcends time and space.

However, I think the more we patronize people, places, and things that abuse God's possessions, the harder it is to have spiritual victory. Everyone knows the story of poor Lot, Abraham's nephew who chose the fertile plains toward Sodom. He lost his family, his reputation, and then in a drunken orgy had sex with his own daughters. His life is summed up in the New Testament:

[GOD TURNED]THE CITIES OF SODOM AND GOMORRAH INTO ASHES [AND] CONDEMNED THEM WITH AN OVERTHROW, MAKING THEM AN ENSAMPLE TO THOSE THAT AFTER SHOULD LIVE UNGODLY; AND DELIVERED JUST LOT, VEXED WITH THE FILTHY CONVERSATION OF THE WICKED: (FOR THAT RIGHTEOUS MAN DWELLING AMONG THEM, IN SEEING AND HEARING, VEXED HIS RIGHTEOUS SOUL FROM DAY TO DAY WITH THEIR UNLAWFUL DEEDS;) THE LORD KNOWS HOW TO DELIVER THE GODLY OUT OF TEMPTATIONS, AND TO RESERVE THE UNJUST TO THE DAY OF JUDGMENT TO BE PUNISHED. (2 Peter 2:6–9 AKJV)

Amazingly, three times in this passage the apostle Peter calls Lot a just man—he was a Christian. No doubt. I'm confident we'll see Lot in heaven. But my goodness, what a rotten legacy he left. Laughed at in his own town, unable to entertain the angels, scorned by his married children, he literally had to be manhandled out of the city by the protective angels. And then out of his two daughters came the Moabites and Ammonites, a wicked, ungodly people group that vexed the Israelites for generations.

I don't want to be a Lot, do you? I want a different legacy, not just physically, but spiritually. I don't want God to have to send angels to manhandle me out of judgment. I want to be snuggled up in God's bosom, far away from His judgment.

Consider another idea. Right after the famous chapter of faith in Hebrews 11, chapter 12 starts out:

WHEREFORE SEEING WE ALSO ARE COMPASSED ABOUT WITH SO GREAT A CLOUD OF WITNESSES, LET US LAY ASIDE EVERY WEIGHT, AND THE SIN WHICH DOTH SO EASILY BESET US, AND LET US RUN WITH PATIENCE THE RACE THAT IS SET BEFORE US, LOOKING UNTO JESUS THE AUTHOR AND FINISHER OF OUR FAITH; WHO FOR THE JOY THAT WAS SET BEFORE HIM ENDURED THE CROSS, DESPISING THE SHAME, AND IS SET DOWN AT THE RIGHT HAND OF THE THRONE OF GOD. (vv. 1–2)

Notice the two things that hold us back in this race: sin and weights. I would suggest that we can have weights that aren't sin. They aren't black and white, but they're weights nonetheless that hamper us in our ability to run with clarity and focus that race with eternal consequences.

So even if it's not sinful to eat junk food, to patronize ungodly food systems and evil farming methods, could we agree it's a weight? It hampers our ability to witness. It hampers our bodies and brains from functioning at full strength. It hampers our spiritual acuity and the visceral object lessons God wants us to appreciate.

To be sure, releasing all these things will not be easy. As the second verse points out, Jesus endured the cross, despised the shame. If you embark seriously on a creation care journey, you'll be laughed at by family. You'll be the butt of jokes from the pulpit: "Oh, let's not eat this cake here. Betty doesn't like white sugar and white flour and factory eggs."

You might be ostracized by friends. They'll say you've fallen off the deep end, joined the tree huggers. You might not listen to conservative talk radio quite as much. It's not a walk in the park. But as Jesus promises, it's a lighter yoke than the weight that keeps us from running a God-honoring race.

So right now, between you and God, what conversation are you going to have? Is it time to take stewardship of His stuff seriously? Does God care how you handle His stuff? Eventually, all of us have to ask: "Pigness of pigs—does God care?"

I'm confident that for many readers, the themes and information in this book are a revelation. They're the first time you've ever been touched by personal responsibility toward God's creation. It's been sobering, enlightening, and hopefully enjoyable in spots. This is my tenth book, and I've agonized and prayed over it far more than anything I've ever written. It's my coming-out book. I don't know what repercussions this will have on my life.

Numerous times in my public presentations I've addressed groups hooting and hollering approval as I rant against industrial food, but then turn deathly silent—and a few walk out—when I mention I'm a right-to-lifer. So I don't know if this book will torpedo my speaking career or alienate creation worshippers who love me. But I could stay silent no longer and felt God anointing me to broach this subject, this way, at this time.

The still small voice that keeps coming into my mind is the challenge Mordecai placed before his beautiful niece, Queen Esther, in the book of Esther. Coming before the king of the Persians, unasked—even if you were his wife, the queen—was nearly certain suicide. But Mordecai knew Esther was a bridge to connect with the king and stop wicked Haman's plot to exterminate the Jews.

As Esther mulled over her responsibilities, her almost certain death by going to the king without being asked, Mordecai challenged her with these words:

THINK NOT WITH YOURSELF THAT YOU SHALL ESCAPE IN THE KING'S HOUSE, MORE THAN ALL THE JEWS. FOR IF YOU ALTOGETHER HOLD YOUR PEACE AT THIS TIME, THEN SHALL THERE ENLARGEMENT AND DELIVERANCE ARISE TO THE JEWS FROM ANOTHER PLACE; BUT YOU AND YOUR FATHER'S HOUSE SHALL BE DESTROYED: AND WHO KNOWS WHETHER YOU ARE COME TO THE KINGDOM FOR SUCH A TIME AS THIS? (Esther 4:13–14 AKJV)

"For such a time as this." Wow. Mordecai knew God would save the Jews with or without Esther, but he wanted her to be faithful to the full extent of her knowledge, her insights, her connections: "for such a time as this." Esther wasn't better than other Jews. She wasn't a better Christian, if you will. But she was uniquely prepared and placed as a conduit of God's information.

God doesn't need me to save His planet. Goodness, He might start the millennial renovation process tomorrow. But He wants us to occupy, to care, to be faithful servants whether we have one day or centuries. So I count it a privilege to bridge the tension between the Christian and the environmentalist. Further, I think God is pleased when we as Christians catch a spiritual lesson from daily living. This

maintains an attitude of prayer, of worship, of communion throughout the day.

My heart breaks for the Christian testimony when we're universally
perceived as planet destroyers. My heart breaks for gully-scarred hillsides and farmers struggling with antibiotic-resistant super-bugs and
herbicide-induced super weeds. My heart breaks for animals confined in
fecal particulate quarters, unable to express even their most rudimentary
uniqueness. This is not to replace an evangelistic heart toward the lost.
It is to augment it, to put feet and hands on it. And to build God's claim
to everything—my soul, my food, my vocation, my farm. Ultimately,
they're His.

So, friend, what about you? I conclude with Deuteronomy
30:19–20:

> I CALL HEAVEN AND EARTH TO RECORD THIS DAY AGAINST YOU, THAT
> I HAVE SET BEFORE YOU LIFE AND DEATH, BLESSING AND CURSING:
> THEREFORE CHOOSE LIFE, THAT BOTH YOU AND YOUR SEED MAY LIVE:
> THAT YOU MAY LOVE THE LORD YOUR GOD, AND THAT YOU MAY OBEY
> HIS VOICE, AND THAT YOU MAY HOLD TO HIM; FOR HE IS YOUR LIFE,
> AND THE LENGTH OF YOUR DAYS: THAT YOU MAY DWELL IN THE LAND
> WHICH THE LORD SWORE TO YOUR FATHERS, TO ABRAHAM, TO ISAAC,
> AND TO JACOB, TO GIVE THEM. (AKJV)

Acknowledgments

This book has been a long time coming. It's been in my heart for several decades, waiting to be born. First, I want to thank my paternal grandfather, Fred Salatin, who embraced an environmental ethic before 1950 by being a charter subscriber to Rodale's *Organic Gardening and Farming* magazine.

My mom and dad, Bill and Lucille Salatin, both nurtured a love for biblical and environmental truth during the 1950s and 1960s, way before the mother earth movement, hippies, and *Silent Spring*.

I'd be remiss not mentioning all my debate instructors throughout high school and college, without whom I would be unable to articulate this message nor have the faith and confidence to stand on conviction. I deeply appreciate my alma mater, Bob Jones University, which instilled a desire to live in the world as a change agent.

Kate Hartson, editor, and Lisa DiMona, book developer, have given professional insight and encouragement throughout this project. Their expertise definitely made the effort stronger and clearer.

Our daughter, Rachel, always artistic, brought beauty and order to our farmstead. Son Daniel and daughter-in-law Sheri are a dynamo of enthusiasm and inspiration for the staff and Polyface team. And our grandchildren, Travis, Andrew, and Lauryn, inspire legacy thinking and create immediacy to creation care.

Most importantly, I appreciate my bride of thirty-five years, Teresa, who has stood valiantly by my side, letting me be weird, defending me even when it was unpopular, and encouraging me to express the Joelness of Joel.

Index